FAMINE IN SOMALIA

T0323021

DANIEL MAXWELL
NISAR MAJID

Famine in Somalia

Competing Imperatives,
Collective Failures, 2011–12

HURST & COMPANY, LONDON

First published in the United Kingdom in 2016 by
C. Hurst & Co. (Publishers) Ltd.,
41 Great Russell Street, London, WC1B 3PL
© Daniel Maxwell and Nisar Majid, 2016
All rights reserved.
Printed in India

The right of Daniel Maxwell and Nisar Majid to be identified as the
authors of this publication is asserted by them in accordance with the
Copyright, Designs and Patents Act, 1988.

A Cataloguing-in-Publication data record for this book
is available from the British Library.

978-1-84904-575-9 *paperback*

This book is printed using paper from registered sustainable
and managed sources.

www.hurstpublishers.com

CONTENTS

ACKNOWLEDGMENTS

Many people contributed to this book. We are eternally grateful to the whole team that helped us in our research, particularly the field research team, including Guhad Adan, Khalif Abdirahman, Mark Bradbury, Fouzzia Musse, Khadra Elmi, and Desiree Bartosiak. Guhad and Khalif deserve special mention as they contributed to the findings in many ways, from finding the right people to talk to, conducting the majority of interviews with Somalis, and adding their insights throughout the study process. At Tufts, a dedicated team of research assistants led by Janet Kim, Merry Fitzpatrick, and Heather Stobaugh helped us plow through some 500 documents that predicted, assessed, or, in one way or another, reported on the famine of 2011. The research was a collaborative effort of the Feinstein International Center at Tufts and the Rift Valley Institute—particularly its field office in Nairobi, and we are grateful to RVI for their support in the study and its dissemination. We are grateful to the publishing staff at Hurst Publishers, and the detailed feedback on the manuscript from two anonymous reviewers.

The research on which this book is based was supported by the Bill and Melinda Gates Foundation and by the Office of Foreign Disaster Assistance (OFDA) of the US Agency for International Development. We are very grateful for their financial support and for their support in raising some of the conclusions found here in policy-making circles worldwide. At Tufts, we would like to acknowledge Elizabeth Gelzinis, Rosa Pendenza, and the entire Feinstein International Center team for their support of this study. We would also like to thank the Rift Valley Institute team, Save the Children—Ethiopia for their support of field work in Ethiopia, Abdi Aynte and the team at the Heritage Institute of Policy Studies in Mogadishu, and James Oduor and the National Disaster Management Authority for their support of the work in Kenya. For her endless assistance in editing, we would like to thank Joyce Maxwell.

Several individuals were extremely helpful in making connections to specific groups. In particular, we would like to thank Ramadan Assi of the International Medical Corp office in Ankara for helping to introduce us to the head offices of many Turkish agencies, and for his understanding of Turkish and Middle Eastern humanitarian actors more broadly. We would also like to thank Osman Consulting and the UK Muslim Charities Forum for their feedback on the non-Western and Islamic humanitarian actors.

We have benefited enormously from discussions with a number of individuals in the humanitarian community in Nairobi. Due to the constraints of the human subjects rules of research, and our assurances of the confidentiality of the interviews we conducted, we cannot name them here, but they know who they are, and we are grateful for their candor and bravery in the context of a politically fraught humanitarian emergency and response. Any research is of course dependent on the time and patience of the respondents interviewed. We would like to thank many people in the humanitarian community—and hundreds of respondents in Somalia, as well as Ethiopia and Kenya, and other locations too numerous to mention.

Lastly, we would like to thank our immediate families—Joyce, Patrick, and Emma Clare Maxwell; and Kate Wood, Sami Majid-Wood, and Els Majid—for their support for (and tolerance of!) this study, which inevitably took up much more time and required a lot more travel than expected—and hence absence from home. We are grateful to everyone.

Dan Maxwell, Nisar Majid

ACRONYMS

ACTED   l'Agence d'Aide à la Coopération Technique et au Développement (Agency for Technical Cooperation and Development in English)
ALNAP   Action Learning Network for Accountability and Performance
AMISOM   African Union Mission in Somalia
ARRA   Ethiopian Agency for Refugee and Returnee Affairs
BBC   British Broadcasting Corporation
CaLP   Cash Learning Partnership
CARE   Not an acronym—now just the name of an NGO.
CBRWG   Cash Based Response Working Group
CDR   Crude Death Rate
CfW   Cash for Work
CHF   Common Humanitarian Fund (UN)
CVMG   Cash and Voucher Monitoring Group
DARA   Not an acronym—a humanitarian evaluation organization in Madrid
DFID   Department for International Development (UK)
EW   Early Warning
EWS   Early Warning System
FAO   Food and Agriculture Organization (UN)
FAOSTAT   FAO Statistics database
FEWSNET   Famine Early Warning System Network
FSNAU   Food Security and Nutrition Analysis Unit for Somalia
FTS   Financial Tracking System (OCHA)
GAM   Global Acute Malnutrition
GCC   Gulf Cooperation Council

GPPI	Global Public Policy Institute (Berlin)
HAP	Humanitarian Accountability Partnership
HEA	Household Economy Analysis
HF	Humanitarian Forum
HPG	Humanitarian Policy Group
IASC	Inter-Agency Standing Committee on Emergency Response
ICAI	Independent Commission on Aid Impact
ICISS	International Commission on Intervention and State Sovereignty
ICRC	International Committee of the Red Cross
ICU	Islamic Courts Union
IDP	Internally Displaced Person
IGAD	Inter-Governmental Authority on Development
IHH	Humanitarian Relief Foundation (Turkish acronym)
IJA	Interim Juba Administration
INGO	International Non-Governmental Organization
IPC	Integrated Food Security Phase Classification
IRIN	Integrated Regional Information Network (Previously part of OCHA)
LEGS	Livestock Emergency Guidelines and Standards
MOU	Memorandum of Understanding
MSF	Médecins sans Frontières (Doctor Without Borders in English)
NDMA	National Drought Management Authority
NGO	Non-Governmental Organization
NRC	Norwegian Refugee Council
OCHA	Office for the Coordination of Humanitarian Affairs (UN)
ODI	Overseas Development Institute
OECD	Organization for Economic Cooperation and Development
OECD/DAC	OECD Development Assistance Committee
OFAC	Office of Foreign Asset Control
OFDA	Office of Foreign Disaster Assistance
OIC	Organization of Islamic Cooperation
OSAFA	Office for the Supervision of the Affairs of Foreign Agencies
PKK	Kurdistan Workers' Party
PMT	Population Movement Tracking
PSNP	Productive Safety Net Program
QRA	Qatar Relief Alliance

R2P	Responsibility to Protect
RUF	Ready-to-use Foods
RUTF	Ready-to-use Therapeutic Food
RVI	Rift Valley Institute
SAM	Severe Acute Malnutrition
SCS	South Central Somalia
SFG	Somali Federal Government
SNA	Somali National Army
SNM	Somali National Movement
SRCS	Somalia Red Crescent Society
SRDF	Somali Relief and Development Forum
TFG	Transitional Federal Government
TIKA	Turkish International Cooperation and Development Agency
TNG	Transitional National Government
UAE	United Arab Emirates
UCT	Unconditional Cash Transfer
UN	United Nations
UNDP	United Nations Development Programme
UNCHR	United Nations Commission for Human Rights
UNHCR	United Nations High Commissioner for Refugees
UNICEF	United Nations Children's Fund
UNOSOM	UN Operation in Somalia
USAID	United States Agency for International Development
WAMY	World Association of Muslim Youth
WFP	World Food Programme
WFP-FAIS	WFP Food Aid Information System
WHO	World Health Organization

PROLOGUE

This book is the end result of a long period of collaboration. Both of us were based in Nairobi in the late 1990s and early 2000s working on food security and livelihoods in the Greater Horn of Africa in the world of international non-governmental organizations—Nisar with Save the Children and the Food Security Analysis Unit (FSAU); Dan with CARE International. We had since gone our separate ways: Dan focusing on food security and humanitarian action, and eventually teaching at Tufts University in Boston; Nisar on the exploration of Somali transnational livelihoods, while working for a PhD with Mark Duffield at the University of Bristol—and hence inhabiting a Somali social and political world removed from the narrower walls of humanitarianism. This study provided an opportunity for us to work together in developing a different kind of analysis of Somalia, one informed by a socio-political perspective.

When the famine in Somalia was declared in July 2011, Dan was called on to provide technical assistance to some of the agencies engaged in the response—a unique venue from which to observe the humanitarian catastrophe and the response. In 2012, along with several other colleagues, we were both asked to help evaluate the unconditional cash transfer response to the famine. In addition to being a chance to follow up in detail on one of the more innovative responses to the famine, this evaluation raised a number of questions: by 2012, there was a mountain of information and data about the famine: reports, assessments, evaluations, and a small but growing peer-reviewed literature. This information was mostly devoted to the formal, Nairobi-based, UN-led humanitarian response to the famine, as seen through the eyes of Western analysts and aid workers. While this provided many insights, this whole category of analysis did not address—and, indeed, often failed to ask—

many questions about other aspects of the famine: First, is it even possible to make sense of this mountain of information and data—to learn something from it? Could the lessons learned from this information help prevent another catastrophic collapse like the one that occurred in late 2010 and early 2011? Second—and more to the point—what happened in areas where the Western, UN-led response was not able to reach (which of course included the most hard hit epicentre of the crisis)? How did people in the epicentre of the crisis deal with the famine? This area was controlled by Al Shabaab, and was largely a "no go" area for Western humanitarian agencies. What were the more localized causes of the famine, and what were the responses of the local community, the private sector, and the Somali diaspora in these areas? Did the experience in these areas tell a story that is substantially different from the story of the formal humanitarian response?

And third, there were a large number of humanitarian actors engaged in the response to the famine who seemed unfamiliar to the established Western, OECD donor-funded humanitarian community. Some of these organizations were Somali, but rather than being dependent on Western donors or NGOs for the funding of their operations, they instead looked to Islamic networks or donors in the Middle East and the Gulf states. Indeed, there were many donors and agencies from the Middle East and from Turkey that were very engaged in the response to the famine that were not recognized as "the usual suspects" in a major humanitarian emergency in the Horn of Africa. For that reason, the Western (mostly Nairobi-based) humanitarian community began referring to these agencies as "non-traditional" or "emerging" humanitarian actors. In fact, they were, for the most part, neither. Some of these agencies had been in existence for as long as organized humanitarianism has existed; others had been working in Somalia for decades, but not necessarily in the humanitarian space. Some were indeed new—to Somalia or to famine response. But partly because they spoke their own languages, and partly because many of them based their operations in Mogadishu and not in Nairobi—and hence were not part of the formal coordination system based in Nairobi—and in part because of their mostly Islamic roots, this group of actors constituted almost another kind of "humanitarian community" in the response to the famine. Although there were joint attempts to coordinate assistance, these two groups operated somewhat independently of each other, and to some degree, each was critical of the approach and the ethos of the other. So a third question was about this group of humanitarian actors: What were their motivations, their responses, and their impacts? What did their experience teach them, and was it different from what the Western humanitarian agencies learned from the crisis? What do the two different groups (which admittedly included great heterogeneity internally) have to learn from each other?

These are the questions that we set out to address with this book. But beyond these questions was a nagging sense that, in many ways, we did not have to know the answers to these questions to have prevented the famine of 2011. So why didn't we prevent it? We don't ask these questions in the first person plural to be precious. In our view, researchers and analysts were equally implicated in the failure to prevent, mitigate, and respond to the famine as were humanitarian Somali leaders and policy-makers, Western donor agencies, and front-line humanitarian aid workers. Hence, part of the title of this book: *Collective Failures.*

In many ways, researching and writing this book has evoked a sense of déjà vu. We have learned a lot, but some of what we heard about Somalia and about famine prevention in our interviews, we already knew before the crisis. So why did this happen yet again? What changed? Are we—as a humanitarian "community of practice"—somehow congenitally incapable of learning from the past? We don't believe we are—but the evidence suggested that we might be. All this motivated a three-year quest to get to the bottom of some of these questions.

The research and writing has been an uncomfortable journey. It has required confronting the fact that roughly a quarter of a million human beings lost their lives in this famine. When the mortality study that announced this figure came out in early 2013, it was met with hostility in many quarters: it stood accused of exaggerating the figures, or of using flawed methods. As we explain in Chapter 4, we believe that the findings of that study are the best record of the mortality that occurred. It might not be precisely correct—as its authors note, it is based on estimates that extrapolate from the data that was available at the time. But we have asked ourselves: What if they missed the correct figure by half? Would we be happy if "only" 130,000 people died in the famine rather than 260,000? (And of course, that is not to mention the statistical truth that if you are going to put wide confidence intervals around an estimated figure that would include 50 percent less than the estimate, it by definition has to include a figure that is roughly 50 percent higher as well—or nearly 400,000 in this case.)

But these figures are abstractions. The fact remains that an obscene number of people lost their lives in this famine and that represents the ultimate failure of both a profession to which we have devoted much of our working lives, and a society with which we have long engaged. Millions more survived, but many of them have been unable to recover their livelihoods, having lost their livestock or having been forced to sell their land to survive; and many remain stuck in the purgatory of IDP settlements in Somalia or the somewhat saner but nevertheless often dehumanizing refugee camps in Dadaab or Dollo-Ado. To borrow the words of our friend and colleague Alex de Waal, this famine was a scandal that should never have happened, and perhaps the only redemption for a catastrophe like this is to learn from it to ensure that it never happens again.

But it has also been uncomfortable in other ways. Many of the humanitarian actors were friends and colleagues. We have had many disagreements about the interpretation of what happened and why. Reflecting on the impact of a famine from the relative safety and material comfort of our quasi-academic, quasi-humanitarian perspective raises all sorts of ethical dilemmas: the roots of the humanitarian imperative lie in the notion of some kind of shared experience as human beings—a shared humanity, if one may say so without sounding pretentious. Yet the objective reality is that we live in separate and mostly non-overlapping universes. Beyond the ethical considerations are the hard-nosed foreign policy choices made by donor governments that essentially ignored the need for a robust international response in Somalia that might have required negotiating access with "terrorist" organizations. From 2008 until the famine was declared in 2011, counter-terrorism objectives clearly trumped humanitarian or famine-prevention objectives. For a period of time after the famine was declared, humanitarian objectives received more attention, but this was short-lived, and highlights the other part of our title: *Competing Imperatives*. Of course, it is by no means clear that even with a good analysis of what happened and why, humanitarian objectives would necessarily receive the same policy attention as political or security objectives if some similar set of circumstances were to recur in the future. And lastly, there is the uncomfortable reality to confront that, ultimately, much of the human suffering in Somalia was caused by the direct predations of fellow Somalis: the policies and practices of Al Shabaab; but also of "gatekeepers" associated with the more powerful clans and even the government of the day in 2011. These predations were tempered by solidarity within clans and, during the height of the crisis, even across clan lines. But the famine clearly was not just the result of bad weather, unfavorable markets, and the policies of external actors.

So what do we hope to achieve by writing a book about this? First, we believe that you cannot learn from the past if you don't understand it—this book is our best attempt to document what happened and why. But second, and perhaps more importantly, we believe that—despite structural constraints and a political economy of aid in Somalia that complicates learning—evidence and learning can inform better policies, better programs, a more humane perspective, and, in this case, foster a stronger effort to prevent future famine. But it will only do so if we choose to make it do so. Conducting research, writing books, disseminating findings—all that is fine, but whether or not it makes any difference depends on what we decide to do with that research, that knowledge, and those findings. It is our profound hope that this analysis contributes to the quest to relegate the scourge of famine to history once and for all.

Dan Maxwell, Nisar Majid

1

INTRODUCTION

Declaration of a Famine in Somalia

On 20 July 2011, the United Nations declared a famine in South Central Somalia. By the time of the declaration, the crisis was affecting over 3 million people. Some half a million children were malnourished, nearly 200,000 of whom were severely malnourished; the proportion of malnourished children in some areas of South Central Somalia was over half the entire population of those aged under five. Tens of thousands could be assumed to have already died.[1] Hundreds of thousands were displaced by the crisis, both internally and as refugees in Kenya and Ethiopia. There had been many warnings about a food security crisis of major proportions in the Greater Horn of Africa—and specific warnings about Somalia—for nearly a year before the famine was actually declared. But a complex set of factors coalesced that both led to the famine and compromised efforts to mitigate its onset.

At face value, the real-time declaration of famine—based on rigorously collected and analyzed data, declared according to criteria that most famine experts had accepted, and made in real time as the crisis was unfolding—was itself unprecedented. In many ways, the declaration confirmed that analysis of acute food security crises had progressed significantly since the catastrophic famine that affected much of the Greater Horn of Africa in the mid-1980s and other, more recent crises as well. The declaration was not without controversy, yet broadly speaking there was a consensus on both the criteria and the evidence. The declaration, and the information behind it, came mostly from the United Nations. The fledgling Transitional Federal Government (TFG) in Mogadishu had little early warning capacity, and hence little in the way of either early warning or a declaration of emergency came from a Somali authority.

But evidence-based early warning and the ability to detect famine as it unfolded were about the only successes that the international humanitarian community could point to in July 2011. Despite early warning going back to the failure of the *deyr* (short) rains in October/November 2010, not enough had been done to mitigate the onset of the crisis or to prepare for the impending disaster. The controlling local authority in all of the famine-affected area—and indeed much of the area affected to a less severe degree—was Al-Shabaab, an Islamist group with self-acknowledged ties to Al-Qaeda, and which had been officially labeled as a terrorist group by the United States and other Western countries. Al-Shabaab had also done little to raise the alarm or prevent the onset of crisis, and its repressive policies had done much to exacerbate the problem. Although there was some evidence that Al-Shabaab was divided internally about how to respond to the impending crisis, its actions exacerbated the crisis and led directly or indirectly to the absence of a number of the international humanitarian agencies that could have both mitigated the crisis and been in a position to respond rapidly. These included the World Food Programme (WFP). This was the first major food security crisis in recent memory in which WFP was not present in the areas most affected, a factor that was to have significant consequences for the response. And for much of late 2010 and the first half of 2011, Western donors were reluctant to provide funding for anything in South Central Somalia for fear that such funds might be diverted into the hands of Al-Shabaab. As a result, little was done to mitigate the looming—and predicted—crisis. Competing imperatives were at the root of the delay.

Background: Somalia in the Public Imagination

Somalia has occupied a prominent place in the public imagination and in public and foreign policy circles for many years, particularly in view of its association with state collapse, terrorism, and maritime piracy, as well as with humanitarian emergency and famine. However, a close scrutiny of these subjects reveals as much about the role of external actors as it does about Somalia itself. Somalia has become an arena in which competing policy discourses are played out, reflecting Somalia's internal tensions and divides as well as those within the United Nations, Western donor countries, and other regional and emerging global actors—including Saudi Arabia, several of the Gulf states, and Turkey.

In governance terms, it is worth stressing that Somalia presents far from a homogeneous picture; since the mid- to late-1990s, the Northwest (Somaliland) and to a lesser extent the Northeast (Puntland) have been far more stable and less violent than the south.[2] Even in southern Somalia, the notions of "failed" state and "anarchy" do little to explain the political predicament.[3] Ken Menkhaus, for example, points to the evolving nature of governance "systems" and "orders" in Somalia since the early 1990s and highlights the disastrous impact of external military intervention in 2007 and 2008.[4] As recently as the early to mid-2000s—some ten to fifteen years after the collapse of the Somali state—a number of prominent scholars were highlighting the resilience and innovation of the Somali economy and its politics. Referring to Somali society, Peter Little offered a definition of resilience as the capacity to deal with hardships without collapsing.[5] Parts of Somali society did, however, collapse catastrophically in 2011, while other parts managed to contain the worst effects largely through their own means. The arrival in Somalia of the global war on terrorism in the wake of the September 11, 2001 attacks in the United States—and particularly the rise of the Islamic Courts regime in Mogadishu in 2005—was arguably the start of the process that ended with the famine, a discourse we pursue in this book. The concept of "resilience" has since been re-invented by the international humanitarian and development community to justify new forms of external engagement in the post-famine context. This notion and its application in Somalia changed quickly from one of apparent strength to something lacking, which can be built back by external actors.

We explore all these themes in this book. Although the events of 2011 were unusual and the loss of human life was extreme, our research suggests that Somalia offers much that can be learned from, and much that is relevant to other parts of Africa and the wider world in an era of globalization. We apply this to the understanding of famines in the twenty-first century; to the changing landscape of humanitarian action, where Islamic donors and agencies are increasingly active with their own claims and ways of working, but which are poorly understood; to schisms within Somali society, including an increasingly engaged diaspora; and a history of patriarchal, lineage-based competition and socio-political hierarchies. Although terrorism and famine describe aspects of Somali society and politics, elements of innovation, flexibility, opportunism, and adaptation are also part of the reality of Somalia today. We explore both sides of these arguments in this book.

The 2011–12 Famine in Retrospective

We know a lot about this famine. First, we know the major causes: the well-publicized drought was a major causal factor—including the lowest recorded levels of rainfall in nearly fifty years in some of the affected areas in both Somalia and neighboring Kenya and Ethiopia. The drought had a severe impact on crop production and on livestock mortality, reducing both food availability in the affected area and the value of the main assets—livestock and labor—that people had to sell to purchase food. But drought (and climatic factors more generally) was only one of several causes. The drought coincided with a global spike in the price of basic food grains that was independent of the local production shock in the Horn of Africa. Somalia imports most of its food even in relatively productive years—through both commercial imports and humanitarian food aid. The increasing global prices for food led to a reduction in the amount Somalia imported and, together with other market factors, this drastically increased the price of food at exactly the time when the value of what people had to sell declined.

Beyond the "natural" and economic causes of the crisis, the ongoing war between Al-Shabaab and the TFG—supported by the African Union Mission in Somalia (AMISOM) and many Western donor countries—was another major factor leading to the famine. The fighting and the resultant displacement of the civilian population exacerbated the impact of the drought and the food price shock. In addition, the repressive rule of Al-Shabaab had undermined the ability of Somali communities to look after themselves and to access outside help when they needed it. The counter-terrorism measures of Western donors and agencies, combined with the antipathy of Al-Shabaab towards humanitarian aid (and food aid in particular), politicized the humanitarian effort, and consequently put extreme constraints on the space for any kind of humanitarian action—be it of a preventive or responsive nature. This "collapse of humanitarian space," as some observers have labeled it, did not happen suddenly: it occurred over several years.[6] But it was a major factor complicating any potential response to the worsening crisis.[7] Further exacerbating the complications in preventing or responding to the crisis was the absence of WFP and most other agencies with the capacity to deliver food assistance. All these factors aggravated a longer-term erosion of livelihoods and environmental degradation in South Central Somalia. Beyond these factors lurked the marginalization of major population groups within Somali society: although the drought and the food price crisis affected much of the Horn of Africa—and Al-Shabaab controlled nearly all of South Central

Somalia—it is no accident that the main casualties of the famine were from the more marginalized clans of the riverine and inter-riverine areas of the Lower Shabelle, Bay, and Bakool regions (the same groups that were the main casualties of the 1992 famine).

Second, we know that this crisis was well predicted. The El Niño Southern Oscillation (ENSO) is a well-recognized phenomenon related to surface temperatures in Southern Hemisphere oceans, and has a well-known effect on rainfall in the Horn of Africa. The year 2010 was marked by El Niño, with above average rainfall, and in the Horn of Africa an El Niño year is typically followed by a La Niña year, which produces the opposite effect: drought or greatly diminished rainfall. Thus for nearly a year prior to the declaration, the drought was predicted, and then documented, by the Food Security and Nutrition Analysis Unit for Somalia (FSNAU) and the Famine Early Warning System Network (FEWSNET), the global food security early warning system funded by the US Agency for International Development. The price spike was not as well predicted, but its effects were also tracked, and its impact was already notable by late 2010. Given WFP's absence, a crisis that might have prompted a major food aid response under other circumstances instead simply failed to elicit any proportionate response for a period of nearly ten months.[8] And not only was WFP not present in most of the area affected by the famine but there was effectively no contingency plan for how a major crisis would be handled in its absence.[9]

Third—and most tragically—we now know that roughly a quarter of a million people lost their lives in the crisis, and indeed most of this loss of life happened while little was being done to mitigate the crisis.[10] A sizeable humanitarian response was scaled up rapidly after the declaration, which helped to prevent further loss of life, but much of the damage was already done. We know that—in addition to long-standing displaced populations— large numbers of additional people were displaced by the famine, both within Somalia and internationally with people crossing into both Kenya and Ethiopia in search of food and safety. During July 2011 alone, an estimated 65,000 Somali people were displaced, followed by 50,000, 48,000, and 73,000 displaced people during August, September, and October respectively.[11] Refugee camps in neighboring countries were inundated: new arrivals doubled from May to June and increased almost threefold during July in Dadaab, Kenya, and fivefold in June at Dollo-Ado, Ethiopia.[12] Large numbers of children were malnourished; people's livelihoods were disrupted or destroyed. Most of these people were from two distinct social groups—the Rahanweyn and the Somali Bantu, from the riverine and inter-riverine areas of southern Somalia, "minority" and "marginalized" groups—the same groups that comprised the majority of famine victims in the 1991–2 famine.[13]

Perhaps more surprisingly, we now have good evidence of how many people lose their lives every year even when there isn't a headline-making famine or humanitarian emergency. The number of people killed by a famine is the "excess mortality" (the number of human deaths beyond a "baseline" figure considered to represent a more "typical" situation). A retrospective study of the famine revealed a shockingly high "baseline mortality" level in South Central Somalia—roughly 50 percent higher than the average figure for Sub-Saharan Africa, which in turn is considerably higher than for the industrialized world.[14] This high baseline mortality level is one piece of evidence of the protracted livelihoods crisis in southern Somalia both before and after the famine—a phenomenon aptly titled "the normalization of crisis" in the late 1990s.[15]

We know that the actions of Al-Shabaab in blocking (humanitarian) access, limiting mobility, and imposing heavy taxes on affected populations were partly responsible for the crisis. But we also know that the counter-terrorism policies of Western governments and donor agencies were partly responsible for the delayed response. Both the local authority (Al-Shabaab) and international actors (donors in particular but also humanitarian agencies) had internal policy debates about the best response to the impending famine that delayed many preventive or responsive measures. Throughout much of late 2010 and the first half of 2011, not only was little funding available for work in Somalia but the threat of criminal liability prevented much of the mitigative action that might otherwise have been possible. The fledgling government of the day—the TFG—controlled very little territory (including within Mogadishu), was riven with internal factionalism, renowned for its extreme levels of corruption, was mostly concentrated on the transition itself, and did little to predict, highlight, or respond to the worsening conditions.[16]

We know that, after the famine was declared, the international community responded with a large-scale emergency intervention that helped to bring the extreme levels of mortality under control. Given the absence of most major food aid actors, the international humanitarian community rapidly scaled up one of the largest cash transfer programs in a single country in humanitarian history up to that point. A combination of factors enabled this to be successful, reflecting the innovation, resilience, and dynamism that also characterize Somalia, including cellphone networks that cover much of the country, an informal banking system (known as *hawala*) that enabled the transfer of funds to remote locations, and a system of traders and markets that responded to the increased demand that the cash transfers enabled. We also know that major responses of other kinds were made available in Mogadishu, in the refugee camps at Dadaab, Kenya, and Dollo-Ado, Ethiopia (although these were also highly problematic, particularly in the first weeks of people's arrival). These interventions saved lives, but also no doubt served as aid magnets (for people in need as well as profiteers and opportunists). Some agencies responded with cash programs that included the condition of working to receive the cash—even in a famine—to send the message that the international community was still willing to invest in infrastructure and other community-level needs in the affected areas. Although earlier crises in Somalia were addressed with large infusions of food aid, it was mostly absent from the acute phase of the response to this famine, except in Mogadishu and in the refugee camps or border areas. Only one agency, the International Committee of the Red Cross, was able to make large-scale distributions of food aid in the famine-affected areas in the second half of 2011, but thereafter, their food aid operations were also brought to a halt by Al-Shabaab.[17] A snapshot of the crisis is provided in Figure 1.1, tracing the levels of excess mortality, the level of international funding for the response, and the numbers of people receiving food assistance in what was acknowledged to be an extreme food security crisis. As often happens in famines, mortality peaked well before the humanitarian response was fully scaled up. This rapid scale up doubtlessly helped to bring the mortality under control, but several other factors no doubt contributed as well.[18]

Unanswered Questions

However, there is also much that we did not know in the aftermath of the crisis. Given the restrictions imposed by Al Shabaab and the counter-terrorism measures meant to contain the organization, much of the response was limited to the periphery of the actual famine. The impact of the famine was widespread, covering large parts of South Central Somalia—almost all inside the areas Al-Shabaab controlled. As a result of these restrictions, much of the affected population in these regions was beyond the reach (or at least the direct reach) of the humanitarian effort. These were the areas where mortality was the highest. However, even after the famine had ended, we knew relatively little about what actually happened in these areas. Likewise, with the emphasis on drought, food prices, and conflict as the causes, and the lack of external intervention, relatively little was known about the internal dynamics that led to the famine.

Figure 1.1: Mortality, Funding, and Aid Recipients: 2010–12

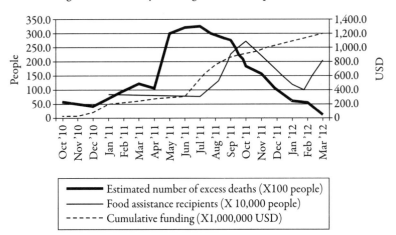

Data: Checchi and Robinson (2013); Food Security Cluster; OCHA Financial Tracking Service.

A number of "new," less well-known, or "non-traditional" humanitarian actors were operating in various areas affected by the famine—particularly Mogadishu.[19] Many were from the Middle East and Turkey; most had Islamic roots and identities. Given the limited access of Western and northern humanitarian agencies, these agencies filled an important gap. But they had their own motivations for engagement beyond merely filling a void left by the standoff between Al-Shabaab and Western donors and agencies. However, at the time of the famine, the rest of the humanitarian world knew relatively little about the challenges those agencies faced, or the impact that they had, and even less about the objectives of the donors who funded their efforts. Their intervention in Somalia in 2011 presaged a much larger global presence—by 2013, for example, Turkey was the fourth largest humanitarian donor in the world.[20] A range of Somali and non-Somali Islamic agencies had been engaged in Somalia for some time before the famine, albeit mostly not in a humanitarian role. What can be learned from their experience?

The aftermath of the famine has seen a major shift in the policy discourse about ways of working in low-rainfall, conflict-affected, chronically at-risk areas of the Greater Horn of Africa (and the Sahel). Much of this discourse comes together under the rubric of "resilience," or the policies and programs that might enable at-risk communities to withstand and "bounce back" from repeated exposure to drought and other natural and man-made hazards. However, it is not clear to what extent the lessons learned from the famine—and indeed from repeated crises in the Greater Horn of Africa—inform this policy imperative to equip communities and institutions to become more resilient in the face of ever-tightening cycles of disaster.

The 2011 crisis was region-wide, affecting parts of Kenya, Ethiopia, and Djibouti as well. But only in Somalia did the crisis deteriorate to the extent of becoming an actual famine. This book does not attempt to analyze what happened in other countries, except for the extent to which factors in other countries affected what happened inside Somalia. This necessarily includes examining the refugee centres in Kenya and Ethiopia, particularly Dadaab (Kenya) and Dollo-Ado (Ethiopia). It necessarily includes the foreign and security policy and military action of both countries along the borders of Somalia, as well as the foreign policies and counter-terrorism measures of countries that would, under other circumstances, have mounted a more vigorous effort at famine prevention. To the extent possible through secondary sources, it includes understanding the policies of—and debates within—Al-Shabaab itself. And it necessarily includes an understanding of Somali politics and clan dynamics, and the way in which these also determined some of the outcomes of the crisis.

This book attempts to address these questions in the context of the broader research literature on Somalia and of what we know about famines. The book does not offer a new theory of famine, but rather uses existing theory to examine the course of this particular crisis, and to interpret new insights and factors not previously included in the explanation of famine. Ultimately, this book is an attempt to come to grips with a collective failure—of both local governance and international humanitarian protection and response—and it is an attempt to ensure that we understand it well enough to prevent it from happening again.

Research Questions

In light of what we know about the Somalia famine and its unique aspects, and about famines and famine theory more generally, this book attempts to address several questions about what we don't know, which were highlighted in the prologue: first, in the areas reached by the humanitarian response (mostly outside of the epicentre of the crisis), a lot is already recorded and known. But questions remain: Why was the response so late? Moreover, as there is a long history of early warning and late response, and a lot of knowledge about the causes of this problem, why did it happen again? What must be done to prevent this well-known and easily recognized problem? Is there something new to be learned from Somalia in 2011?

Second, much of the analysis of food insecurity and famines is focused on livelihoods: the way in which individuals, households, and communities use the resources at their disposal to earn a living and the choices they make—or are forced to make—to provide for themselves. Livelihoods are often categorized in terms of groups that share similar characteristics and strategies for making a living, and "livelihood groups" are often the main category of social analysis in early warning and food security analysis. Some livelihood groups were hit harder than others in Somalia. But in Somalia, a major determinant of vulnerability both within and between livelihood groups is the extent to which households or communities are tied into broader social networks, and these networks are often defined in terms of social identity. A comprehensive livelihoods analysis would take these factors into consideration but this is a complex task, and rarely undertaken. Differences in the wealth and risk diversification within such groups or networks were a major determinant not only of the extent to which people were affected by the crisis but also led to significant exploitation of some groups in the context of the response. What was the impact of the famine when viewed through the categories of social and political identity? In the context of Somalia, this analysis focuses mostly on the notion of clan or lineage.

Third, crises such as the one that affected Somalia in 2011, typically elicit a large-scale response from the international humanitarian community. The Somalia famine eventually did as well, but as noted, the response came very late, and limited access to the epicentre of the famine prevented a robust effort at mitigation or humanitarian response in the areas most affected by the crisis. What happened in these areas? What can be learned about the local or community-led responses to these kinds of crises? Can knowledge about these responses help to improve overall famine prevention and response? Similarly, what was the role of the "emerging" or non-Western humanitarian actors? What can we learn from their efforts to improve overall famine prevention and response, particularly in a politically fraught and polarized context?

In the aftermath of the 2011–12 crisis—as in the aftermath of major regional crises in the past—efforts have been made to address the underlying causes of famine. During 2012 and 2013, one widely held proposition was that, had there been more emphasis on "resilience programming" and more focus on enabling local communities to withstand recurrent shocks, both natural and man-made, the famine wouldn't have occurred, or at least the impact would have been considerably reduced. This is a bold claim that perhaps reflects a preoccupation with "technical fixes" at the expense of addressing political constraints. But what are the lessons that could or should be learned from the famine? Do they provide evidence to support the current policy discourse on resilience? And what do they say about the prospects for preventing future famines?

Analysis of past emergencies suggests that the best way to prevent famines from recurring is to ensure that the people who are responsible for preventing them are accountable to the people who actually suffer their consequences. This analysis was revisited early on in the Somalia famine as well.[21] But has anyone assessed accountability for the 2011–12 famines in Somalia? If not, why not? And what does that say about the prospects for preventing future famines? And what parties should be considered in an assessment of accountability? Much of the focus has rightly been on international actors, but ultimately, Somali actors were also to some degree responsible for the events of 2011–12. Finally, what are the key lessons from the Somalia famine of 2011–12 that could be learned from to prevent and mitigate future famines, or to protect people better when famine does strike? These are the questions this book intends to address. It is not an attempt to "expose" or blame—it is rather a modest attempt to understand: a clear understanding of the past is the best hope for shaping a different future.

Brief Outline of the Book

The remainder of the book examines a number of themes. Chapter 2 briefly reviews what we know about famines and famine theory. This includes the technical definition of famine and the development of famine measures. Somalia plays a unique role in this measurement, given that the current definition of famine comes from an instrument developed by the Food Security and Nutrition Analysis Unit for Somalia.[22] Chapter 2 also reviews the so-called "Early Warning/Late Response" problem that was identified two decades ago,[23] but which continues to manifest itself in "slow-onset" food security emergencies, including in Somalia in 2011. The chapter provides a brief overview of famine response including food aid and the history of food aid in Somalia, as well as the rise of cash programming in humanitarian emergencies. Overall, the chapter explores the reasons why famines persist in an era when technical capabilities suggest they should be consigned to history.[24]

Chapter 3 provides background information specific to the Somalia context. It gives an overview of recent Somalia history, focusing on the period since the civil war that began in the late 1980s, including the rise and fall of the Islamic Courts and the rise of Al-Shabaab. It provides a brief review of the famine of 1992–3, the cycle of crises that have ensued, and the basis of the "normalization of crisis" label that has stuck to Somalia for the past decade and a half. Chapter 3 also briefly reviews Somali socio-political dynamics relating to different clans and livelihood groups. Given the long history of humanitarian assistance in Somalia, the chapter also examines the political economy of aid in Somalia in relation to different actors including government, donors, and international agencies, the business community (especially private sector contractors to the aid industry), Somali NGOs, militias and militant groups, and ordinary citizens—for whom aid is part of the calculus in their livelihood choices and influences mobility and migration. The chapter also examines the withdrawal of WFP and other agencies from South Central Somalia, and provides a brief overview of the conflict and the main actors. Chapter 3 highlights some of the internal factors that did not in themselves cause the famine, but which exacerbated its effects. Finally, Chapter 3 also traces the rise of Al-Shabaab, the impact of the counter-terrorism legislation intended to contain it, and the limits this put on effective humanitarian action as the crisis worsened.

Chapter 4 examines the early warning information in greater detail, and outlines factors that set the stage for the famine. It tracks the course of the worsening crisis, including a deeper analysis of the impact of Al-Shabaab's governance and policies—and the restrictions of counter-terrorism measures—which together frame much of the delay in preventing and responding to the crisis. The chapter outlines the regional dimensions of the crisis, and describes in detail its impact in terms of livelihoods, food security, displacement, malnutrition, and mortality.

Chapter 5 presents a Somali narrative of the famine, taken from interviews conducted in different parts of Somalia and refugee camps in Ethiopia and Kenya. These "voices" reflect a human view of the famine and reveal the nuanced and varied ways in which people manage in such extreme times. Chapter 5 also explores the role of the Somali diaspora, Somali mosques, and the Somali private sector, all of which are inter-connected and have become increasingly active players in Somalia, particularly if compared with the previous famine of 1992.

Chapter 6 provides an interpretation of many of the issues that arise from the narratives in Chapter 5. This includes a deeper exploration of Somali clans and socio-political identity, and changes in livelihoods in the time frame preceding the famine, and how this affected vulnerability. Chapter 6 analyzes various factors of resilience and coping in the context of the famine, particularly exploring social connectedness as the key to understanding vulnerability. The chapter concludes with an exploration of several mechanisms of social exclusion in Somali society, including the "gatekeeper" phenomenon.

Chapter 7 is a review of the response of the UN-led, Western humanitarian community. The chapter begins with analysis of the late response and the lack of contingency planning. It then examines the "distancing" of the aid effort over time, as humanitarian agencies withdrew managers from Somalia and moved to Nairobi from the mid-1990s onward, and the increasing "bunkerization" of aid agencies in Somalia, leading to the "remote management" of much of the humanitarian assistance effort during the famine and some of the problems this caused. Chapter 7 also examines the evidence on the humanitarian response to the famine, including the unconditional cash transfers (UCT), and cash for work (CFW) food aid in the accessible areas along the Kenyan and Ethiopian border and in the capital, Mogadishu. Finally, the chapter briefly reviews some of the major evaluations of the response, in an attempt to begin to gather the evidence on what was learned.

Chapter 8 considers the "non-Western" humanitarian actors and the shifting international dynamics around the crisis. This includes the engagement of these donors and agencies in the Somali crisis, especially Islamic agencies, Middle Eastern and Turkish donors and humanitarian agencies, and the blurring of boundaries between state action and non-governmental humanitarian action, and the private sector. It examines the differences in "reach"—both humanitarian and political—of traditional and new humanitarian donors and actors.

Chapter 9 picks up the story line in 2012, in the aftermath of the famine. A new government was formed in Somalia in 2012, with much greater international legitimacy and a different focus domestically. The chapter briefly sketches Somali politics in the aftermath of the famine, the new government, and the declining reach of Al-Shabaab. It also reviews the pivot of the international community to the "resilience" agenda and offers a critical analysis of the policy discourse around resilience—what it means and how it plays out—and considers the way in which the lessons learned from the famine inform the current policy discourse and programmatic action around resilience (or not). Lastly, the chapter briefly outlines the "malaise" of humanitarian action in Somalia—a phenomenon that preceded the famine but which has grown acutely worse in the period since 2012.

Finally, Chapter 10 focuses on the difficult question of "so what?" This includes asking some familiar questions about the nature of humanitarian action: Why was famine not prevented? Why was the response so late? Why were key vulnerable populations missed in the response? It also involves asking some hard questions about accountability for famines: Why is it so difficult to hold actors accountable in famines? How are competing policy imperatives (or, at least, competing objectives) managed in crises in fragile states (in this case, counter-terrorism objectives and humanitarian objectives)? Where does accountability for learning about crises lie, and why, paradoxically, do learning and accountability seem to be at odds with each other?

But it also involves asking some specific questions about this particular famine: What did we learn about the way that famine-affected populations beyond the reach of conventional humanitarian response deal with crises? What did we learn from 2011–12 in Somalia? How generalizable are these lessons? How does the engagement of rising, non-Western actors inform future policy and planning? How should "established" or Western humanitarian actors and "new" or non-Westerns actors engage with each other? And what are the implications of all this for our general understanding of famines? For famine prevention and response? For Somalia? For the "international humanitarian community"? The famine that affected large areas of South Central Somalia in 2011–12 was the result of numerous factors. The drought was a major factor, driving the decline in production, the increase in livestock mortality, and the collapse of rural labor and commodity markets. Simultaneously, rising food prices—both domestically and globally—combined with the loss of income from labor and livestock drove a disastrous drop in people's ability to access food. In the absence of major humanitarian actors, with local governance by a repressive insurgent group that did not want humanitarian assistance (especially food aid), and with counter-terrorism laws in donor countries that further restricted the actions of humanitarian agencies, a famine may seem in retrospect to have been all but inevitable. Yet a famine need not have been the outcome had local Somali actors and the international humanitarian community been better prepared for this set of factors, and had mitigation efforts been more rapid and more appropriate. It is towards the goal of better understanding what happened in Somalia before, during, and after the famine, and of preventing such a catastrophic event in the future, that this book is offered.

2

THE PROBLEM OF FAMINES

"For almost a century, there has been no excuse for famine."[1] So begins a famous critique of our understanding of famine and, in particular, of the repeated failure to foresee and prevent the catastrophic loss of human life and the destruction of human livelihoods that famines cause.[2] But Alex de Waal wrote that critique in 1997, describing the continued occurrence of famine as a "scandal" nearly fifteen years before the Somalia famine of 2011–12. Advances in theory and understanding, in famine early warning, in humanitarian response, and in a broader sense of accountability—highlighted in the "Responsibility to Protect" doctrine that was adopted by the UN General Assembly in 2005—led many observers to hope that humanity had finally put an end to the scourge of famine. Indeed, in early 2011, referring to improvements in humanitarian action, one of the authors wrote, "Mortality in acute food security and nutrition crises has been reduced, which is a significant achievement. But relatively less progress has been made in recovery from crises."[3] But mortality was already beginning to spike in Somalia before these words were even off the printing press.

This chapter provides some important background to the analysis of Somalia 2011–12. First, it briefly reviews famine theory—what we know about famines and what causes them. Second, it provides a discussion about what famine actually is, and why "famine" is such an emotive and politically fraught term. The development of famine measures—and agreeing some kind of a consensus definition of what constitutes a famine—was actually a major achievement (but not one without controversy and dissent). We briefly trace

15

this discussion because Somalia was not only the site of the development of the instrument that defines famine and provides the current definition of the thresholds for declaring famine but also because Somalia became something of a test case for the controversy that continues to surround the definition.

Third, the chapter provides background to one of the most persistent and baffling problems about contemporary famines and food security crises: although improved early warning systems may predict these crises, there is a repeated failure to intervene in time to prevent them—the phenomenon Margie Buchanan-Smith and Susanna Davies[4] described in 1995 as the "missing link" between early warning and response, or what Stephen Devereux[5] calls "response failure." Early warning and a very delayed response certainly characterized the Somalia famine of 2011–12, but this was not a new phenomenon.

Fourth, the responses to famines have changed, and this chapter very briefly reviews what we know about these responses, both by the international mechanisms of humanitarian action and by affected communities themselves. Fifth, famine experts agree in principle that accountability for acts of commission and omission in famines holds the key to ending this problem, yet the issue of accountability for famines remains unsolved—and almost untouchable. And in summary, we again address the question of why famines continue to persist in a world that knows how to prevent them. All of these themes are necessary to understand what happened in Somalia in 2011–12.

Understanding Famine

Famines were long considered simply to be food shortages that resulted in people starving—usually the result of something that disrupted food production: droughts, crop disease, or in some cases, wars or other political factors. More recently, the understanding of famines revolved around economic processes that led to destitution, distress migration in search of food or employment, increased malnutrition, and ultimately, increased mortality. Contemporary understandings of famine note a difference between factors that trigger a famine and the policies or public actions that either serve as a pre-cursor to, or fail to prevent, famines.[6]

In 1798, Thomas Malthus offered perhaps the most enduring theory of famine. Malthus believed that population growth outpaces improvements in agricultural production, ultimately leading to shortfalls in food availability. Some people would necessarily starve as a result. Famines were thus a "check" on population growth.[7] Until fairly recently, this view still predominated in understanding—and predicting—famines. In 1981, Amartya Sen stood this understanding of famines on its head by observing that access to adequate food (not aggregate food availability) was the real problem. He introduced the notion of food "entitlements"—food that people could actually access through their own production, through trade, or through some kind of transfer. It was the failure of entitlements—rather than an outright shortage of food—that explained the occurrence of famine.[8] While entitlement theory still largely applies, a number of improvements have been added to it, focusing on different causes and triggers. And though much of the focus continues to be on conflict and natural disasters, David Keen proposes that famines may be the result of intent, not just accident, and that some groups in society actually profit from famine.[9] On the other hand, Luka Deng points out that particularly in conflict or complex emergencies, wealthy people—people with otherwise perfectly adequate entitlements—may actually be more vulnerable since their wealth may make them targets, a point more broadly developed in livelihoods analysis by Sue Lautze and Angela Raven-Roberts.[10]

De Waal took this notion further by suggesting that the emergence of an actual famine is inevitably the result of human decisions, and proposed that those responsible for either creating the circumstances for famine or for failing to prevent it should be held accountable for their actions. De Waal also introduced the notion of "political contracts" between governing authorities and the populations they rule as the means to prevent famine.[11] In an earlier book, de Waal highlighted the nature of famine-coping strategies by demonstrating the extreme lengths to which famine-affected populations would go to protect their productive assets and ensure that they could recover after a famine. In the cases he examined, this turned out to be a higher priority than either the avoidance of extreme hunger or even elevated mortality. Subsequent work by Sen reframes famine more along the lines of Keen and de Waal as a violation of rights, noting the links between access to adequate food and good governance.[12] A controversial—and often misrepresented—claim in Sen's 1999 book is that famine cannot happen in democracies. His point was that democratic institutions, such as freedom of expression and association, an independent press, and the right of recall, would hold leaders accountable for their actions (and in the case of famine prevention, for their inaction as well)—in many ways building on the "political contracts" notion suggested by de Waal.

While different theories have focused on different causal factors, actual famines are almost always caused by multiple factors. Natural disasters are often thought to be the primary cause (or at least the primary trigger), but natural disasters usually only result in famines when other underlying social or political factors have made large sections of a given population vulnerable, and when public policy or collective action fails to address that vulnerability. Famines may be the outcome of war or the result of government actions or policies, based on a misunderstanding of the situation, or intentional policies to marginalize and control a portion of the population. In its more extreme form, famine and the manipulation of humanitarian assistance have been used as instruments of war.[13]

Drought and other natural disasters are the most straightforward of hazards to predict, and so drought-triggered famines should be the most straightforward to prevent. Drought and natural disasters remain an important causal factor in contemporary famines, but they are rarely the sole cause. In the 1943 famine in Bengal—Sen's primary case study in his 1981 book—the collapse of "entitlements" was brought about by rapid food price inflation in the context of a world war. Sen's point was to show that certain groups of people—in this case, mostly landless laborers whose wages were stagnant in the face of rapid wartime food price inflation—could not afford to buy food even if it was relatively plentiful in the market. Other factors may aggravate famines that occur in wartime. The famine in Biafra during the Nigerian civil war from 1968 to 1970 resulted from a prolonged military blockade. The aid effort mounted by well-meaning humanitarians to address the famine caused by the blockade probably prolonged the war and worsened the effects of the famine.[14]

Other factors have been recognized more recently as contributing to increased vulnerability to famine, or to the failure to prevent or respond to famine. These include pandemics, global and local market dynamics, and politics. Deng demonstrated how global interests in petroleum resources exacerbated agricultural production shortfalls, displacement, and the manipulation of aid during the civil war in Sudan that led to the Bahr el Ghazal famine in 1998—one of the last major famines of the twentieth century.[15] Many famines have been triggered or exacerbated by the policies or actions of governments, even in the absence of war or violent conflict. British policies on land tenure and faith in free-market policies to resolve food shortages underpinned the great famine in Ireland in the mid-nineteenth century—although the crisis was triggered by a potato pathogen.[16] Some of the worst famines of the twentieth century occurred in the Soviet Union and China as the result of state-induced revolutionary changes, but without militarized conflict (albeit with plenty of coercion).[17] The collapse of preferential trade with the Soviet Union and the policy of *juche* (self-reliance) triggered a famine that killed an estimated 1 million people in North Korea in the late 1990s.[18] De Waal and Alan Whiteside noted the advent of so-called "new variant famines"—crises altered by the dynamics of the HIV/AIDS pandemic, which both increases the vulnerability of communities to famine and in many cases undermines the capacity of state institutions to prevent it or respond.[19] The point is that almost all actual famines have multiple causes and that, usually, a complex series of events serve to trigger famines.

These studies have also led to an understanding of famines as a process (not just an "event"), with logically defined markers that allow analysts to predict with some degree of certainty when and where conditions are likely to lead to famine. This, in turn, should enable government policy-makers and humanitarian agencies to intervene in time to prevent actual famines from occurring. That famines have continued to occur despite these improvements in analysis, and in the ability to mitigate and prevent them, was the scandal to which de Waal referred in 1997—and which is even more scandalous today.

Defining Famine

Famine is broadly understood as "an extreme crisis of access to adequate food, manifested in widespread malnutrition and loss of life due to starvation and infectious disease."[20] But the word "famine" is controversial, in part because, at least until recently, no commonly accepted technical definition existed of what actually constitutes a famine; and in part, because the term evokes an emotive and political "hot-button" response that other, similar terms, such as "hunger," "food security crisis," or "humanitarian emergency," do not.[21]

Although "famine" is commonly used to describe inadequate availability of or inadequate access to food, the currently accepted technical definition of "famine" revolves around levels of malnutrition and mortality, as well as severe food insecurity. More comprehensive definitions also include measures of morbidity or illness, food consumption, and destitution. Some definitions of famine—particularly the perception of people directly affected by it—do not focus so much on mortality but rather on the widespread experience of hunger and destitution.[22]

The technical means of describing famine have evolved significantly since the mid-nineties, but mostly revolve around two factors: the prevalence of wasting—low body weight compared to height (most frequently in children under the age of five years but also sometimes in adults), referred to as global acute malnutrition or GAM; and the crude death rate (CDR), expressed in numbers of deaths per 10,000 population per day—in the population as a whole, and sometimes specifically in children under the age of five years. But even these technical measures carry with them a degree of controversy. Numerous attempts have been made to suggest thresholds for determining when famine conditions exist, but none was ever widely accepted.[23] Widespread malnutrition and documented mortality in a limited area of eastern Ethiopia in early 2000 led to competing claims of "famine!" (from critics) and "famine averted!" (from authorities and agencies responsible for the humanitarian action to prevent and respond to the crisis).[24] Both parties (critics and defenders) based their conclusions on the same data. To address this controversy—and precisely because the use of the term is so fraught—Paul Howe and Stephen Devereux proposed a "famine scale" based on both the severity of conditions (malnutrition and mortality) and magnitude (numbers of people affected).[25] They suggested that a CDR greater than one person per 10,000 people per day and a prevalence of GAM greater than 20 percent should be viewed as constituting "famine conditions," with higher death rates and a higher prevalence of malnutrition indicating more severe manifestations.

While the Howe–Devereux scales were not widely adopted in operational terms, they led directly to the formulation of the scale that has been widely adopted by governments, donor agencies, and operational humanitarian agencies—the Integrated Food Security Phase Classification (IPC),[26] which is now being adopted and implemented in more than thirty countries.[27] This classification system also includes thresholds for what constitutes relatively "normal" (i.e., non-crisis) conditions, and for various degrees of stressed or crisis-affected conditions of a lesser magnitude than famine, up to and including famine itself. It is a data-amalgamation protocol that takes disparate indicators of human wellbeing—including livelihood stress, food consumption, malnutrition, and mortality—and combines them to provide a "current status" assessment of population groups, typically defined in terms of their livelihoods, that is comparable across dissimilar contexts.

With specific regard to the technical definition of "famine," the IPC emphasizes three thresholds, all of which must be met simultaneously: a CDR greater than two people per 10,000 people per day; the prevalence of GAM in children under five years of greater than 30 percent; and more than 20 percent of households with effectively no access to food and no ability to cope. Various modifications to these thresholds have been suggested. Helen Young and Susanne Jaspars noted the exponential relationship between malnutrition and mortality (as the prevalence of malnutrition increases, the likelihood of death increases exponentially). They suggested a famine threshold for mortality of five per 10,000 per day, though the IPC threshold remains at two. Young and Jaspars also suggested not only considering severity and magnitude but also considering the duration or longevity of a crisis as a classifying indicator.[28]

In actual famines, the conditions are sometimes considerably worse than the thresholds stipulated by the IPC. Helmut Kloos and Bernt Lindtjorn reported GAM as high as 73 percent in some places during the famine in Ethiopia in 1984.[29] Deng reported CDRs of twenty-six people per 10,000 per day during the Bahr el-Ghazal famine in Sudan in 1998. So the thresholds in the IPC are relatively conservative—but in some ways deliberately so because the purpose of the IPC is not just to provide a retrospective classification, but also to provide information for decision-making on response, much like the classifications given to hurricanes and cyclones. The IPC, and the institution that developed it—the Food Security and Nutrition Analysis Unit for Somalia (FSNAU)—played a crucial role in the run-up to the famine of 2011, and that was the first time the IPC was used to declare a famine in real time.

There is a wide gap between external definitions of famine—such as the IPC and other definitions noted here—and the more local or context-specific definitions given by people who actually experience famine. This is a theme explored in depth by de Waal in Sudan in the 1984 famine, and more recently by Mulugeta Handino in the context of the "green famines" of Southern Ethiopia.[30] However, to date, relatively few attempts have been made to incorporate the more local definitions of famine into broader famine analysis or discourse—a topic we return to in Chapter 10.

The Early Warning/Late Response Problem

Research and practice in the past thirty years—particularly since the great famines in the Horn of Africa in the mid-1980s—have focused on famine prevention or mitigation, rather than simply on providing assistance to victims once famines have occurred. The ability to predict famine—famine early warning—is a key component of this effort, and major resources have been invested in early warning systems since the 1980s. Much of this originally came together in a USAID-funded program now called the Famine Early Warning System Network (FEWSNET), but many early warning systems are also now in place—some national, some localized, some (like FEWSNET) global.[31] FEWSNET now covers some thirty chronically risk-prone countries in Africa, Asia, and Central America/the Caribbean. Major improvements have been achieved in forecasting climatic patterns, production trends, and market factors that determine people's access to food, and hence to warning when things are going seriously wrong. Other, related forms of early warning, such as conflict early warning, may not exclusively track food security but may also have implications for famine.

Despite impressive improvements in early warning, Buchanan-Smith and Davies[32] noted over twenty years ago a "missing link" between early warning and the early response necessary both to prevent and mitigate famine. They noted manifestations of this "missing link" in a number of African countries that had suffered slow-onset, drought-triggered food security crises: information was available about the problem, but policy-makers and agencies did not intervene until a full-blown emergency (some of which reached the magnitude of famines) was underway. In their original analysis, Buchanan-Smith and Davies suggested that although sometimes there actually were information constraints, there were four main explanations for delayed responses in slow-onset food security crises even when adequate information had been available. Sometimes the inability to respond quickly was the result of the limited capacity of humanitarian agencies operating on the ground; sometimes bureaucratic delays, "inertia," and red tape; sometimes institutional factors and a lack of trust between the people who produce the information and those who have to act on it; and frequently, political considerations or interference were the reasons for delayed responses. A similar phenomenon was noted in 1999–2000 in Ethiopia, although in the 2002–3 crisis in Ethiopia, early warning did lead to effective government, donor, and agency action to avert a major crisis whereas in 1999 it had not.[33] The "Mandera Triangle" crisis of 2005–6 in the Kenya–Somalia–Ethiopia border area was yet another example of the problem, with some six months elapsing between early warnings of the crisis and the scaling up of the response—during which time the opportunity to intervene to protect livelihood losses and improve the chances for rapid recovery were lost.[34]

Writing about the Sahelian crisis of 2005, Kent Glenzer noted that existing early warning and response systems are forever limited to—indeed designed to produce—"partial success."[35] That is, the system will produce an analysis, it will raise an alarm, and it will eventually mobilize some resources that will save some people's lives and protect some people's livelihoods. But as it is constituted, early warning systems cannot protect everyone's life and livelihood—because they never trigger a response until after some people have died and some livelihoods have been destroyed. This is because early warning/response systems as they are currently constructed exist to meet the needs of the responders, not the needs of the people the system ostensibly exists to protect; and because the humanitarian response system can't decide whether the greater policy priority is to prevent "under-coverage" or "leakage"—that is, whether to focus on providing adequate assistance to people who need it, or on making sure no aid is wasted, stolen, or diverted by people who don't actually need it. The implication is that the bottom line concern of the current "system" is simply to contain the damage, not to prevent it.

Although their book was written in 1995, Buchanan-Smith and Davies's analysis remains very relevant today, and Glenzer's hard-hitting critique provides important insights beyond the original analysis. Somalia in 2011 was without doubt the most tragic manifestation of the "early warning/late response" problem in recent history, but it was not new news.

Famine Mitigation and Response

Since at least the 1970s, public efforts have been increasingly devoted to improving responses to famines to limit human mortality. Governments and donors have invested not only in establishing early warning systems but also in developing strategic food reserves. This has been accompanied by the rapid growth of humanitarian agencies that can quickly intervene to prevent or mitigate famines. In the 1980s and 1990s, significant resources were invested in strategic grain reserves in risk-prone countries like Ethiopia. By the early to mid-2000s, these grain reserves were replaced by greater reliance on cash contingency funds—a trend that was partially reversed after the food-price crisis in 2008, in which the food value of cash contingency funds plummeted in the face of rapidly rising food prices. However, even where emergency reserves existed, they didn't necessarily prevent famine, and were often subject to political manipulation.[36]

In their work examining the Great Lakes region of Central Africa and responses to famine and food security crises, Simon Levine and Claire Chastre found that, even as recently as the mid-2000s, humanitarian agencies were limiting their programming to a handful of interventions that were often based on assumptions rather than analysis—often ignoring information and analysis even where it existed. The responses were mostly limited to in-kind food aid for household-level food insecurity, and "seeds and tools" for presumed production shocks. At best, these interventions were having only a limited impact on addressing the problem.[37] Famine response and mitigation interventions have since expanded rapidly, though some innovations are often neglected in favor of the older, institutionalized interventions that are more likely to be funded.

Historically, the earliest famine-response mechanisms were the Indian Famine Codes, the policies of the British Raj in response to the famines that plagued colonial India. Dreze and Sen note that some of the mechanisms in the Famine Codes are still in use, including reducing restrictions on labor mobility, stabilizing food prices through market interventions, and creating public employment schemes (food-for-work schemes or, more recently, cash for work), that enable affected populations to earn a minimum wage to afford to buy food.[38]

From the 1950s until the 1990s, the default response to any kind of food security crisis was food aid, usually provided in-kind to the recipient, and very frequently donated in-kind primarily as a means of reducing domestic surpluses in exporting countries.[39] As surpluses in donor countries began to dry up in the early 2000s, donations of cash—either for the local or regional purchase of food aid, or for direct transfer to recipients to enable them to purchase the food of their choice (or to meet other urgent needs)—have become more common.[40] A much wider range of livelihood interventions are now available to prevent or mitigate the slide into famine, including livestock interventions in pastoral livelihood systems,[41] more sophisticated means of addressing agricultural livelihoods, and micro-finance interventions. Contemporary nutrition programs in famines or acute food security crises focus on "ready-to-use" therapeutic and supplementary foods, and on community-based program management, rather than the more expensive in-patient care that was also very inconvenient for mothers or other caregivers of malnourished children.[42] All these intervention options were to play an important role in the response to the Somalian famine, but even more so were the coping strategies and social connections of Somali communities affected by the famine.

This rather different story told by the study of "coping strategies" has also grown out of famine studies, and includes reliance on migration, increased natural resource extraction, consumption of wild foods, and a variety of social obligations within and between communities. These are explored in greater detail in Chapter 5. In relation to migration, rurally based livelihoods have become increasingly trans-nationalized in many parts of the world over the last twenty to thirty years.[43] The engagement of diasporas and the role of remittances have become increasingly important elements of this trans-nationalization of livelihoods—a process in which Somalis and Somalia are at the forefront.[44] Nearly one out of six Somalis is estimated to be in the diaspora.[45]

Accountability for Famine

An underlying concern for accountability runs throughout the recent work on famines—beginning with Sen and certainly de Waal, Devereux and many others discussed in this chapter. That is, if governments, donor agencies, and humanitarian agencies know so much about famines and famine prevention, the very existence of a famine reveals some error of either commission or omission that enabled that famine to occur. To put it in the blunt words of the most radical perspective, famines are crimes for which individual policymakers, leaders, and other responsible parties should be held criminally accountable.[46] Even from more moderate perspectives, the lack of accountability for famine prevention is the critical factor that must be addressed—including in areas ruled by non-state actors, or in states with weak or nonexistent democratic institutions—if famines are ever to be relegated to history. Accountability is not just about response—it is primarily about addressing the underlying conditions that make famine a possibility, and especially about arresting the downward spiral of livelihoods and vulnerability that make famine a real possibility. In other words, accountability requires those in positions of responsibility not only to address how to improve productivity and the resiliency of livelihoods but also to ensure that social protection mechanisms are in place during non-crisis times and ensuring their timely use for prevention and mitigation, and for response once famine threatens. This is also what makes the term "famine" so politically explosive, and explains in part why people are often reluctant to use the term. On the other hand, when the word is used—as the evidence from Somalia in 2011 will show—it also has a kind of political mobilizing power that other language—"food security crisis" or "humanitarian emergency"—does not.

The discussion about accountability for famines evolved mostly in the 1990s and early 2000s. Although largely a separate discourse relating more to the prevention of genocide and mass atrocities, the "Responsibility to Protect" (R2P) doctrine and the broader discussion about humanitarian protection were welcome developments that at one point were widely believed to give more clout to famine accountability. The notion of R2P was suggested in the report by the International Commission on Intervention and State Sovereignty (ICISS), which the Canadian government had commissioned in 2001,[47] partly in response to the 2000 "Millennium Report" of the then secretary general of the UN, Kofi Annan.[48] Annan's report highlighted the Rwanda genocide and the atrocities committed in the Balkan wars, and not famines *per se*. The roots of this discussion went back to the provision of assistance in Iraqi Kurdistan and indeed Somalia in the early 1990s.[49] Changing the definition of famines to include the notion of criminal culpability provided the link to R2P. The recommendations of the ICISS report were widely considered, and fed into a UN World Summit resolution in September 2005 that endorsed the obligations of each country regarding the prevention of mass atrocities and the obligations of R2P. The UN Security Council authorized a peacekeeping force in Darfur in August 2006, referring to the same doctrine. The R2P doctrine has been invoked several times since, although never in specific response to famine.[50]

Accountability is not simply about scapegoating or playing a "blame game"—real institutions of accountability send a firm message about expected norms of institutional behavior in crises, and accountability is not only about results: it is also about learning, improvement, and prevention. Howe and Devereux proposed an "accountability matrix" that recognizes the roles of various stakeholders (governments, donors, agencies, early warning systems) and assigns each a specific function.[51] They propose that, in the aftermath of famines, each stakeholder's role should be examined and some form of "proportionate accountability" assigned. Haan et al. attempted an initial analysis of accountability for the Somalia famine.[52] This is a theme we explore in greater detail in the final chapter.

So Why Do Famines Persist? [53]

In a review of famine theory and empirical research in 2007, Devereux speculated as to why famine persisted in the twenty-first century and divided such crises into "old" famines—climatic, environmental, and disease-related famines that resulted from some kind of production failure—and "new" famines—political crises, with an emphasis not only on causal factors that might include production shocks and/or the market failures explored by Sen but also on political shocks, and the failure to prevent such crises, or response failures.[54] Somalia in 2011, as it happened, was all these and more.

Much of the machinery for famine prevention is still modeled on the "old" understanding of famines. Indeed, much of the analysis of Somalia in 2011 still tends to focus on drought, which remains one of the major hazards for famine in the Horn of Africa. But the drought also affected Kenya and Ethiopia and no famine occurred in those countries—indeed, there was barely any elevated mortality (aside from the camps in Dadaab and Dollo-Ado where Somali refugees congregated and where mortality was quite horrendous). The real causes always seem to be found in the political realm rather than in the more comfortable technical realm—hence the discussion about accountability, but also the difficulty of ever having an accountability mechanism that has any real authority. In Somalia in 2011, causes included the actions (or inaction) of the Somali TFG, Al-Shabaab, and other local authorities, as well as the actions of neighboring governments, donor agencies, and regional bodies. It also includes the actions (or inaction) of humanitarian donors and agencies, and even local communities and the diaspora. The multiplicity of actors that cause (or prevent) famine makes attributing accountability difficult, but it also makes the search for learning even more important. We also address these themes in the remainder of this book.

3

SOMALIA AND EXTERNAL INTERVENTION IN THE GREATER HORN OF AFRICA

1970–2010

Introduction

The Horn of Africa generally, and Somalia in particular, has been the scene of recurrent political volatility and violent conflict, as well as periodic droughts and famine, over the last forty years. The region has significant geopolitical importance and was part of Cold War rivalries. Somalia remains a landscape within which regional and global powers regularly intervene—with maritime piracy and counter-terrorism being the primary stimuli over recent years. These factors, functions of both external intervention and internal factors—and the interplay of the two—have caused several humanitarian crises and large-scale movements of populations over time, which in turn are associated with enormous influxes of foreign aid.

Given this complex history, a full understanding of the context of the 2011 famine requires understanding many factors. These include the history of the Somali state and its collapse in the early 1990s; repeated crises and their humanitarian impact; international intervention and the political economy of aid—developmental, humanitarian, and military; displacement, migration, and the formation of a regional and global diaspora; and the rise of Islamic extremist groups and counter-terrorism measures aimed at them. This chapter briefly outlines this history. Appreciating this interplay of factors—internal and external, natural and man-made—is key, and some would argue that external intervention by foreign powers in late 2006 and the resultant political and humanitarian crisis provide a useful starting point leading up to the famine of 2011. The chapter provides short accounts of the famines in the mid-1970s and early 1990s in order to provide some comparison with that of 2011. Finally, it traces the rise of the militant group, Al-Shabaab, and the counter-terrorism measures intended to contain it.

State Formation and Collapse

"Greater Somalia" was divided between Ethiopia, France, Britain, and Italy during the colonial era, with present-day Somalia administered by Britain and Italy. Somalia became independent in June 1960 and had a democratic government before General Siad Barre orchestrated a coup in 1969.[1] The Siad Barre government initially embarked on a scientific socialist path, nationalizing all major industries including commercial farming with the support of the USSR. However, the Ethiopia–Somalia War of 1977–8 marked a major turning point, with the USSR switching its allegiance to Ethiopia at the last minute, leading to the defeat of Somalia.[2] Under the new patronage of the United States and the West, the Somali state became increasingly dependent on foreign aid, and this, together with the rise of militarized opposition groups, contributed to the eventual demise of the state.[3]

Collapsing and Stateless Somalia

During the mid- to late 1980s, under widespread allegations of large-scale corruption, the regime of Siad Barre came under increasing pressure from the World Bank and the United States to make structural changes to the economy. The Somali National Movement (SNM) was increasing its military opposition, partly because of certain clans' exclusion from state-based patronage networks. The withdrawal of donor funds that the government had been heavily dependent on and the rise of different clan-based opposition groups ultimately led to civil war, initially with the central government targeting SNM strongholds in the north (present-day Somaliland) from 1988 to 1990. The civil war then spread to the south with the government falling in 1990.[4] Menkhaus et al. divide the last twenty-five years of Somalia's history in to the following five periods: the war years, 1988–92; large-scale UN intervention, 1993–4; localized armed conflict (not civil war), 1995–2006; a short period in 2006 under the Islamic Courts Union in the south; and war (insurgency and counter-insurgency) from late 2006 following the Ethiopian military occupation of Mogadishu.[5]

The UN Intervention

While international intervention had long featured in Somalia, it ramped up with the collapse of the state. Lobbying from humanitarian agencies for a peacekeeping mission contributed to the UN military intervention, which lasted from December 1992 to May 1993 and was followed by the UN Operation in Somalia (UNOSOM), Phase II of which began in May 1993.[6] The objective of UNOSOM II was "to provide Somali society with a 'window of opportunity' to resolve the factional and clan conflicts that led to the collapse of the state and which were the root cause in the famine."[7] However, by late 1993, the UNOSOM program was considered "adrift." Menkhaus argues that US policy was driven by media images (first of war and famine), and then by dead US soldiers (the infamous "Black Hawk down" incident). He further attributes the influence of hardliners and intra-US political dynamics rather than those involving senior UN officials.[8] This experience was significant for its peace enforcement role in the context of the failure of international intervention during the Rwandan genocide in the following year.

Aid and the Rise of the Private Sector

Humanitarian and military intervention in Somalia in these war years had a major and important unforeseen consequence: it recapitalized the local economy, particularly in Mogadishu,[9] the trading hub for most of the south. The looting of property and international aid, as well as the small- and medium-scale trade opportunities that arose with the presence and resources of UNOSOM, contributed to the rise of a new business class.[10] The period under UNOSOM—a time of huge resource transfers—is noted for stimulating the NGO sector in Somalia, which had been largely absent during government years.[11]

The private sector has been the engine of growth in the Somali economy since the early 1990s, with the Somali *hawala* and telecommunications companies emerging as particularly noteworthy.[12] The evolution of *hawala*s, driven by the demands of a growing diaspora and trade-based economy at the time, reflects how crises create new opportunities and development, even in the absence of a central state. These businesses have evolved through clan- and Islamic-based social networks.[13] Many of them have significant charitable arms, financing infrastructure and other longer-term projects as well as supporting people in times of humanitarian emergency (see Chapter 5).

The Post-UN Period

The roughly ten years following the departure of the UN was often described as "no war, no peace"—a period in which Somalia was largely forgotten in international relations. It was, however, notable for innovation and growth as well as increasing inequality, poor social indicators, and occasional humanitarian emergencies.[14] Observers note that in the middle of this period, developments in Somalia were taking place in a context of "globalization" and "localization," where the scale and pace of globalization is defined in relation to increasing transnational movements of people, goods, and information; the instantaneous global movement of finance and capital; the telecommunications revolution; and the proliferation of various non-state actors (including NGOs).[15] In turn, localization is described in relation to global trends in the demand for democratic participation, the decentralization of political power, and the rising prominence of civil society. In line with these trends, Somalia was becoming a major trading hub for the wider region, and the Somali diaspora was growing and extending its influence—sending back to Somalia ever-increasing remittances. Another trend was the rise of both militant Islamic groups and Islamic charities in Somalia, arriving in part to fill the major gaps in social services.

This period also saw the emergence of new and varied forms of order and authority, from the secessionist state of Somaliland and the autonomous regional state of Puntland (both in the north of the country), to a variety of combinations of customary law, sharia courts, municipalities, business leaders, neighborhood watch groups, and civic movements in the south.[16] Southern Somalia has a significantly different social, ecological, and economic context and a different history from other parts of the country. In short, there is a much greater ethnic diversity with substantial inequalities between social groups. Access to productive agricultural land has been a significant driver of conflict (both important factors in vulnerability to famine).[17] The private sector and remittances were major economic drivers in the south, particularly in Mogadishu and other key urban centres. Roland Marchal, for example, described Bakhara market, in Mogadishu, as the "mother of all markets" linking Somalia with global and regional markets.[18]

These developments in economy and governance were used to challenge the "almost pathological" descriptions of "chaos" and "failed" statehood that came to prominence in Somalia following the events of September 11, 2001.[19] While the welfare indicators and public services admittedly declined, Tobias Hagmann argued that Somalis and Somalia were "ditching their aid-dependent state and foreign patrons and determining their own future."[20] Within this more stable period, the dwindling international aid resources reinforced local resource competition, and influenced claims to local representation.[21]

2006 and the Brief Reign of the ICU

The period from 2006 onwards marked the latest trajectory for the country, with increasing violence, instability, and foreign intervention associated with the full-scale arrival of the "War on Terror" in Somalia and the wider region.[22] For a brief period in the second half of 2006, the Islamic Courts Union (ICU)—which grew out of alliances between businesses and local courts—enforced peace and the rule of law in Mogadishu and large parts of southern Somalia, the first time that one single authority had managed anything like this since the Barre government.[23] However, soon the hardliners within the Courts were worrying Ethiopia, which had backed the incumbent TFG. While the Courts initially gained respect and support from local people as they brought security to Mogadishu and other areas, this was relatively short-lived. Soon, as Menkhaus put it,

> Somalis were torn between their desire to support a movement that brought calm to the capital for the first time in 15 years, and fear that the same movement was beginning to replicate many of the same authoritarian tendencies at home and ill-considered clashes with Ethiopia that had proved so disastrous under the Siad Barre regime.[24]

The ICU regime proved to be short-lived. Ethiopia attacked Somalia in late 2006 and quickly toppled the ICU, but the invasion had many unintended consequences. While it achieved the objective of chasing the Islamic Courts out of the capital, the most radicalized element of the Courts, the Al-Shabaab (youth) movement took on the role of main opposition to the newly re-installed TFG. The Ethiopian invasion also led to the mobilization of the diaspora and many others in support of Al-Shabaab, seen as defending against a traditional enemy.[25] Fierce fighting between Al-Shabaab and the TFG and Ethiopian (and eventually African Union) forces led to the large-scale flight of people from Mogadishu, most of whom took refuge around Afgooye, northwest of the city. Conditions in Afgooye were so bad that it was dubbed the "world's worst humanitarian crisis" in early 2008. It also led to the flight of financial capital to Nairobi, Kenya.

The History of Humanitarian Crisis and the Political Economy of Aid

Humanitarian emergencies of varying degrees of severity underscored the vulnerability of Somali populations to various hazards throughout this period, some of which were "natural" (flooding and drought) and some of which were man-made (conflict or displacement). Several need to be understood to put the 2011–12 famine in perspective.

"Abaar": The 1974–5 Drought in Northern Somalia

In the early to mid-1970s, just prior to the Somalia–Ethiopia War, a prolonged drought affected much of the Sahel; it brought about a large-scale famine in Wollo in Ethiopia and also affected Somalia. The worst of the drought's impact was in 1974, but Siad Barre's socialist experiment, combined with political opposition mainly from northern clans, turned the drought into a famine. During the nationalization process, the government closed certain trade routes and introduced tight export controls in the northern port of Berbera. The government had also introduced price controls and cereal rationing, both of which seriously affected food availability in markets. This left over a million drought-affected pastoralists in northern Somalia with little alternative but to buy exorbitantly priced food on the black market.[26] Some 250,000 ended up in relief camps, with many more receiving government assistance of one kind or another. International relief organizations did not play a major role in responding to the crisis, but the Barre government did receive assistance—notably from the USSR and Sweden, as well as a few other countries. An estimated 18,000 people died in the famine, along with an estimated 1 million head of cattle and half a million small ruminants.[27] Given the extent of the losses, Gunnar Haaland and Willem Keddeman suggest that some large-scale redistribution of livestock took place between those who survived the drought without large-scale animal losses and those who had lost practically everything.[28]

The interpretation of this disaster varies widely—Ismail Ahmed and Reginald Green attribute most of the negative outcomes to the unintended impacts of the Barre regime's attempts to socialize the economy of Somalia. Basil Davidson, on the other hand, notes that the government played a vital role in protecting life and dealing with the post-famine consequences of a large number of pastoralists losing their livestock and claims that the episode had a "happy ending."[29] It is true that the loss of "only" 18,000 people is considerably less than in subsequent crises and likewise true that the Barre government handled most of the relief effort itself. The contrast at the time with the way in which the Ethiopian regime of Haile Selassie bungled its attempt to deal with the effects of the same drought, was notable: the Wollo famine of 1974 resulted in the deaths of an estimated 250,000 people, and was ultimately a significant factor in the overthrow of the emperor by the Derg a year later.[30]

However, little doubt remains that the experimentation of the Barre regime in centralized management of the pastoral economy was at least partly to blame for the exacerbation of the impact of the drought, and indeed the "happy ending" Davidson refers to included the resettlement of 100,000 former pastoralists in riverine areas of South Central Somalia—a fate enthusiastically embraced, Davidson implies, by the herd-less pastoralists. Ahmed and Green suggest they were coerced into becoming farmers by the Barre regime that was eager to sedentarize northern clans to keep them under control. Either way, some 100,000 former pastoralists from the Darood clans were resettled in the Lower Shabelle and Middle Juba Valleys—among the most fertile of the riverine areas of the south, and traditionally inhabited by Rahanweyn and Somali Bantu groups. The displacement of these groups from some of their traditional lands was to play an increasingly important role in the impact of both the 1992 and the 2011 famines.

Few other parallels exist between the famine of 1974 and the famines of 1992 and 2011; the focus in 1974 was on northern pastoralists within a relatively stable political context, whereas the following two famines were focused in the south, among similar ethnic population groups and where conflict and insecurity provided much of the context. The refugee crisis that followed the Ogaden (i.e., Ethiopian–Somali) War in 1977–8 would provide more parallels—both in terms of the scale of the crisis, the political nature of the causes, and the manipulation of aid.

War and Famine, 1991–2

Over 200,000 people are estimated to have died in the famine of 1992 in southern Somalia.[31] The dynamics of this famine were driven by the collapse of the central state and the resultant civil war, which disadvantaged particular population groups. However, de Waal emphasizes that the process of rural impoverishment began in 1988 with forcible land alienation, drought, and a breakdown of basic social services that were part of the more general decline of the government during the 1980s.[32]

An important parallel between the famines of 1991–2 and 2011 was their geographic and social focus on the riverine and inter-riverine areas of southern

Somalia, in contrast to the focus on northern camel pastoralists during the 1974–5 famine. The agricultural and agro-pastoral areas of the Juba and Shabelle river valleys, and the rain-fed inter-riverine areas, were home to the majority of the famine-affected populations in both of these more recent famines,[33] the Rahanweyn and Somali Bantu. De Waal describes these two groups as, respectively, second-class and third-class citizens in Somalia. They have had little political representation over time, as well as limited opportunities in government employment and in education. These groups also differ culturally from the majority Somali clans and speak a different dialect.[34]

Drought was not a major cause of the 1991–2 famine; rather, "the famine had its origins in the collapse of the state and the general disintegration of law and order that contributed to an economy of sustained plunder."[35] De Waal, who has written most extensively on this famine, identifies complementary causal factors including battles between the more powerful clan-based militias, where local assets including food stores and livestock were looted. In addition, these minority groups were least able to access relief resources because of their status and the control and diversion of aid by more powerful clans and militias.[36] De Waal also distinguishes between dynamics in the Shabelle Valley and Juba Valley, as well as between the valleys and the Bay region. He notes that the riverine valley areas, where the Somali Bantu are primarily located (along with Rahanweyn clans), were hit earlier than the Bay region, in part because many people had been displaced from Mogadishu to these relatively rich agricultural areas. These areas then became the focus of conflict and looting between competing groups. In addition, these areas were known to be highly productive, as they remain today, and therefore also attracted seasonal laborers, increasing the numbers and depleting food stocks.

While the fighting in the river valleys took place during much of 1991, Bay region was relatively calm, and famine only developed in Bay much later in the year and into 1992, after fighting resumed. Within Bay region, a very large and heavily populated region, home of the Rahanweyn, the famine was localized, with estimates of up to 40 percent of villages affected.[37] De Waal notes that it was "fear, not hunger [that] drove the people away."[38] There was large-scale displacement from the most-affected areas, but little change in others. The major centres hosting displaced populations were Mogadishu, Baidoa, Lower Shabelle, and Kismayo. Relatively few famine-displaced from the river valleys and Bay region went to Kenya or Ethiopia—most of the displaced in Kenya were urban populations from the major clans.

In terms of humanitarian responses to the 1992 famine, de Waal highlights local efforts and the interventions of the Somalia Red Crescent and the

ICRC. In contrast, he is highly critical of the failure of the United Nations,[39] and presents a mixed picture of international NGOs. De Waal credits the impartiality of the ICRC and the importance of its partnership with the Somali Red Crescent Society and other local committees and voluntary groups. This approach is contrasted with that of the UN, identified as taking minimal physical and institutional risks and limiting its presence on the ground.[40] This provides a very interesting parallel with the nature of the humanitarian response in 2011. Looting and diversion of aid, particularly food aid, was a major problem and challenge from 1991 onwards that affected all organizations. Food aid operations were subject to direct diversion, where militia groups targeted communities that had received aid, making vulnerable populations difficult to reach and contributing to the war economy.[41]

Humanitarian Crises in the Post-UN Era

An El Niño event affected the Greater Horn of Africa in 1997–8, resulting in widespread flooding in both the Juba and Shabelle river valleys and a widespread relief effort to address the aftermath. The subsequent La Niña event had consequences for other parts of the Horn of Africa more than for Somalia. The rains failed in Ethiopia in 1999 and early 2000, resulting in a widening crisis that came to a head in 2000, and which affected much of the Somali National Regional State (or the Ogaden). The effects of this drought were relatively less severe in Somalia itself, although pastoral groups in the border areas and in Somaliland were badly hit. One of the main results in Ethiopia was that food assistance was significantly delayed, largely because of political constraints—a theme that was to repeat itself several more times in the Horn of Africa.[42] However, when food aid deliveries eventually caught up, excess food aid found its way from eastern Ethiopia into grain markets in the Bay, Bakool, and Hiraan regions of Somalia, leading to a collapse of sorghum prices there.[43]

The "Mandera Triangle" drought affected parts of northeastern Kenya, southeastern Ethiopia, and southwestern Somalia beginning in 2004 but intensifying quickly in the aftermath of the failure of the *deyr* rains in late 2005.[44] By 2005, a handful of interventions operating in Ethiopia and Kenya were beginning to incorporate the notion of "crisis modifiers"[45] or other means of rapidly mitigating a worsening situation due to drought or other hazards. However, the Mandera Triangle drought was the primary exemplar of early warning and late response in the early twenty-first century: large-scale improvements had been made in pastoral early warning—going back to the 1999–2000 drought—but without the concomitant links to contingency planning or mitigation. A range of interventions to protect pastoral livelihoods was in place, but not implemented.[46] These interventions were subsequently codified as the Livestock Emergency Guidelines and Standards.[47]

Scattered rainfall failure, seriously compounded by the impact of the 2008 global food price crisis, led to a major scaling up of emergency food assistance in 2008 and 2009—the largest-scale food aid operation Somalia had seen since the 1991–2 famine. The United States was among the largest, most consistent donors of food aid in Somalia during this period. Menkhaus describes the period from 2007 to 2008 as "a calamity of enormous proportions for the country, arguably as bad as the disastrous civil war and famine of 1991–92."[48] Menkhaus is very critical of foreign political intervention in this period, describing it as achieving exactly the opposite of what the United States and its allies wanted in terms of ousting the Courts.[49] This period had profound implications for the famine of 2011. The fragile economy of southern Somalia collapsed.[50]

The Political Economy of Aid

Simons argues that the "avalanche of aid" that started in the 1970s was a major factor in the Siad Barre regime's shift from a focus on national interests to self-survival and self-enrichment.[51] Large amounts of bilateral aid from this period led to a swollen civil service. The Somalia–Ethiopia War of 1977–8 led to an enormous inflow of refugees, estimated at 1.5 million people, and an equally enormous inflow of aid—particularly food aid—to support them.[52] This aid response ultimately provided (illicit) income and opportunities for government officials, employees of aid agencies, profiteers and opportunists, as well as the refugees themselves. Simons argues that all became, to some degree, "dependent" on this source of income. Inflating the figures for need and diverting resources became common practice and sometimes happened on a large scale. By the 1980s, developmental and humanitarian aid to Somalia accounted for over 70 percent of the state's resources.[53] This legacy led Somalis to adopt certain attitudes: "aid should be supplied without conditions," and "a lack of accountability is considered innate to foreign aid."[54] Lee Cassanelli notes that foreign aid, including refugee relief, development aid, and military assistance, has long been a target of Somalia's power seekers and opportunists.[55] In the admittedly resource-scarce environments that humanitarian emergencies in Somalia take place, humanitarian aid is a significant resource, one frequently fought over and diverted from its intended use, a practice that has long been tolerated and considered part of the price of doing business. The report of the

UN Monitoring Group for Somalia and Eritrea emphasized the full depth of this problem in 2010 by suggesting that up to half the food aid in South Central Somalia was being diverted to unintended uses or recipients.[56]

The Normalization of Crisis in Somalia

The combined effect of repeated shocks, delayed responses, and ever-shortening recovery periods between shocks, underpinned by a growing environmental crisis, led to the slow-motion weakening of livelihoods across virtually all areas of South Central Somalia. Repeated annual reports of high levels of malnutrition and food security had already—in fact, years before—led to the notion of the "normalization of crisis" in Somalia. This is a state in which the international humanitarian community, as well as development agencies, donors, and the fledgling state in Somalia, simply tolerated extreme levels of human deprivation that would have motivated all of them to move rapidly in other circumstances.[57] Mark Bradbury argued that the combined impact of beliefs about "aid dependency" and arguments about "local solutions to local problems" led to a reduced interest in humanitarian problems and greater interest in "sustainable development" even in wartime and put the primary onus for this development on local communities themselves. This provided the pretext for international withdrawal from places like Somalia and denial of responsibility for humanitarian emergencies there.[58]

Displacement, Migration, and Diaspora

Displacement and migration have long been features of the Somali landscape connecting Somalis within the region (Somalia, Ethiopia, Kenya, and Djibouti) as well as farther afield. The oil boom in the Middle East in the 1970s and 1980s (where large numbers of Somalis went to work), the Somali–Ethiopian War, and the 1988–92 Somali civil war are all major episodes involving mass outmigration and generating new remittance flows and connections.[59] Over 1 million people were displaced during the Somali civil war, mostly within the country, but many fled to Kenya, resulting in a major shift in Somali demography. Today, many cities in North America, Europe, and Australia are known for their large Somali populations. By 2001, UNDP was reporting that one in six Somalis were in the diaspora (in both neighboring as well as more distant countries).[60] Much of this movement has been enabled through kinship ties, through which families remain connected in their new transnational form—and this also has clan-based identity patterns. The diaspora are sometimes described as "near" (generally East Africa and the Middle East) and "far" (generally Europe, North America, and Australia).[61] These locations have implications for their disposable remittance income.

Migration and the emergence of a large Somalian diaspora are very much associated with the "major" clans—not the Rahanweyn and Somali Bantu, who did not have the same access to education and employment opportunities, or to the networks that enabled migration to the Middle East and later to Europe, North America, and elsewhere. There is limited research on the links between clan identity and migration patterns, and there are certainly representatives of both of these social groups in various diaspora locations—but their relative numbers and wealth are much more limited than for the "major" clans.

The role of the diaspora was increasingly prominent and recognized through the 1990s and 2000s. By 2008, the value of remittances to Somalia from the diaspora was an estimated $500 million to $1 billion per year. This accounts for the largest single portion of the economy.[62] The diaspora is increasingly recognized for its involvement in all walks of life, from development and humanitarian to social and political work.[63] While this diaspora was too young to play a significant role in the famine response in the early 1990s (and in fact, at that point, largely comprised social or clan-based groups other than those most affected), the "trans-nationalization" of Somalis and Somalia would become a more significant feature of the 2011–12 response. It is important to recognize that while this engagement and response is crucial to Somalia in economic terms, many who send money become marginalized groups in their new "host" countries, whether as asylum seekers and refugees or longer-term residents. They are often associated with welfare dependence and unemployment and are affected by loneliness, racism, family tensions, and the difficulties of adjustment.[64]

Against this background, the internal and external political situation was shifting significantly. To put the famine of 2011 in context, it is important to understand these shifts and, in particular, to understand the role of Al-Shabaab and the counter-terrorism regulations that attempted to contain and undermine it.

The Role of Al-Shabaab

Harakat al-Shabaab al Mujahideen (Movement of Warrior Youth, Al-Shabaab) first came to prominence during the brief rule of the ICU government. The movement grew out of the multiple failings of different ideologies to make a viable Somali state, including the failure of democratic governance; of clanism; and of Somali nationalism, Marxism, and wardlordism.[65] In many ways, it was hardly surprising that Islam, and Islamic fundamentalism and jihad, would emerge as a dominant political organizing rubric out of the corrupt, chaotic, and often externally manipulated politics that has characterized at least the southern half of Somalia in recent decades (the area where, perhaps not surprisingly, Al-Shabaab has been most influential). Stig Jarle Hansen notes that, "By the late 2000s, Islam was the only belief system in Somalia that had not been discredited, and citizens went to religious leaders with their needs for protection."[66] Al-Shabaab's rise challenged the established order in Somalia on many fronts, including its engagement with the international community in general and humanitarian aid agencies in particular. Al-Shabaab to some degree also challenged the clan system; to some degree it was hostage to the clan system (as is nearly any political actor in Somalia); and to some degree, it tried to turn it on its head—by promoting some of the marginal clans and by recruiting fighters from those clans.

However, over time, its use of suicide bombing as a tactic inside Somalia, its brutal enforcement of its version of Islamic law, its unaccountable police force, and its generally repressive rule have undermined its popularity and legitimacy. Nevertheless, Al-Shabaab—and the role it played in the famine of 2011—is more complex than the one-dimensional accounts in the popular press.[67] Al-Shabaab was by no means the only armed non-state actor resisting the TFG in the period leading up to the famine, nor the only Islamist group. Hizbul Islam, formed by the union of smaller groups in 2009 (before being largely absorbed into Al-Shabaab), and other groups were also active. Yet Al-Shabaab was by far the biggest, and the focus of most of the international attention.[68]

Al-Shabaab had played a role in subduing various warlords and clan-based militias in southern Somalia during the rise of the ICU government in 2006. But the Ethiopian invasion of Somalia in late 2006 set the stage for the rise of Al-Shabaab's power—without that external threat, the ground would not have been ripe for such a radical movement. Indeed, the Ethiopian invasion also helped to radicalize Al-Shabaab and certainly paved the path to its ascendance as a political/military force within Somalia.[69] Between 2006 and 2008, the group's membership grew substantially from a few hundred to several thousand, and its links to Al-Qaeda became more prominent. Much of the emphasis has been on Al-Shabaab's international role and, in this case, its antipathy towards international humanitarian aid. But initially it had a nationalist agenda as opposed to the clan-based loyalties that had dominated Somalia.

Over time, it gradually took on an internationalist jihadist agenda as well. These objectives correspond to some degree to the origins of the individual members—and Al-Shabaab did and does have foreign fighters and foreign operatives, some of whom have Somali origins, some not.[70]

Al-Shabaab Rule

Al-Shabaab was initially a fighting force, and questions remain as to whether it initially aimed to administer territory.[71] Nevertheless, in the aftermath of the war against the Ethiopians, Al-Shabaab was the de facto local authority in much of South Central Somalia including Mogadishu. A 2010 Human Rights Watch report labeled life under Al-Shabaab rule as entailing "peace and security—for a price."[72] After the chaotic warlord period, and the war against the Ethiopian army, the early period of Al-Shabaab rule was indeed more peaceful, with better security at the local level compared to what had previously been the case. However, Al-Shabaab maintained order and security through a climate of fear, public executions, and arbitrary interference in people's personal lives, from regulating dress to the contents on cellphones. They were especially harsh about restricting the freedom and role of women. Women were barred from commerce or other activities that would put them in contact with men other than their husbands.[73] Yet, at the same time, Al-Shabaab fighters were also implicated in rape and violence against women and girls—referring to rape victims as "temporary wives."[74] Al-Shabaab implemented harsh punishments for crimes (including amputation for theft and the death penalty for apostasy). It also violated numerous elements of international humanitarian law, such as the use of indiscriminate attacks and human shields (however, the same Human Rights Watch report that documents these abuses by Al-Shabaab also documents many of the same practices by the TFG and AMISOM).[75]

Much of the information about Al-Shabaab came from cities that were accessible to journalists and other observers. In rural areas, a number of other factors shaped Al-Shabaab's rule, particularly during the famine and in the period leading to it. First, information was restricted: a number of informants from Islamic NGOs and the private sector (who would have been in a position to help) claimed that little information was coming out of some of the worst hit areas under Al-Shabaab control in the lead up to the famine, contributing to a later response than may otherwise have been the case. While the group did set up a "Drought Committee" in 2010, which provided some support to selected people, its role was very mixed.[76] Second, mobility was restricted. As the food security situation deteriorated, Al-Shabaab imposed restrictions on people moving out of their areas, including to access aid provided by Western donors. People who did attempt to leave in search of employment or aid had to take longer routes out of Al-Shabaab-controlled areas to avoid being stopped, which would have increased time and cost. Tales of being stopped were common among refugees in Dollo-Ado, and people reported resorting to walking through the bush to avoid Al-Shabaab checkpoints along the roads.[77] Third, in some areas, Al-Shabaab blocked trade in areas retaken by Kenyan or Ethiopian/AMISOM forces, areas which saw higher food prices as a result. Much of North Gedo was affected by such a blockade in mid-2011.[78]

Taxation

Probably no issue undermined Al-Shabaab's legitimacy (and worsened the impact of the famine) more than its taxation policies. Al-Shabaab relied heavily on the export of charcoal extracted from southern Somalia to the Persian Gulf via the Kismayo port. This unsustainable practice, which has existed since the early 1990s, reportedly earned Al-Shabaab millions of dollars in profits.[79] However, from relatively early on, Al-Shabaab raised a considerable part of its revenue from taxing not only the urban business community but also rural production.

In relation to the rural economy, crop production was taxed during the planting season as well as during the harvest—many interviewees reported having being charged to plant their fields. At harvest, the usual time for contributing *zakat* to the poor,[80] Al-Shabaab took over the role claiming it would redistribute *zakat* (respondents often reported not seeing any evidence of such redistribution). Al-Shabaab also claimed ad hoc contributions over time, justifying this as "jihad" or as defense against a forthcoming attack. Even weddings were taxed.[81]

Livestock owners were also subject to the same set of taxes—*zakat* contributions and ad hoc contributions as well as a transaction tax on all market exchange. In the urban economy, both small and large businesses were taxed. While many of these practices appear to have been widespread and affected nearly all businesses in Al-Shabaab-controlled areas, taxes served to identify willing supporters. The wealthy and those who were less (ideologically) sympathetic were also targeted for contributions. A rural household "tax" was required as well, with the threat that one of the sons might be taken as a fighter if the tax was not paid, "a thinly veiled form of forced conscription."[82]

These taxation measures altered the redistribution mechanisms within society by extracting a significant proportion of household and aggregate wealth, and they also contributed to the reduction in the number of wealthy households in many areas (as these people left), which in turn shrank the wider social safety net during the crisis of 2011.[83] Some evidence can be found that the increased taxation on rural production contributed to riskier cropping and livestock production practices that ultimately made people more vulnerable to the crisis.[84] These risky cropping practices primarily involved the increased planting and production of sesame over several years in Bay region, which may have contributed both to reduced stores and lower production of sorghum in these areas.

Significant numbers of people had begun moving out of Al-Shabaab-controlled areas into Dadaab, Kenya, throughout 2010, prior to the famine, for a variety of reasons, including Al-Shabaab's taxation and recruitment practices, and people's low expectations for the future in terms of the economy and "opportunities."[85] Migrants included not only vulnerable people at risk in the famine but also better-off people who had traditionally been part of the local safety net by providing opportunities for casual employment or even through outright assistance.

With revenue streams from the taxation of trade and exports, Al-Shabaab as a whole was relatively less dependent on aid, but local Al-Shabaab leaders could personally profit through locally enforced "taxation" methods.[86] Starting in mid-2010, the group reorganized and extended its reach beyond major urban centres under the direction of its own "humanitarian coordinators" and "head of the Office of Zakat." These regional coordinators began imposing strict controls, including aggressive taxation efforts. In 2011, Al-Shabaab lost control over both the Bakhara market in Mogadishu and the port in Kismayo. This increased pressure on other sources of revenue, and indeed during this period Al-Shabaab's attempts to extract greater revenues out of aid agencies became more pronounced.

Counter-Terrorism in the Greater Horn of Africa

At least since the embassy bombings in Nairobi and Dar es Salaam in August 1998, and particularly after the attacks in the United States on September 11, 2001, counter-terrorism objectives have been a major impetus behind international engagement in the Greater Horn of Africa. The United States based a Combined Joint Task Force in Djibouti beginning in 2002, with the aim of preventing Somalia from being used as a base for terrorism. Outside of Somalia itself, but among Somali-speaking populations in Kenya and Ethiopia, the objective of the task force was to "win hearts and minds through the delivery of humanitarian and developmental aid"—part of a broader counter-terrorism strategy.[87] Islamic jihadist groups had long been suspected of taking advantage of the relatively "ungoverned spaces" of South Central Somalia as a conducive operating environment. But for a number of years the concern was limited to relatively small groups, such as Al-Itihaad al-Islamiya and other groups with a jihadist agenda but largely local grievances. With the demise of the ICU government in the aftermath of the Ethiopian invasion, Al-Shabaab rapidly increased its influence in South Central Somalia by being the only group to resist the Ethiopians successfully. In the beginning, Al-Shabaab was believed to hold mainly a Somalia-focused agenda, but its engagement against the Ethiopians as well as the increasing presence of foreign jihadis eventually broadened its agenda.[88]

In February 2008, the US Department of State listed Al-Shabaab as a Foreign Terrorist Organization. The US Treasury Department, which operates the Office of Foreign Asset Control (OFAC), followed suit. The OFAC listing makes any transaction with a proscribed organization a crime. In Somalia, this included the incidental diversion of assistance that subsequently fell into Al-Shabaab's hands. The diversion of aid has long been a part of the war economy in Somalia—one that the aid business has struggled to control. Later in the same year, in October 2008, Al-Shabaab forced two US-based NGOs to withdraw from South Central Somalia, including CARE International, which had been one of the major providers of emergency food aid in Somalia since the 1992–3 famine. The management and logistics of food aid in South Central Somalia had long been fraught with difficulties, and few agencies had the capacity—or the stomach—to take on such a role. CARE's expulsion took place during a serious food security crisis, due in part to high food prices globally. When CARE was expelled, WFP was able to take over most of the food aid operations that CARE left, and no major gaps in food distribution occurred immediately—a situation that was dramatically different later on when WFP was also forced to withdraw. The UN Security Council adopted Resolution 1844 later in 2008, which sanctioned individuals or organizations threatening "the peace and stability of Somalia, by opposing the TNG or AMISOM" and which particularly targeted Al-Shabaab.[89]

In November 2009, the United States shut down its entire food aid pipeline to South Central Somalia. This was justified on the fears of food falling into

Al-Shabaab's hands and was therefore framed as complying with OFAC regulations. At the time, WFP was investigating charges that some of its transporters had been diverting large amounts of food aid, thus providing some grounds for the United States to be worried about OFAC compliance. However, the timing of the shutdown suggested to some observers that more than just aid diversion was involved. Al-Shabaab had been on the OFAC list for almost two years by the time food aid was shut off, and for years it had practically gone without saying that some amount of food aid was going to be diverted—certainly aid diversion in Somalia was not new news in 2009. However, the shutdown of food assistance into areas controlled by Al-Shabaab coincided with a planned offensive by TFG and AMISOM forces, and at the time there was an effort to enlist humanitarian agencies to provide support to civilians in areas retaken by the TFG. Of course, no link could ever be confirmed between the aid cut-off and the AMISOM offensive. Whatever the motive, WFP's pipeline was cut by 40 percent overnight. In the end, the TFG/AMISOM offensive failed to recapture any significant territory in 2009 or early 2010.

WFP later suspended all of its operations in South Central Somalia, officially citing security threats, though privately there were also concerns about its inability to control where its assistance went, and legal fears about the consequences of it ending up in Al-Shabaab's hands.[90] In early 2010, the UN Monitoring Group confirmed what everyone already knew: large amounts of food aid had indeed been going astray in South Central Somalia, although the level of diversion they reported came as something of a shock.[91] They claimed as much as half of the food aid in South Central Somalia was being diverted from its intended purpose. At the time funding was cut, WFP itself sought to downplay the notion of any dispute with its major donor, but the UN humanitarian coordinator for Somalia subsequently accused the United States of politicizing its assistance, making operations more difficult—even in places that the UN or other humanitarian agencies could still reach.[92] At a minimum, by making operating in Al-Shabaab-controlled areas impossible, donors were seen as undermining the principle of impartiality. It is worth noting that the handful of international agencies still able to operate in the most fraught contexts in South Central Somalia by this time were those that unfailingly prioritized this principle (underlining a point made by de Waal in reference to the 1991–2 famine).[93]

In June 2010, the US Supreme Court upheld the US government's attempts to prevent the Humanitarian Law Project from engaging in training on international humanitarian law and conflict resolution to two listed terrorist organizations, maintaining that this constituted "material support" to these organizations.[94] The Court found that even this kind of assistance could help to "legitimate" terrorist organizations, or enable other resources to be used for terrorist activities.[95] The case had nothing directly to do with Somalia, but the implications were immediately obvious to anyone working on Somalia at the time. UN Security Council Resolution 1916, passed in March 2010, created a so-called humanitarian "carve-out," stating that the provisions of its earlier resolution did not apply to "urgently needed humanitarian assistance in Somalia." Some observers believed that this sufficiently acknowledged the difficulties—and the relative priority—of delivering humanitarian assistance in Somalia.[96] But while this created some space for some agencies and some donors, it didn't fully address the problem. US agencies and any agency receiving US funding were still quite worried about US law—irrespective of any UN resolutions.

None of the issues that arose in Somalia in 2010 were new: the politicization of aid, the diversion of food and other aid, the limited humanitarian access, the deteriorating security situation for humanitarian agency staff, or the increasing tendency towards the remote management of aid. But the events of 2009 and 2010 helped to set the stage for the famine of 2011: first, neither of the two major food aid agencies was able to operate in South Central Somalia—the only agency still operating there with the capacity to move food aid on any scale was the International Committee of the Red Cross. Second, and perhaps equally tellingly, the stage had been set for a long-running standoff between donors and agencies around the interpretation and implementation of counter-terrorism laws that would have a significant effect on humanitarian action. This went far beyond its impact on food aid alone and would not really be addressed until the famine had already claimed tens of thousands of lives—and in fact the underlying issues are still far from resolved.

It was, of course, perfectly within both the letter and spirit of international humanitarian law for a donor to require guarantees that assistance not be diverted by or to a belligerent party in a conflict. But the strict interpretation of this requirement tended to fly in the face of twenty-plus years of some degree of relative acceptance of the realities on the ground in Somalia (as well as other countries such as Afghanistan and South Sudan, where some degree of aid diversion had long been tolerated as part of the cost of engagement), and raised the specter of criminal punishment for individuals and agencies associated with diverted aid. The counter-terrorism laws were the most clearly stated in the case of US assistance, but Canada, the UK, Australia, the EU, and many Western European donor countries all had statutes of some kind and all listed Al-Shabaab as a terrorist group by 2010. But in the end, the US statutes were those that caused the most concern. Preventing the "leakage" of aid was seen in humanitarian circles as not only being impossible to guarantee, given the circumstances, but also as directly undermining the principle of impartiality because it made working in any area under Al-Shabaab influence—let alone Al-Shabaab control—nearly impossible. This included almost all of southern Somalia and large areas of central Somalia as well. Much of this area was already in a humanitarian emergency throughout this period.[97]

Setting the Stage for Famine

Nothing that happened in the time period from 2006 to 2010 necessarily preordained a famine in 2011, but almost all the bits of the history discussed here contributed to both the emergence and the severity of a crisis that really began to bite in late 2010. The combination of natural and man-made hazards in the Somali context, the political economy of aid, the constant attempts to "capture" aid by various Somali actors, the rise of Al-Shabaab and its policies, and the concomitant rise of counter-terrorism regulations intended to contain groups like Al-Shabaab, all played a part in setting the stage for the famine of 2011–12. The next chapter lays out the early warning of 2010–11 and describes the dimensions of the famine.

4

THE WORSENING CRISIS, THE DELAY,
AND THE IMPACT OF THE FAMINE

Early Warning 2010–11

As noted in Chapter 2, the development of early warning systems is one of the great achievements in famine prevention. Building on the observation that famines are the result of predictable trends, early warning systems have sought to identify and track these trends since the 1970s. These include rainfall and weather patterns where drought is a major hazard, but follow food production and prices more generally, as well as patterns of employment, income, and access to adequate food by vulnerable groups, and other trends related to the ability of vulnerable populations to earn an adequate livelihood.

The Somali famine had multiple causes, some of which were very straight-forward to predict—in particular, the La Niña-related drought in the Horn of Africa—some of them less so, particularly the food price volatility and the course of the fighting between the TFG/AMISOM and Al-Shabaab. Some of the main complicating factors were well known well in advance of the crisis and in fact, did not vary much in the run-up to the crisis (the policies of Al-Shabaab, the absence of WFP and other major food aid actors, the counter-terrorism restrictions). In the Real-Time Evaluations undertaken, early warning (EW) information was generally considered "accurate and timely" across the region.[1] The main sources of this information were the FEWSNET, which is global, and the Somalia Food Security and Nutrition Analysis Unit (FSNAU). They collaborate closely to produce Somalia-specific information.

However, by 2013–14, some of the key parties involved in the response were beginning to express doubts retrospectively about the quality and certainty of that information, suggesting that the information was inadequate, contradictory, and probabilistic,[2] or didn't lead to decision-making. FEWSNET and FSNAU published regular reports and continued to do so over the period from August 2010 to the declaration of the famine. Beyond their regular reporting, they issued sixteen additional special bulletins or other early warning flashes over that period. These began with reporting the severity of the short season (*deyr*) rain failure (September–December 2010) in much of the Greater Horn of Africa, but became more specific and more alarming over time.[3] Some fifty briefings were given to donors, UN agencies, and other partners by the two EW organizations between August 2010 and the declaration of famine in July 2011.[4]

In late 2010 and early 2011, the epicentre of the evolving crisis appeared to be in the central regions of Galgadud and Mudug, rather than the riverine and inter-riverine areas in South Central Somalia that were ultimately the hardest hit by the famine. This understanding of the situation—that central Somalia was more affected than the south—continued right up to the point the famine was declared.[5] It was not until a month or so prior to the declaration of famine that the focal point of the widening crisis was identified as actually being Bay, Bakool, and Lower Shabelle regions, rather than in Mudug and Galgadud. Given the amount of information made available, it is difficult to argue that early warning information was insufficient. However, had a major response been mounted earlier, it might have focused disproportionately on areas of central Somalia that, ultimately, were less badly affected. This problem was identified early on in the post-crisis analysis of EW information, but it should be remembered that all of South Central Somalia was firmly controlled by Al-Shabaab, and regular information collection, while it did continue, was more difficult to update in these areas.

However, other, more complex explanations emerged for the locus of the humanitarian disaster shifting to other regions. These relate to the identity, livelihoods, and resources that distinguish the more powerful Hawiye clans in the Central Regions State where the crisis initially seemed to be concentrated from the Rahanweyn and Somali Bantu groups that were ultimately more severely affected. The groups in the Central Regions were able to mobilize significant responses through their own means, including temporary hosting by urban kin of struggling rural pastoralists (the former had more remittance or other non-rural income), as well as mobilizing significant diaspora and business-related resources. The diversification of these clans, in itself a reflection of their political power, made this possible—and made it possible to get these resources into Al-Shabaab-controlled areas.[6]

In addition to being able to raise significant resources and negotiate assistance through Al-Shabaab, it was rogue members of the same clans that were later enriching themselves through the capture of humanitarian aid that was arriving in Mogadishu to support the IDPs coming from the Lower Shabelle and Bay regions, who were largely made up of the Rahanweyn and Bantu.[7]

In retrospect, information on terms of trade for food probably provided the clearest and most sustainable indication of how bad the situation was. The terms of trade is an appealingly simple measure of wellbeing, requiring little information other than simply noting prices and daily wage rates in local markets. It is a measure of the relative value of what people could sell compared to the price of the food they needed to buy. In Somalia, ordinary people either had livestock or their own labor to sell, and they had to purchase staple foods. With good rains in the first half of 2010, the demand for labor was high and the price of food was relatively low. Given these conditions, the demand for livestock was high as well. The failure of the *deyr* rains led to a rapid decline in demand for labor and an increase in the price of food locally, which coincided disastrously with a global spike in food prices. Somalia is dependent on food imports even in good years; in a bad year locally, a global price spike—as already witnessed in 2008—could have devastating effects. The terms of trade for both small ruminants to food, and labor to food, collapsed in late 2010 and didn't recover until after the famine had been declared. The global Food Price Index maintained by the UN Food and Agriculture Organization was increasing rapidly in the latter half of 2010 and peaked at an all-time high in early to mid-2011. This coincided with a collapse of the value of items Somalis had to sell. Figure 4.1 depicts the kilograms of grain that a day's labor would purchase in the three hardest hit regions of Somalia.[8]

Note that whereas a day's labor would purchase an average 6–8 kilograms of grain during the first eight months of 2010, this figure drops to about 2.5 by early 2011. Figure 4.2 depicts the same information for small ruminants—sheep and goats. These are the most commonly kept livestock by lower-income people, and by both pastoralist and agro-pastoralist livelihood groups.

The sale of an average goat in Bay region in mid-2010 would have purchased 300 kilograms of grain; by early 2011, a goat was worth only about 50 kilograms. Even in the Lower Shabelle region where the decline was less precipitous, the value of a goat in 2011 was only half of what it had been in 2010.

Figure 4.1: Terms of Trade: Labor and Grain, 2010–12

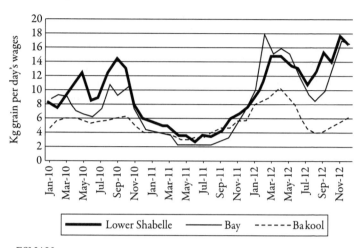

Data: FSNAU.

Figures 4.2: Terms of Trade: Goats and Grain, 2010–12

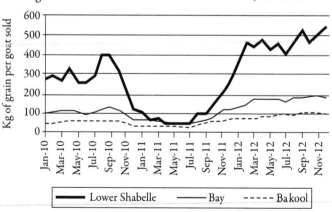

Data: FSNAU.

The key point is not so much the severity of a drop in terms of trade as it is the longevity of a drop as resources and coping strategies are quickly exhausted during periods of poor terms of trade. Figures 4.1 and 4.2 make it clear this began with the failure of the *deyr* rains in 2010, and continued right through to the declaration of famine (at which time the global price of food began to drop; local conditions began to change soon thereafter with the return of the *deyr* in September–October 2011). The precipitous decline in late 2010, combined with the duration of this decline, is what spelled disaster for the lowest-income groups across South Central Somalia—and even for many better-off people. This resulted in many reports of widely differing perceptions of the context and the severity of the crisis locally. Hence, many agency staff interviewed in 2013–14 reported confusing and contradictory information about local conditions coming from local partners.

For a number of years, the preference among donors has been growing for "hard data"—that is, information not about predicting future trends, but about real, measurable current conditions.[9] The emerging consensus is that nutritional status is the best single indicator of humanitarian wellbeing, as it captures a wide range of causal factors. But several problems have emerged with this: one is that the prevalence of malnutrition can—and frequently does—reflect multiple causes; without more comprehensive analysis, saying with certainty what the drivers of poor nutrition are in any given situation can be difficult. The second is that nutritional status is a "lagging indicator"—it is only detected after a problem has become very serious. The third is that collecting rigorous nutrition information is an expensive and time-consuming exercise, so sometimes shortcuts are used and sometimes, nutritional information—and especially mortality information—is just not available. With regard to Somalia in 2011, Rebelo et al. note that:

> Decision-makers were unable to clearly demand very large-scale early action due to the confusion and lack of clear nutrition surveillance data or information, or triggers for action between the Deyr and Gu FSNAU reports at a time when, in retrospect, it appears that nutrition status and food insecurity were deteriorating at an unprecedented rate in a very short period ... Given the uncertainty about the situation, the balance of risk versus needs often tipped in favor of the former for decision-making, delaying response.[10]

And early warning information, like any prediction of the future, is, of course, always probabilistic. This concern was raised in donor reports and repeatedly in interviews as an objection to the information available in 2011,[11] but it is self-evident that projections of the future are never certain.

Probability-based climate predictions were made as early as August 2010 (indicating a relatively high likelihood of individual and consecutive poor seasons) and progressed through increasingly dire scenarios and situation analyses over the following months. These early warnings were being raised in the midst of extremely high levels of food insecurity in many parts of southern Somalia, and where the prevalence of malnutrition was already beyond accepted "emergency" thresholds. In terms of early warning and its relation to activating a response, Somalia—like much of the Horn of Africa—presents a classic case where information on humanitarian indicators routinely exceed humanitarian-emergency thresholds, another manifestation of the "normalization of crisis."[12]

Regional Dimensions of the Crisis

By mid-2011, an estimated 13 million people were affected by the food security crisis in the Horn of Africa. Some 4.3 million of these were Kenyans, where malnutrition rates among children in the most affected areas were generally above emergency threshold levels. The government of Kenya was slow to declare an emergency, but a robust, if delayed, response that included significant private as well as public and international funding, combined with lower levels of chronic vulnerability and an existing public safety net, largely avoided excess mortality among Kenyan populations.[13] In addition, Somali pastoralists in northeast Kenya were able to move relatively freely to access water, pasture, and other resources. These resources included aid, as many Kenyan Somalis moved some of their family members to the Dadaab refugee camp.[14]

Likewise, Ethiopia experienced severe drought in the southern and eastern parts of the country. By mid-2011, an estimated 4.5 million Ethiopians were affected by an acute livelihood/food security crisis. Oromiya and Somali regions were the most severely affected and likewise saw increased food insecurity and malnutrition, stress migration, dependence on water trucking, livestock deaths, and risk of disease outbreak. But like Kenya, no major loss of human life occurred among Ethiopian populations during the drought. Ethiopia has a better-developed social protection system—the Productive Safety Net Program or PSNP—along with early provision of an emergency water supply, which were credited with scaling up quickly enough to avert a disaster.[15] In both Kenya and Ethiopia, the main livelihood groups affected by the drought were pastoralists, who to some degree were also able to cope with conditions by moving their herds. This is in contrast to the more agricultural and historically marginalized populations in Somalia that comprised the majority of famine victims in 1992 and 2011. Both Kenya and Ethiopia saw major influxes of refugees—and the plight of the refugees was very different from that of the citizens of Kenya and Ethiopia.

But Somalia was by far the worst hit country, with agro-pastoralist, riverine-farming, and displaced populations being the most affected communities.[16] The back-to-back failure of the rains caused a widespread shortage of water and, subsequently, the worst annual crop production of the previous seventeen years, as well as the loss of grazing for livestock. The shortfalls in crop production, combined with high global food prices, led to record high cereal prices with near-record low livestock and wage prices. As a result of this combination of factors, along with the restrictions of Al-Shabaab, large numbers of children were malnourished, livelihoods were disrupted or destroyed, and a disturbingly high number of people lost their lives. By July, more than half of the entire country's population was affected by crisis. This included 750,000 famine-affected, 3.3 million in need of immediate life-saving assistance, and a total of 4 million in crisis.[17] The Somalia famine resulted in excess mortality of an estimated 258,000 people between October 2010 and April 2012. This overall mortality includes 133,000 children under the age of five. Excess mortality began in late 2010 and peaked in May–September 2011.[18]

Al-Shabaab and Counter-Terrorism Measures

The interactions between Al-Shabaab, the TFG, foreign governments, and aid agencies are critical to understanding the famine and the events that led to it. As noted in Chapter 3, the US State Department listed Al-Shabaab as a "specially designated global terrorist" group in 2008. Many other governments, in particular the Australian, British, and Canadian, quickly followed suit, as did the UN Security Council.[19] In light of these sanctions and the historical role of the UN in the conflict, the humanitarian arm of the UN was perceived by Al-Shabaab as being "political" (i.e., not impartial).[20] This perception made it increasingly difficult for the UN humanitarian agencies to negotiate or maintain humanitarian access, as the UN was seen by Al-Shabaab to be the "most spy-friendly agency."[21] Critical to understanding the famine itself is an understanding of the role played by Al-Shabaab in some of the factors that led to the crisis, in blocking access to aid agencies, and in controlling movement and information during the famine. But equally important is an understanding of the role of counter-terrorism policies put in place to control and undermine Al-Shabaab.

The Timeline to a Famine

In July 2009, Al-Shabaab set up the Office for the Supervision of the Affairs of Foreign Agencies (OSAFA) to monitor the activities of international organizations operating in Somalia—particularly UN agencies and NGOs. Almost immediately, it ordered the closure of several UN offices for engaging in activities "hostile to Islam."[22] By this time, Al-Shabaab controlled significant territory in South Central Somalia, much of which was badly affected by a food security crisis resulting from erratic rainfall and high global food prices.

Al-Shabaab had a long-standing antipathy towards food aid, believing that it was being "dumped" in Somalia, wrecking Somali markets, and undermining self-reliance; it specifically blamed WFP for using food that was spoiled or expired. But the basis of Al-Shabaab's antipathy towards humanitarian agencies ran much deeper than just the food aid issue. Other major disagreements existed, such as the empowerment of women that many agencies explicitly promoted (as well as other areas that Al-Shabaab saw as anti-Islam) and, above all, the fear that aid agencies were integrated into Western intelligence networks. Two US NGOs had already been forced to leave South Central Somalia in 2008 on suspicions of involvement in the killing of Adan Hashi Ayro (an Al-Shabaab leader killed by a hellfire missile from an American drone)—a role the NGOs strongly denied.

Nevertheless, some analysts suggest that, for a period of time, good working relations existed between Al-Shabaab and foreign humanitarian agencies—mostly in 2007–9 after the Ethiopians withdrew and before the AMISOM/TFG offensives of late 2010 and early 2011, when Al-Shabaab controlled significant parts of the territory in which the agencies were working.[23] The transformation of Al-Shabaab from an insurgent movement into a political force that controlled territory meant it had to govern that territory. In this context, the issue of taxation arose,[24] and also of the relationship with, and control over, humanitarian agencies and resources. In many cases, Al-Shabaab provided better security for aid distribution than the TFG or the warlords had, and prevented some of the criminal looting of aid that had been rampant in warlord-controlled areas.[25] But a governance role also meant that Al-Shabaab had to confront the clan system more directly, and required a stronger internal police force. The "Amniyat" or secret police became a force unto themselves—reputedly feared even by Al-Shabaab leaders.[26]

In 2010, Al-Shabaab created a "Drought Committee" within these local administration systems. It was established largely to demonstrate Al-Shabaab's awareness of the risk of drought and its decision to expel humanitarian organi-

Figure 4.3: Map of Somalia Showing Famine-Affected Areas

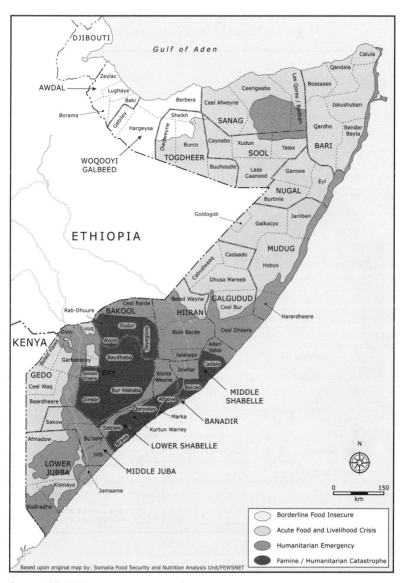

Source: FSNAU.

Figure 4.4: Map of Al-Shabaab-Controlled Areas

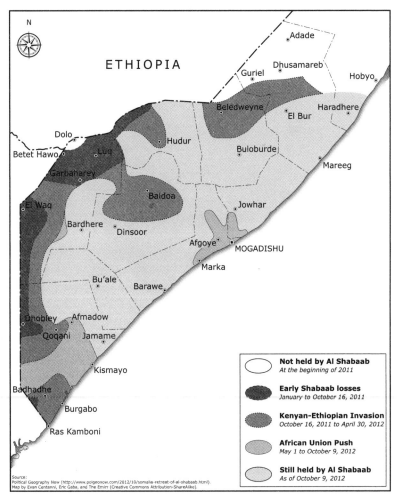

Source: Political Geography Now.

zations in regions under its control. Marchal notes that Al-Shabaab was trying to "regain the sympathy of the population."[27] Taxes collected from salaries, rented homes, and use of public properties were given to the Drought Committee which then distributed cash, food, or clothes to those affected by drought. When these contributions were not enough, Al-Shabaab requested "voluntary contributions" from traders and businesses. However, these efforts did not appease the populace, which grew increasingly discontented with Al-Shabaab's (lack of) response to deteriorating conditions. WFP withdrew from South Central Somalia in response to a variety of threats in late 2009 and Al-Shabaab banned it from returning in early 2010. Seven other agencies were banned in September 2010, further reducing alternate sources of assistance.

A major internal leadership struggle between October 2010 and February 2011 badly weakened Al-Shabaab and undermined central command and control, meaning that it entered the humanitarian crisis of 2010–11 as a weakened and increasingly threatened movement.[28] Negotiations over humanitarian access with a central authority, and which local commanders would subsequently respect, became increasingly difficult. AMISOM started a major offensive on February 22, 2011 in Mogadishu that would eventually drive Al-Shabaab out of the city. But this effectively focused TFG and international attention on military action at the very time the humanitarian situation was spiraling out of control.

Separate offensives against Al-Shabaab by several militias with external support from Kenya and Ethiopia were launched in the first half of 2011, forcing Al-Shabaab into a multi-front war in the run-up to the famine.[29] The fighting in Mogadishu reached a climax in May. In June, an Al-Qaeda leader was killed in Mogadishu, apparently as the result of an accidental wrong turn, not by a strategic strike by AMISOM forces; Osama bin Laden was killed in Pakistan in May. Overall, "the spring of 2011 was thus a time of trouble for Al-Shabaab."[30] Not only did the increased fighting cause more displacement and intensify the humanitarian crisis, it also meant that both Al-Shabaab and the TFG were focused on the fighting, not on the humanitarian crisis—except as a potential source of resources and an opportunity for the manipulation of power.

In August, Al-Shabaab pulled out of Mogadishu, although it continued to conduct hit and run raids in the city. During the response to the famine in the latter half of 2011, both Ethiopia and Kenya invaded Somalia. Kenya invaded Al-Shabaab territory west of the Juba River in Somalia. While the public objective of the incursion was to respond to the kidnapping of Western tourists and aid workers from Kenya, the speculation was that Kenya wanted to create a "buffer territory" in pursuit of their economic goals. Shortly thereafter, Ethiopian forces invaded the Bay, Bakool, and Hiraan regions of Somalia. These military offensives allowed AMISOM to capture territory near Mogadishu, including the Afgooye Corridor.[31]

Thus internal leadership struggles and external assaults from AMISOM and the fledgling Somali National Army, as well as militias connected to neighboring countries, put Al-Shabaab on the defensive and combined with deteriorating relations with humanitarian agencies just at the time that conditions were taking a decided turn for the worse in late 2010 and early 2011. These combined both to worsen the impact of the crisis and make humanitarian access more difficult.

Negotiated Access and Relations with Humanitarian Agencies

As the depth of the food security crisis became clear in mid-2011, Al-Shabaab announced that any group, whether "Muslim or non-Muslim" could provide assistance to the civilian population as long as such groups had "no hidden agenda."[32] But when WFP tried to re-enter South Central Somalia, Al-Shabaab made it clear that they were still banned. They went on to say that while the drought was a problem, the UN famine declaration was "utter nonsense, 100% baseless and sheer propaganda."[33] Al-Shabaab publicly framed engagement with aid agencies in terms of efficiency or security, styling itself as a "government in waiting." Co-opting aid agencies furthered its self-image and demonstrated that it had something positive to offer civilians.[34] At the same time, limiting humanitarian access was seen as part of its "propaganda campaign against the West" and reflected Al-Shabaab's deeply held suspicion of aid agencies as spies or as the enemies' conspirators.[35] Pointing to "misconduct" and "illicit activities," Al-Shabaab's Office for Supervising the Affairs of Foreign Agencies expelled most UN agencies (including UNHCR, WHO, and UNICEF, which had, up to that point, managed to maintain a somewhat separate identity from the more political arms of the UN in Somali, and from WFP) and other major international organizations on November 28, 2011.

Throughout this period, Al-Shabaab not only tried to prevent population movement out of affected areas but also forcibly relocated displaced people within their areas of control or, in some cases, forced people to return to their areas of origin in time for the rains in 2011 so that they could plant crops and help to alleviate the food crisis. Menkhaus notes that these forced relocations amounted to a "death sentence" for some people who were already severely weakened by both the drought and the displacement.[36] While some agencies were granted permits to work in areas under their control, access was granted only through direct negotiation with Al-Shabaab. As part of the access negotiations, aid agencies were required to complete registration forms and, allegedly, to pay fees and sign off on other documentation that laid out general conditions for access, including pledges not to proselytize.[37] In some cases, additional "taxes" were demanded, based on project type or size, and Al-Shabaab attempted to co-opt or control the delivery of aid, especially if activities included distribution of goods. Agencies had to disclose project details (specific activities, budgets, and staff members' names) and their activities were monitored closely. Consequences for breaking rules included expulsion, additional taxes, and attacks on aid workers. Agencies that still had access grappled constantly with the question of whether to accede to Al-Shabaab's ever-tightening control over aid in order to maintain what little contact they had with affected populations.

Counter-terrorism Constraints on Mitigating the Worsening Crisis

This period saw protracted negotiations over how to operate in South Central Somalia within these constraints, and steeply declining US contributions to the humanitarian effort. Internal differences existed between USAID, the State Department, and the Treasury Department over the best way to handle the Somalia crisis. OFAC was portrayed as just a bureaucracy doing its job, but it was pushing a very hard line on Somalia in 2010 and 2011, and this had a chilling effect on the willingness of US agencies (and to some degree, other agencies and US citizens working in other agencies) to engage in Somalia. A number of agencies noted that they had the contacts and the capacity to work in South Central Somalia in early 2011, but were very worried about the possible legal consequences.[38]

In the midst of a good deal of legal ambiguity, the impact on the response in Somalia was entirely unambiguous: according to the Financial Tracking Service of OCHA, the US contribution to the humanitarian response in Somalia went from $237 million in the 2008 fiscal year to less than $100 million in 2009, to less than $30 million in 2010.[39] After the expiration of contracts in October 2010, almost no US funding was renewed for South Central Somalia until the time of the famine declaration. Funding support from other donors continued, albeit at a relatively low level, and with their own set of constraints.[40]

Throughout this time, US officials argued that the constraints to humanitarian access were Al-Shabaab's policies and actions, not counter-terrorism laws in the United States or other donor countries, and they gave verbal assurances that they would not punish agencies for small amounts of aid that might go astray.[41] But no funding was available from US sources, and agency lawyers believed that the laws were clear and the consequences for breaking them severe—and verbal assurances to the contrary meant little. Many agencies were basing their decisions about where to work not on the basis of need, or even staff security, but on the basis of legal and reputational considerations.[42] At stake was not just the operation of a given agency in Somalia: accusations of "helping terrorists" could destroy the reputation of an agency globally. So the standoff over the interpretation of policy continued throughout the time when a major effort at mitigating the worsening crisis should have been mounted.[43]

Thus a good deal of confusion existed about the precise nature of the statutes, and ambiguity about their consequences. The ambiguity in the system made it plausible for the US government and other donors to paint the agencies as the ones dragging their feet. While both USAID and the State Department issued verbal assurances that they did not intend to prosecute humanitarian agencies, neither the Departments of Treasury nor Justice did so—and no government agencies were willing to provide clear, written assurances. In this context, many agencies simply closed down operations or maintained only a minimal presence—despite having some capacity and at least some degree of access.

Behind the scenes, several agencies made efforts to find a way out of the impasse. Testifying before the Senate Committee on Foreign Relations' Subcommittee on Africa on August 3, 2011, (after the famine had been declared), a senior US humanitarian agency official noted that good faith efforts had been made to resolve the impasse between USAID and humanitarian agencies, but that, "The blame for the delays and obstacles ultimately lies with the nature of the restrictions themselves."[44] He went on to narrate several years' worth of effort to resolve the issue, which ultimately ran out of steam right as the contracts for the 2010 fiscal year were expiring at the end of September 2010, after the first warnings of the impending crisis had been issued, and indeed as the *deyr* rains that year were already beginning to fail. A deal was eventually reached, but only weeks before the famine was declared. The official went on to say, "The eight months that were lost were a period in which the humanitarian community was well aware of the prospect of severe drought and famine. This was the very period when the US government's UN and NGO partners could have been working full-tilt to prepare for the coming calamity."[45]

Given the acknowledged gravity of the situation after the famine was declared, an OFAC license was granted, exempting humanitarian assistance from some of the conditions previously imposed.[46] The license was issued on July 28, 2011, eight days after the famine was declared. The declaration itself appears to have been the determining factor in changing policy, although a renewed push on public advocacy had been made by some agencies and the US NGO umbrella organization, Inter-Action, in May and June 2011.[47] But the point is that humanitarian objectives became an equal policy consideration to counter-terrorism objectives only after the famine had been declared. For the most part, US foreign policy objectives during this period revolved around ensuring the transition to a legitimate, representative government, containing Al-Shabaab, and countering the presence of Al-Qaeda in the Horn of Africa.[48]

The OFAC license lifted the threat of sanctions against individuals and agencies provided that humanitarian operations were carried out in good faith, but still required rigorous reporting of any diversion of assistance. It only applied to funding provided through USAID, so it didn't cover private funding or funding from other donors (although agencies could apply for a stand-alone license for such assistance). And it was not binding on the Department of Justice, meaning that it still provided no real guarantee against prosecution, particularly under the "material support" statutes upheld in the 2010 Supreme Court decision.[49] This ongoing ambiguity persisted well into the post-famine period. Nevertheless, the OFAC license freed up the space for a robust US response to the famine—albeit a late one. The United States became a major donor to the cash transfer program, as well as playing its more traditional role in providing food aid and other humanitarian assistance.

None of this, of course, is to imply that counter-terrorism measures alone were the reason for the worsening crisis. As noted in Chapter 3, the actions of Al-Shabaab were also an ever-increasing constraint on both the humanitarian agencies and the populations they controlled as the drought worsened, food prices shot ever higher, and mortality increased.[50] And other internal factors exacerbated these factors. But many international agencies were no longer operating in South Central Somalia by late 2010, and those still there were operating almost entirely by "remote management" or working solely through local partner organizations, and were thus very worried about their ability to control events on the ground, for which they were nevertheless legally responsible. The ambiguity about legal culpability, the reputational risks, and the risks to staff safety and security all led to a good deal less engagement and mitigation than might have been the case—Al-Shabaab's obstructions notwithstanding.

Ashley Jackson and Abdi Aynte note various missed opportunities that could have been used to negotiate improved humanitarian access during the crisis. They suggest that humanitarian leaders could have taken a principled stand on engagement with Al-Shabaab over access, and against the counter-terrorism restrictions. And they suggest that agencies could have collaborated and shared information to stand united in their negotiations for access—points that some in the humanitarian community strongly contest.[51] Lastly, the TFG could also have helped the humanitarian effort; the lack of national policies only compounded problems of access.[52] Nevertheless, the point of Jackson and Aynte's analysis was that the blockage of access to aid agencies was not as universal as it was portrayed at the time, and that it was possible, albeit difficult, to negotiate humanitarian access with Al-Shabaab, even at the height of the crisis. But humanitarian agencies faced the "impossible choice" of conceding to at least some of Al-Shabaab's demands in order to access badly affected civilian populations under their control, as otherwise they would be forced to withdraw. If they withdrew, they were violating everything they believed in regarding the humanitarian imperative; if they acceded to Al-Shabaab's demands, they not only persisted in reinforcing long-standing structural problems with aid in Somalia but also ran the risk of being charged with crimes. Jackson and Aynte's point is that this need not have been the case.

Andrew Seal and Rob Bailey suggest that both the inadequate funding and the counter-terror policies may have been strategic maneuvers to "undermine" Al-Shabaab:

> Inadequate funding was a direct and inevitable consequence of donor anti-terror legislation. So was the failure to provide an enabling legal environment for humanitarian agencies to operate without the threat of prosecution. This strategy also had serious consequences for the presence, operational capacity and access of agencies on the ground.[53]

Thus the efforts to weaken Al-Shabaab are likely to have made the famine worse in parts of Somalia.

The Impact of the Famine

The impact of a famine—the damage to and loss of human life and livelihoods—can be described and measured in many ways. The data and evidence in this section represent the best efforts of external analysts to collect and analyze the limited information that objectively characterized the impact of the 2011 famine in Somalia. The emphasis here is on the damage to livelihoods; the displacement of people because of the drought and the livelihoods crisis, conflict and insecurity, or other causes; the resulting severe food insecurity and malnutrition; and the loss of human life (politely referred to as "excess mortality").[54] The experience and impact of the famine from a Somali perspective is examined in Chapter 5.

The precise evidence for the famine declaration is presented in detail elsewhere.[55] Here we make reference to the declaration, and briefly depict the levels of key indicators at the time of the declaration, but do not recount in detail all the evidence presented specifically for the declaration. For purposes of completeness, the impact of the refugee influx into Dadaab and Dollo-Ado are included here, but otherwise the data are only for Somalia, even though, as made clear above, this was a crisis that affected the whole Horn of Africa region.

FSNAU used the Integrated Food Security Phase Classification to declare the famine.[56] While in general the IPC calls for a "convergence of evidence" approach to amalgamate the analysis of disparate kinds of data and evidence, three key thresholds had to be surpassed to declare a famine. These include a prevalence of GAM of greater than 30 percent,[57] a CDR[58] of more than two deaths per day per 10,000 people, and that at least 20 percent of all households in the affected area face extreme food consumption shortfalls with limited or no ability to cope. All these are described below.

Livelihoods

The severity of the 2011 crisis had profound implications for the livelihoods of many hundreds of thousands of households, in addition to the impact of mortality, malnutrition, and displacement. Although significant subdivisions exist, the main livelihood groups in South Central Somalia are pastoralist (livestock herding), agro-pastoralist (mixed farming and livestock keeping), riverine (agriculture—both small-scale and mechanized), and fishing—in addition to urban-based livelihoods, particularly trade. Each livelihood group interacts differently with the market and is vulnerable to climatic shocks and food price changes in different ways. Figure 4.3 depicts overall grain production in Somalia, reflecting the impact of the back-to-back failure of the rains in late 2010 and early 2011 (the failure of the *deyr* rain in 2010 was reflected in a poor harvest in early 2011, and these figures are recorded at harvest). This

Figure 4.5: Total Grain Production, Somalia, 1996–2011

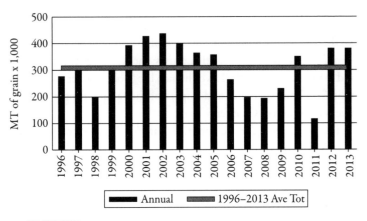

Source: FAOSTAT.

of course had an impact on aggregate food availability in the local market, but equally importantly, this collapse of agricultural production spelled disaster for smallholder farmers who depend on their own production for consumption, for landless people or people who depend on seasonal wage labor in agriculture to supplement other forms of income to enable them to buy adequate food, as well as for pastoralists who depend primarily on purchased food. The demand for seasonal labor in agriculture—particularly in the irrigated farms of the riverine areas that often serve as a labor magnet in other crises—plummeted in late 2010 and early 2011, as did the daily wage that laborers could earn.

Livestock, probably the most important asset for the two dominant livelihood groups in Somalia, took a huge hit in 2011, with levels of vulnerability varying by animal type. Camels are the least vulnerable to drought and are also associated with particular clan identities or groups, whereas cattle are the most vulnerable. Differences in livestock ownership reflect different clans or social groups. While precise figures on livestock losses are extremely difficult to obtain, the evidence suggests cattle deaths were very high across South Central Somalia, especially in the Lower Shabelle and Bay regions, with very high concentrations of cattle being brought into the Shabelle Valley from other regions. Some of the losses were due to the sale of drought-affected animals before they died. But most were due to the deaths of animals—particularly cattle. As grazing dried up along major livestock marketing corridors, markets collapsed and herders couldn't sell animals at any price because traders couldn't get them to regional markets without grazing en route. Available figures show a large increase in the export of hides and skins in 2011.[59]

Much of the Lower Shabelle River, a significant water source for thousands of cattle and other livestock, dried up.[60] Livestock losses were estimated at 30–50 percent of herd size in some locations, to as high as 65 percent for cattle pastoralists from Lower Juba. These losses have major implications for recovery.[61] Losses reported in interviews were even higher in some areas and for some specific clans and social groups, such as the Jiddo in Lower Shabelle and the Dabare in Bay region.[62] Beyond actual losses, huge costs were incurred in keeping livestock alive. And sometimes, despite the investment in water trucking or the purchase of fodder, animals ultimately died anyway (see Chapter 5).

For rural-based populations, the collapse of both agricultural labor opportunities and the market for small ruminants meant an immediate switch to a variety of coping strategies. The extraction of natural resources is both a normal, seasonal activity, as well as one that can intensify in times of extreme difficulty. This was the case in 2011. This was best documented in the Lower Shabelle region, where cutting trees for firewood, construction poles, and charcoal production expanded as a distress-coping strategy with a significant incoming population adding to the already-significant pressure on natural resources.[63] But natural resource extraction intensified everywhere.[64]

The Shabelle and Juba Rivers are critical natural resources in good years and bad in southern Somalia, mitigating the impact of unpredictable rainfall on agriculture and providing a permanent water source for humans and animals. Lower Shabelle in particular is a critical "safe haven" in terms of access to agricultural labor, water, and pasture for people and livestock from the immediate surroundings as well as a much larger catchment area across southern Somalia. In 2011, this was again the case. However, limited maintenance of canal irrigation infrastructure in recent years as well as the construction of a dam upriver on the Shabelle in Ethiopia limited the potential of this area to absorb people and animals in 2011.[65]

While the relative impact among different livelihood groups has been well examined by FSNAU, the different impacts among other social groups remain largely underexplored. Relatively little analysis has been done on why some people and social groups survived and others did not, or how some social groups or livelihood groups coped where others did not. Nisar Majid and Stephen McDowell suggest that the major victims of the famine had particular livelihood and socio-political characteristics that were not well understood.

Farmers and agro-pastoralists who rely heavily on rain-fed crop production were significantly affected, as were cattle-rearing pastoralists who lost significant amounts of their herds because of a lack of grazing and water.[66]

Food Security

Most of the food security data for the declaration of the famine was based on the decline in agricultural production, the steep drop in the wage labor rate and prices received for livestock, and the rapidly increasing price of food—all of which led to the disastrous drop in the terms of trade depicted above—and in the observation of increased levels of coping. Some analyses measure the contribution of different sources of food or income to total household food security, and then compare that to "minimum food needs" (meaning the amount of food required to enable the household to survive) and "minimum livelihoods needs" (meaning the amount of food and income required for the household to survive without sacrificing productive assets). Whereas a baseline assessment showed a typical household in South Central Somalia being able to meet about 200 percent of its minimum food needs, by mid-2011 this had dropped to about 50 percent of minimum food needs for the most badly affected groups.[67]

Acute food insecurity was the driver of much—though not all—of the high levels of malnutrition and mortality. By mid-2011, terms of trade for the purchase of food were at record-low levels, and programs to address the lack of access to adequate food were scaled up quickly after the famine was declared. Once the response ramped up, various program monitoring mechanisms reported extremely high levels of food insecurity.[68]

Displacement

Movement of populations in Somalia has ebbed and flowed, both internally and externally, for the past two decades. The Ethiopian invasion and occupation of 2007 and 2008 resulted in a huge new spike in internal displacement and in many ways set the stage for the famine of 2011.[69] But during late 2010 and early 2011, after two failed rainy seasons and the worst harvest since the 1992–3 famine, food insecurity and conflict led to an exceptionally large-scale population displacement.

Internal Displacement

Figure 4.6 depicts internal displacement during the period that framed the famine. Robinson et al. break down the time frame into three distinct periods:

Figure 4.6: Internal Displacement in Somalia, by Cause, 2010–12

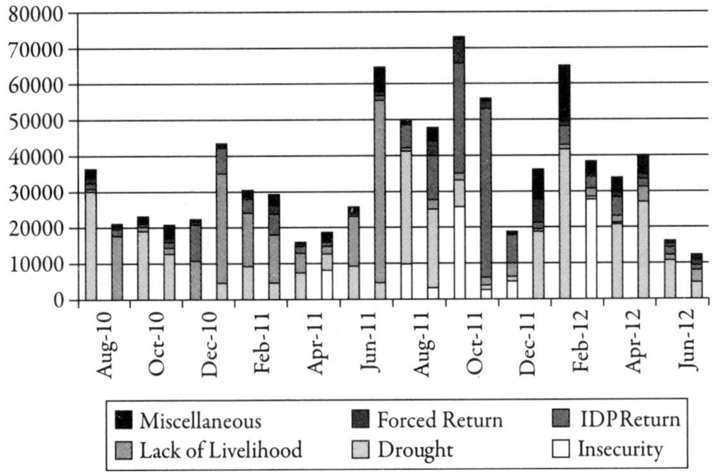

Data: Robinson et al. 2014 (UNHCR Data).

the "pre-famine" period from August 2010 to April 2011, the "famine" period from May to October 2011, and the "post-famine" period from November 2011 to July 2012.[70] During the pre-famine period, most internal displacement occurred either from or within the urban areas, and insecurity—mostly the result of fighting between Al-Shabaab and AMISOM/TFG—accounted for three-quarters of the displacement. However, drought-related displacement spiked notably when the failure of the *deyr* rains was felt from December through February and through the failure of the *Gu* rains (April–June).

So many people moved during this whole period that analyzing total numbers of internally displaced people doesn't really reveal much. Not surprisingly, the hardest hit areas (Lower and Upper Shabelle, Bay, and Bakool) also had the most restricted access for humanitarian assistance. Most of the assistance available was concentrated in Mogadishu, creating a pull factor. Renewed fighting between Al-Shabaab and AMISOM/the Somali National Army increased displacement again in the "post-famine" period, which caused some of the factors leading to food insecurity and malnutrition to extend well into 2012. The famine was officially declared over in February 2012.[71] Note that much of the forced return of IDPs was during the short rains in 2011 and in preparation for the long rains in 2012 after the famine was declared over.

Refugee Movement

During this period, movement out of the country increased dramatically, with an average of 4,000–7,700 refugees arriving every month in Ethiopia and Kenya, respectively. Over the course of the crisis, some 150,000 new refugees arrived in Kenya, and nearly 120,000 in Ethiopia, peaking at nearly 27,000 new arrivals in July 2011.[72] Figure 4.7 shows new arrivals at Dadaab and Figure 4.8 shows new arrivals at Dollo-Ado, by region of origin. Note that the registration of new arrivals in Dadaab was suspended after October 2011 (concurrent with the Kenyan invasion of Somalia). Thus, no services were available to new arrivals. The Refugee Consortium of Kenya reported a drop-off in new arrivals from nearly 1,000 per day to fewer than fifty. This high-lighted a "fundamental disintegration of hospitality" on the part of Kenya,[73] forcing would-be refugees to find other means of survival. Ethiopia main-tained its "open door" policy throughout this period, but refugee authorities and humanitarian agencies in both countries struggled to keep up with the influx. Agency staff later regretted not making better use of information about refugee influxes to assist in early warning and understanding the evolving conditions inside Somalia.[74]

In Ethiopia, Somali refugee numbers had been stable since the 1980s and 1990s in the Jijiga and Gode zones. However, in 2011, approximately 20,000 additional Somali refugees arrived at camps in the Gode and Afder zones, in addition to the influx into camps in Dollo-Ado.[75] Dollo-Ado was already host to some 40,000 refugees in two camps (Bokolmayo and Melkadida)—mostly the families and relatives of men who had fought against Al-Shabaab in mili-tias aligned with Ethiopia in 2007–9. The small stream of incoming refugees increased steadily in early 2011, with new arrivals averaging 5,000–10,000 per month from January to April. But then the rate of new arrivals increased dra-matically—an increase not foreseen by either UNHCR or the Ethiopian Agency for Refugee and Returnee Affairs (ARRA).[76]

The refugees arriving in Dadaab for most of this period were from the Middle and Lower Juba regions, with a spike from the Bay region at the height of the impact of the *gu* rains failure. The biggest number arriving in Dollo-Ado were from the nearby Gedo region, but also from Bay and Bakool, with steady numbers from Mogadishu (Banadir region) as well. Most of the people displaced from Lower and Middle Shabelle—the other two hard-hit regions—went to Mogadishu.

Most of those who fled in search of humanitarian assistance were women and children, while men often remained behind to care for any remaining

Figure 4.7: Refugee Arrivals in Dadaab, by Region of Origin, August 2010–July 2012

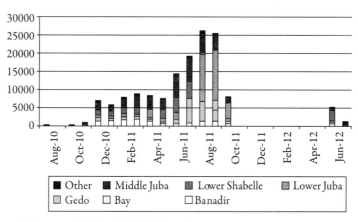

Data: Robinson et al. 2014 (UNHCR Data).

herds or other assets. Those who arrived at their destination were in poor health, dehydrated, and malnourished after several days or weeks in transit.[77] What these figures cannot depict are the conditions they faced upon arrival, wherever that might have been: Dollo-Ado, Dadaab, Mogadishu, or some other location where IDPs congregated. Basic services in Dollo-Ado were completely overwhelmed with a fivefold increase in new arrivals during the months of June and July. Unfortunately, despite attempts to meet needs (including opening two additional camps), the situation in Dollo-Ado remained bleak following the influx of new arrivals, with the prevalence of GAM reaching as high as 50 percent in the new camps,[78] and remaining "unacceptably" high for several months up to the end of 2011.[79] The CDR reached 1.9 in one of the new camps, and had CDR been measured separately for the transit camp, it probably would have been higher.[80] The transit camp had been built to house a maximum of 2,000 people, and it was intended that people would stay there only a few days—during June and July 2011, the population in the transit camp exceeded 15,000 and some people reported staying there longer than a month.[81] Indeed, this was the reason that Ethiopian authorities quickly opened up two new refugee camps, at Kobe and Heloweyn.

Dadaab, a town in the semi-arid Northeastern Province of Kenya, has been host to the world's largest refugee camp. It was first constructed in the 1990s. Most who seek refuge there are Somali, fleeing the long-standing conflict in their home country. In 2011, an additional 152,000 Somalis fled to Dadaab,

Figure 4.8. Refugee Arrivals in Dollo-Ado, by Region of Origin, August 2010–July 2012

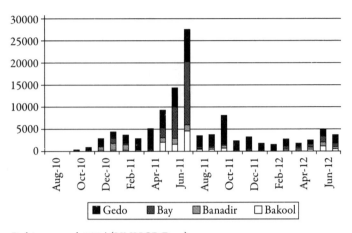

Data: Robinson et al. 2014 (UNHCR Data).

pushing the refugee population to 443,000. Just as in Dollo-Ado, Dadaab experienced an unexpected influx of new arrivals in June and July, with the number of new arrivals peaking in August. From January to June, new arrivals averaged 9,500 per month, yet the number jumped to 26,000 new arrivals in July—an almost threefold increase in one month.[82] Historically, Dadaab had been predominantly composed of Darod/Ogaden clans from the Somalia/Kenya border area.[83] In both Dollo-Ado and Dadaab, the agro-pastoral Rahanweyn now form a significant population (if not the majority). They were severely affected by the famine but were not previously displaced internationally. This group's origins, social identity, and livelihood base are significantly different from other Somalis, and this affected their vulnerability in 2011 (see Chapter 6).

Malnutrition and Mortality

At the time of the declaration, an estimated 450,000 Somali children were acutely malnourished; nearly 200,000 of these were severely acutely malnourished[84]—and this measure did not count those who had already died from complications related to malnutrition. The prevalence of GAM (which includes both severe and moderate malnutrition) was averaging over 40 percent in southern regions, with severe acute malnutrition (SAM) at nearly 20 percent[85]—indicators that far surpass the necessary criteria for famine declaration. Table 4.1 depicts the prevalence of GAM, SAM, and the CDR by region and livelihood group in mid-2011. Note that the threshold for declaring a famine for GAM was 30 percent and for CDR was two people per 10,000 people per day.[86]

Table 4.1: Prevalence of Global Acute Malnutrition, Severe Acute Malnutrition, and Crude Death Rate, July 2011

Region and Livelihood Zone	GAM, % (95% Confidence Interval)	SAM, % (95% CI)	CDR/10,000/day (95% CI)
Bakool pastoral	55.9 (50.6–61.2)	20.4 (15.2–26.7)	1.9 (1.6–2.2)
Bay agro-pastoral	55.0 (45.8–64.0)	29.8 (22.8–38.0)	1.1 (0.7–1.4)
Gedo agro-pastoral	51.9 (41.8–61.9)	19.3 (13.8–26.3)	1.7 (1.1–2.2)
Gedo riverine	48.1 (38.7–57.7)	25.2 (19.1–32.6)	1.6 (0.8–2.4)
Bakool agro-pastoral	45.9 (42.3–49.6)	16.4 (12.9–20.6)	1.9 (1.6–2.3)
Lower and Middle Juba riverine	45.9 (41.5–50.3)	21.9 (18.9–25.2)	1.2 (0.8–1.5)
Hiraan agro-pastoral	43.2 (37.7–48.9)	16.3 (13.4–19.6)	1.5 (1.1–1.9)
Lower Shabelle (Afgooye) IDP	40.7 (34.5–47.2)	17.7 (13.4–22.9)	4.2 (3.2–5.3)
Lower Shabelle agro-pastoral	40.6 (34.6–46.8)	20.9 (16.2–26.5)	4.2 (2.9–5.5)
Lower/Middle Juba pastoral	39.5 (35.9–43.2)	18.7 (15.8–21.9)	1.2 (0.8–1.7)
Mogadishu IDP	39.4 (32.4–46.9)	15.3 (11.6–19.8)	4.3 (3.2–5.4)
Lower/Middle Juba agro-pastoral	38.9 (34.8–43.1)	17.2 (14.0–20.9)	1.1 (0.8–1.4)
Middle Shabelle agro-pastoral	35.3 (24.9–47.3)	17.1 (10.3–27.1)	2.3 (1.7–2.9)
Lower Shabelle riverine	28.7 (24.4–33.5)	14.2 (11.6–17.3)	5.9 (4.3–7.6)
Hiraan pastoral	27.3 (24.2–30.6)	12.8 (10.5–15.6)	1.5 (1.1–2.0)
Gedo pastoral	23.8 (20.1–28.0)	5.9 (4.1–8.5)	1.2 (0.8–1.6)
Hiraan riverine	20.7 (18.4–23.2)	9.1 (7.2–11.5)	1.4 (1.0–1.7)
Middle Shabelle riverine	19.6 (16.4–23.2)	8.2 (5.7–11.6)	1.7 (1.1–2.3)

Source: Rebelo et al. 2012.

The prevalence of GAM and SAM varied greatly at the time of the declaration, but the highest level of recorded GAM was in the Bakool pastoral zone (55.9 percent) and the highest SAM was in the Bay agro-pastoral livelihood zone (29.8 percent). Broadly speaking, agro-pastoral and riverine livelihood groups, and IDPs, suffered the highest prevalence of malnutrition. But a number of pastoral groups—particularly cattle pastoralists from Middle and Lower Juba—were also hard hit.[87] Rebelo et al. go on to show declining levels of GAM and SAM after the famine was declared, and the response was scaled up.[88]

As already noted, the overall estimated death toll attributable to the famine is 258,000.[89] The largest death tolls are estimated to have been in Bakool, Banadir, Bay, Lower Shabelle, and Middle Shabelle regions.[90] Figure 4.9 depicts the total monthly mortality from the famine over time.[91] Between May and October 2011 in southern and central Somalia, the CDR exceeded 2.0 in several areas and was over 5.0 among a few livelihood groups. The groups with the highest CDRs in July 2011 were Bakool agro-pastoralists, Bay agro-pastoralists, Afgooye IDPs, and Mogadishu IDPs with 2.11, 2.15, 4.02, and 5.68 per 10,000 per day respectively.[92] All these rates surpassed the IPC famine threshold.[93] These generalized depictions do not reveal the social identities and concentrations of mortality and destitution, which were among the Rahanweyn, and particular sub-clans of the Rahanweyn.[94] Some analyses suggest that the most vulnerable population in Lower Shabelle were displaced people, including those from Bay region and other badly affected areas who were trying to reach Mogadishu.[95]

Summarizing the Impact

Some other elements of the impact of the famine should be mentioned as well—while the causes of mortality were not recorded, the likely actual cause of death in many cases was an infectious disease such as measles or a respiratory infection in children made vulnerable by malnutrition. In general, while a significant amount of information was available about malnutrition and mortality in Somalia, less information was available about public health elements of the famine, though we know from other, similar crises that infectious disease is always a major killer.[96]

Mortality dropped off fairly quickly after the declaration. Some have speculated that this was due to the impact of the humanitarian response that followed (the humanitarian response would have included "emerging" and Western agencies from this point).[97] Mortality in famines often crests and

Figure 4.9: Estimated Excess Mortality, October 2010–March 2012

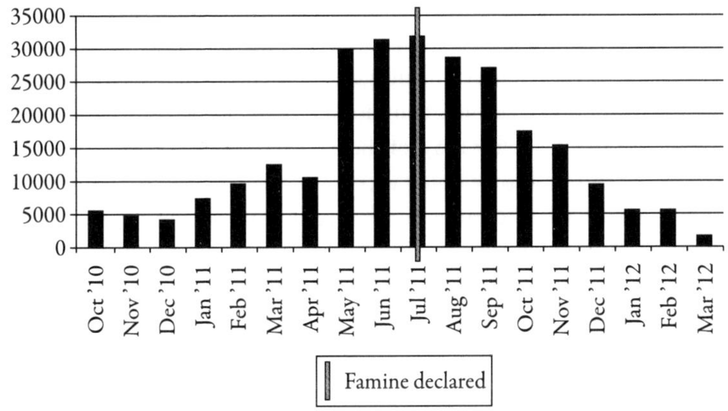

Data: Checchi and Robinson 2013.

declines rapidly as a result of its own dynamics—by definition, those most at risk are more vulnerable and succumb more quickly.[98] Of note, however, is that even before the formal declaration, the price of food had begun to fall, quite independently of any humanitarian effort; and with the prediction and then arrival of a better *deyr* rain, demand for labor began to pick up, so the terms of trade improved rapidly after July/August 2011. This alone no doubt accounts for some of the drop in mortality.[99] All of these factors played a role.

Perhaps the most important point here is that, while all of these elements have been analyzed separately, all the impacts of the famine occurred, and to the same people. So people were also experiencing all the things that can be counted up and analyzed—the malnutrition, the death of their children or other vulnerable members of their families, arriving in a strange place hoping for assistance but instead facing agonizing delays, more deaths, and brutal exploitation at the hands of "black cats"—while Somali individuals and households were trying to limit the losses to their farms or their livestock; while trying to get access to enough food; while mothers were drastically cutting back on their own consumption of food to try to give their children more; while families were being split up—some in search of assistance and others desperately trying to protect their remaining assets; while trying to help their kin and neighbors but watching their own stocks dwindle; while moving away from their homesteads trying to avoid Al-Shabaab, and being harassed and taxed en route; and all the while hoping that the rains would fall. The very length of the sentence required to describe the barest bones of the experience underscores the difficulty of expressing the cumulative experience of a famine with statistics. But it was the numbers that enabled the famine to be declared, and it was the declaration that finally got the attention of the authorities, the donors, and the international community generally—and that enabled a response. But that was after most of the damage had been done. The Somali experience of this multitude of impacts is explored in detail in Chapter 5.

This sequence of events raises profound questions for both the humanitarian community and for policy-makers far beyond the circumscribed realm of humanitarian action. These questions are addressed in Chapters 9 and 10. To provide a better understanding of the actual experience of the famine, Chapter 5 turns to a more qualitative and internal look at what happened, and how people responded and did their best to cope in increasingly awful circumstances.

5

"NO ONE TO CRY TO"

A SOMALI NARRATIVE OF THE FAMINE

Introduction

This chapter tells the story of the famine through the testimonies of Somalis who lived through and were most directly affected by the catastrophic events of 2011.[1] Such narratives have been rare in the analysis of famine, and they serve to capture a Somali "voice" and perspective that is often missing or very limited in humanitarian, policy-making, media accounts, or academic research related to Somalia and Somalis—or to famines more broadly. In fact, in its remotely managed form, humanitarian action has been criticized for its intellectual, emotional, and psychological distance from crisis-affected populations.[2] This is very much the case in South Central Somalia. In addition to the communities most affected by the famine, this chapter presents narratives from those Somalis both within Somalia and abroad—in the business community, the diaspora, and the Somali mosques (in Kenya and Somalia)—who were prominent among the first responders to the crisis and who were little heard or consulted by the international community.

The chapter begins in Bay Region, identifying particular clans and districts in the worst of the famine, areas under the control of Al-Shabaab at the time. The geographic logic of the chapter moves from the epicentre in Bay Region to the Shabelle Valley (also very badly affected), and then outwards to the Juba Valley, in turn linking to Kenya and Dadaab, and then to the Dollo-Ado refugee camps in Ethiopia. Each of the narratives presented here is accompanied by a short explanation to help interpret the key points. Chapter 6 provides further analytical interpretation, but the purpose of this chapter is to offer unfiltered stories of the famine from the perspectives of those most affected by it. These narratives have been partially edited from the original Somali (both Maxatiir and Af-Maay) in which they were spoken, and then written in English by the research team. These narratives are selected from several hundred as both representing the overall famine story and illuminating key themes.

The Epicentre of the Famine

The following four narratives concern the heart of the famine area, among the agro-pastoral Rahanweyn clan[3] from Bay Region, but they also illuminate and describe factors that apply more generally, including diversification, the importance of identity and social networks, and the role of the business community and diaspora.

1. A Rahanweyn-Leysan man from Baidoa District

Our family kept cattle, some camels, and we ran a farm. As a family, we have many people who are able and can work and we sell our labor to farms during the farming period. This is called "ta'ab goosi." We had a good sesame harvest in gu 2010. In general, farming practices in Bay Region have changed [in recent years] and the change was towards growing cash crops—sesame and groundnuts. Before the drought of 2011, livestock numbers increased too much but reduced to almost zero because of the drought, especially for cattle. I had invested to buy ten good-looking cows. I used a good amount of my money for my son's marriage and dowry. Yes, we had a relatively good amount of sorghum reserves. Things were well and in order.

Unfortunately the 2010–11 deyr failed.[4] From February to April 2011, there was a very hot jilaal. We did not have our own water but we were getting some water [brought by tanker] from Baidoa. I don't know who exactly was paying for that water. Because there was no livestock feed stocks from sesame, our cattle and goats had nothing to feed on. We had to give part of the sorghum we had and share it between people and livestock. When the sorghum was finished, we started giving the livestock the grass roof that was on our huts. This stressful situation continued, and we began to reduce the number of meals and amount of food we ate. This was the beginning of January 2011 and onwards. Cattle had started dying by February 2011, and by the end of April they were almost finished. By May, people started becoming displaced, moving to different places. In our case, we divided the family into three groups: one group went to Dollo Ethiopia refugee camp, one group went to Baidoa, especially the weaker ones, and one group stayed or moved with the camels and goats (because there were lactating camels). I was part of the Baidoa group. We moved to Baidoa during June 2011. I went to ask some clan members in

Baidoa to help me and save my family. They helped me with some food, and that was enough for at least a month. I also found some aid that was provided by a Baidoa business group and Al-Shabaab. Later there was some aid from the Red Cross and Al-Shabaab. All my family members are in Baidoa District and I don't have any family members in other countries that I can cry to, but there are some clan members in Baidoa town that I can cry to for some assistance.[5]

Households with large numbers of cattle and farmers were worst affected. The pure farmers were all affected as they had bought a lot of animals the previous years. People with many children, old people, and sick people were also affected very much. Children and old people were those who died most. I have seen a family with more than ten children, and four of them were dead within two days. People who have nobody to cry to, who don't have kinsmen to help, don't have a son or a daughter in the towns or out of the country to help ... these people could not cope with the situation.

The drought affected the following clans the worst: the Gelidle, the Yantar, the Hubeer, and the Jareer from different clans. These are all the strong producers of sorghum in Bay Region. The Yantar and Hubeer had a very bad conflict in 2007–8 which affected their reserves. They had also begun planting more sesame. They were also the worst affected in terms of Al-Shabaab taxation (on farm produce). The Jareer don't have any form of livelihood apart from farming. They always finish their products quickly. They are also farm laborers and there were no farm labor jobs to be had for two seasons.[6]

In our case, we were also affected very much in our village but not many people died. Because, as Leysan, we could not let our clan members die of hunger while we know and have something. The Leysans in Baidoa and even other places were collecting money to help us.

Identity, Diversification—and Crisis

This quote captures multiple dimensions of the lived experience of 2011. The household itself was relatively wealthy and diversified, owning cattle, camels, and goats, as well as practicing some farming. The informant indicates a little-known underlying pattern, where the cash crop, sesame, has been introduced, and the cash returns invested in cattle, whose numbers then collapsed catastrophically in 2011 as people depleted their own savings in an attempt to keep themselves and their cattle, their prime assets, alive. This story captures the progression of the crisis from the first failed rainy season (the *deyr* of 2010–11) through the dry season (*jilaal*) until the failure of the main rainy season (*gu* 2011). At this point, any hope for a quick recovery was lost and families had to divide up and move to areas where they could find help. This excerpt also highlights the role that social networks and clan identity play as a safety net, in this case the Leysan, a relatively wealthy and diversified clan by Rahanweyn standards.[7] The informant contrasts his identity with other clans and social groups in the epicentre of the crisis, including the minority Jareer (Somali Bantus—a heterogeneous group that includes indigenous farming populations and former slaves and who were less able to survive the conditions at the time).[8] The multiple influences of Al-Shabaab are also evident.

2. A Rahanweyn-Elay man from Burhakaba District

I do farming, producing only sorghum. I also depend on wage labor to earn an income, both farming labor and in-town work. There have been no significant farming changes in this district. We know sesame has gained momentum in other areas of Bay Region but it is not suitable in Burhakaba District. Recurrent migration because of droughts and water shortages, as well as the 2006–7 conflict between the ICU and Ethiopia, which was mainly in Burhakaba, has caused major disruptions in this area.

The crisis started as early as deyr 2010–11. When the deyr rains failed, it led to water shortages and reductions in the food reserves. When that previously happened, humanitarian organizations used to do water trucking, but that was stopped by Al-Shabaab. Many people started moving out of the villages as early as February 2011 because of water shortages. They were only moving to villages that have water and to Burhakaba town. Most of them had at least some food reserves. In my case, I moved to Wafdhay, which is our main village. I started collecting firewood, charcoal, and even building logs [for construction] and selling them in Burhakaba to get [money to buy] food and water for the family. In April 2011, the water catchment in Wafdhay dried up and there was nowhere to stay. The gu rain also failed. No rain fell. We had no option but to move out along with many other people. We sold the few food reserves we had and walked to Mogadishu. Al-Shabaab were stopping people from going but we used a long route so that they didn't [find] us. We reached Afgooye IDP camps and Al-Shabaab moved us to Kilometer 50[9] where we had the worst experience. As a family, I lost two of my children there. After two weeks we again walked in a hiding way because there was no help [at Kilometer 50], yet we were forced to be there. We reached Mogadishu. For almost ten days, we were depending on begging in the streets with our children because there was no aid. It was around late May to early June 2011 that we were taken to one of the Mogadishu IDP camps. They bring food every day but after taking photos the food is taken back from all the people and only 20 percent given to us. Some business people and the owner of the camp, plus the NGO staff, are taking the food. We can't complain because they will chase us from the camp. Sometimes the militia would come at night, taking the few things left and raping girls and women.

Over three quarters of the IDPs in Mogadishu are Rahanweyn-Elay. Cattle pastoralists and farmers were the worst affected. Women, children, and elderly people were among the worst affected. Many of them died, either on the way or when they were in the IDP camps. Water shortage, lack of humanitarian assistance, and Al-Shabaab pressure were the main causes. Yes, Al-Shabaab pressure still continues because they are forcing people to pay tax wherever they are.

During the ICU and Hizbul-Islam time (2006), there was too much recruitment into militias.[10] During Al-Shabaab time, there was increased fear and terrorizing of the population. Al-Shabaab stopped all humanitarian assistance while people were dying. The current local authority is corrupt and taking everything for themselves. They work closely with NGO and INGO local staff and share what would have been given to the population. In the IDP camps we got some assistance, but it was the biggest corruption I have ever seen.

Coping, Displacement, Harassment, and 'Gatekeepers'

This interviewee indicates the local variations within Bay Region where, for example, sesame production was not part of the dynamic of the time, and chronic water shortages are a well-known problem. Exploitation of the natural environment, in the form of charcoal production and the collection and sale of "bush products," is an important strategy for earning money for many people in difficult times. But the family is ultimately forced to move and Mogadishu is relatively close, though the interference by Al-Shabaab is also prominent. The interviewee highlights the high death rates, awful conditions, and corruption associated with the IDP camps in and around Mogadishu; "gatekeepers" pervade the humanitarian system in Somalia and are particularly renowned as the "managers" of displaced camps. But "gatekeeper" more generally means anyone who controls access to goods and services or the flow of information or who withholds any of these. They can be in humanitarian organizations, local administration, government agencies, or in the private business sector—particularly those who contract to provide services such as transportation or warehousing for the aid industry; and inevitably, there are gatekeepers among the displaced themselves.

3. A Rahanweyn-Hubeer (Jareer) woman from Qansaxdheere District[11]

I was a rain-fed farmer, also doing farm labor, and I owned some cattle [before the 2011 crisis]. There were major changes in our area leading up to 2011. We once became rich because of sesame and livestock but became very poor after a short time.[12] Also, the increased fear because of Al-Shabaab made many people migrate before the drought crisis. There was also conflict between the Hubeer and Yantar, which made us lose a lot of our food reserves (this was 2007–8), as well as internal conflict between the Hubeer and Jareer-Hubeer, which also made us very poor. The combination of all these problems made us more vulnerable.

From 2009 to the gu rains of 2010, we harvested a lot of cash crops (sesame) and had very few food reserves in the granary or "bakaar." We invested in buying cattle with most of the cash from our sesame. In 2010–11, the deyr failed, followed by a very long and harsh jilaal. There were no reserves in the bakaar. There was a shortage of water during the 2011 jilaal (February–April). The cattle had nothing to feed on and their bodies deteriorated and became very weak. Sesame has no stalks to feed cattle and we had to share the little sorghum we had between people and cattle. From late April to May 2011, cattle started dying. In June 2011 we became displaced because there was no food, no water, and the livestock [were] dying. We left [the area] with some of the cattle still alive but not able to move. One of my children died on the way to Baidoa. We arrived in Baidoa in a congested camp called Bargiyamo. It was full of people of all clans. We received some food and other items from Baidoa people. We got some help from a local organization.

All of my family and relatives have been living in Oflow village but now they were displaced to different places like Dollo, Dadaab, Mogadishu, and some of us are here in Baidoa. The people most affected in 2011 were agro-pastoralists, pure farmers, and labor dependents, and people who owned cattle were worst affected, as when the rain fails their livelihood fails. In terms of clans, the Hubeer, Yantar, Gelidle, and Dabare, as well as Jareer, were worst affected.[13] Households with many children and aged people also. Those who had business and others to cry to were better and have not moved out of the village.

The main causes of the famine were recurrent conflict between different clans in recent years, increased shift from sorghum to sesame growing, investment of sesame earnings in cattle, drought, and cattle diseases. In terms of local authority influence, they only create conflict, impose heavy taxation, and create tensions and terrorize people.

Minorities, Conflict, and Agricultural Change

This woman refers to her identity as Jareer within the Hubeer sub-clan of the Rahanwcyn. She is speaking from one of the two districts associated with the epicentre of the famine (Qansaxdheere and Dinsor). She confirms the recent change in farming practice with short-term gains realized from increased sesame production that are then invested in cattle—high value animals, but which were very vulnerable to the drought of 2010–11. She also points to the recent history of conflict in the area and its repercussions on food reserves. She highlights the weakening of social ties and social re-distribution mechanisms as many of the wealthier and/or more prominent people had left the area because of Al-Shabaab pressures. She stresses the high levels of displacement and its consequences, herself losing a child in the process. But she also points to the help received from local people and organizations, particularly in Baidoa town. She reaffirms the importance of social connections and the importance of having someone outside the rural economy to "cry to."

4. The Business Response: A Rahanweyn Trader in Baidoa

I am a businessman and I have a business in both Mogadishu and Baidoa. I was in Baidoa from February to June 2011. When the IDPs moved into Baidoa, I was among the business people who were helping the IDPs with some money sourced from within Baidoa as well as from ourselves. This was from mid-May 2011.

In the first week of June 2011, I was asked to head a local emergency relief committee that was being planned. I resisted, but I was influenced and pushed by friends and business colleagues. I finally accepted it, but with a condition that I would select the people to be working with me and they agreed. Our work was to coordinate the aid coming in to Bay Region from the diaspora and aid agencies. We were meeting all the agencies on a daily and weekly basis to plan where to go or who to target. We were also the centre of diaspora assistance. Most of the diaspora assistance was sent to me and the Baidoa Mosque Committee. Our committee received more than $800,000. We used all this money to buy food.

The first response was from the Somali community, especially the business people, the local population, and even the first arriving IDPs who were able to share what they had with others. The second response was from the Somali diaspora and the big business companies. In Baidoa, Concern was the first organization, followed by Islamic Relief and other Islamic organizations like Manhal and Zamzam Foundation.

We also received money from a mosque in Nairobi, Kenya ($80,000 in all, received in July 2011); the Somali business community in Mogadishu in July 2011; Rahanweyn groups in Saudi Arabia, Syria, Kuwait, and Dubai (June and August 2011). Money came from the Somali diaspora in Europe, the United States, Canada, Australia, and South Africa.

We faced many challenges including having no knowledge in the humanitarian response and Al-Shabaab policy and restrictions. International humanitarian organizations have given us a lot of problems (they target a number of beneficiaries and don't want to help new arrivals who are dying. They are very rigid).

I will never ever be part of such a committee again because it is full of blame, and I fear that I might have denied somebody food while he/she is in need, which is a sin. I will contribute but not manage.

Business and Religious Networks

Compared to the "major" Somali clans, the Rahanweyn have relatively small business and diaspora populations (particularly compared to their numbers) because of their historical marginalization. That is, they have had fewer opportunities for education and formal employment, which translate over time to processes of urbanization, migration, and the formation of a diaspora.[14] Nevertheless, there was a significant response mobilized by the Rahanweyn through their business, diasporic, and religious networks. The timing of this response is significant, beginning in mid-May, a full two months before the famine declaration and larger international mobilization. Al-Shabaab was fully in charge in this area and attempted to help manage the aid response once it had accepted that the crisis could not be contained. The respondent also highlights what a difficult job it is to manage such resources and be responsible for deciding who does and does not get help. Interestingly, this man acknowledges some of the accountability associated with managing assistance—an admission many formal humanitarian agencies were afraid to make.

The River Runs Dry

The focus shifts to Lower Shabelle for the next two narratives, one of the other loci of the famine but which has a distinct contributory factor and contains different social groups and livelihood patterns.

5. A Rahanweyn-Dubane Man from Qorioley District in Lower Shabelle[15]

I am a member of the Darbane, a sub-clan of the Dubane Digil who live in villages in and around the districts of Qorioley, Buulo Mareer, Golweyn, Kurtunwaarrey, and others. I am married and have four children. All of us survived the crisis and we had no deaths in our family.

I was a farmer before the crisis. My farm is on the bank of the Shabelle River. The river had many canals that relieve it from excess water and irrigate farms far from the river. These canals are now in a bad condition and most of them are blocked. The river now floods more often. This is what happened to my farm before the crisis (in 2010). It was flooded, and I had to wait until the next season for it to dry up, but before I was able to do anything it was again flooded and I had to wait again. By the time the farmland dried up completely, the farm was a bush with big trees that needed clearing. I did not have the means to do this so I started renting other farms.

The crisis came while I was in this situation. It was already harsh jilaal, but then the gu rains failed, and the river waters receded to very low levels. Actually, in some areas the river was virtually dry. There was no rain and no water in the river so I had no harvest. I then took an axe and went into the bushes to cut trees and sell them as building or enclosure material or burn them to produce charcoal. Then every clan started to claim ownership of the bushes in their territory and preventing others from cutting it. I was tortured a few times for trespassing on other clans' territory and cutting down their trees, but I had no choice as I needed to feed my family.

Then my wife went to Mogadishu on her own to see if there was any help available. She went to Badbaado IDP camp in Mogadishu and after a while she sent us fare money for all five of us and asked me to bring the children to Elasha Biyaha near Mogadishu where she would be waiting for us. We jumped on a lorry. No one bothered us until we reached Shalambod, near Marka, where we were stopped by Al-Shabaab. They lectured us, saying that it was a bad idea to take the children to a place where there were many Ugandan, Burundian, and other infidels. They said we were supposed to take the fight to them and this place was not really safe for children. Most of the people were afraid and didn't say anything, but some people talked back to them, saying they had nothing to eat and no one was coming to this area to help so they had to take their children to where they could get help or else they would all die. They said, "If you give us food we will stay with you." Others said that they had sold everything they had, including their land and homes and had no place to return to and asked, "Where will we return to?" Al-Shabaab's reply was that this drought was brought upon us by God and he will take it away and help us. They did not actually order people to get down but many people were afraid and got down.

The lorry took us to Elasha Biyaha, and from there my wife took us to Badbaado camp in Mogadishu, where she was staying. In the camp where we stayed, we were told to get cooked meals every day from a place nearby. Some days people tell me that some people were given cards to get rations of food but this was done in the night and they gave these cards to their own clans, friends, and acquaintances. I was not a friend or a member of their clan so we were never given a card but we were okay as long as we got something to eat every day. My wife used to go to town to do menial work for the well off in the town such as washing their clothes, cleaning, or any other work she could find. We used the money she brought back to buy more food for us and the children.

There are not many jobs for men in Mogadishu, but after a while I started to work pushing a wheelbarrow, carrying things for people. In other times I sold water to the IDPs, fetching it from nearby places. Later, I worked as a security guard in the camp. I stayed in these IDP camps for two years, during which time I saw many tragedies and crimes. We were very hungry most of the time. Many children died of malnutrition and diseases such as cholera. I have seen youths from established communities in Mogadishu come into the camps almost every night and rob these IDPs of the few things they had and rape woman with impunity. In the end, I came back to re-establish myself here (in Qorioley District) but my wife and our four children are still there. I have now cleared my farm and started growing tomatoes and beans. If all goes well, I will bring my children back.

Many people in the area sold their farmland during the crisis. Some have even sold their homes and have nothing to come back to. The people who bought this land are those with money or have some relatives abroad. If a person informs their relatives abroad that because of the crisis cheap land was available, then they will send money and buy the land. This is now causing conflict in the area, as more people return and ask for the land they sold to be returned to them.

Fear of Al-Shabaab, Exile to Mogadishu, and the "Benefits of Famine."

This respondent explains the importance of the canal system along the Shabelle River, and how it has fallen into disrepair (since the early 1990s). He also highlights the almost complete and unprecedented drying up of the river from the Qorioley area downstream during 2011, an important issue as many people and livestock were brought to these areas in 2011 to look for labor, water, and pasture, as is traditionally done in difficult times. He indicates the difficulty of trying to survive by collecting and selling bush products and the competition for resources at the time. As with many people from this area, relatively close to Mogadishu, the family was able to access aid and opportunities that flooded in following the declaration of the famine and media attention in July and August 2011, although some people were forced to sell some of their land in order to survive. People who bought the land were those with relatives in the diaspora, and they were able to accumulate land and other wealth during the famine. The terrible conditions in the IDP camps and the role of "gatekeepers" were reinforced.

6. A Reer Aw Hassan Man from Qorioley District

Before the crisis, I used to depend on my cattle and my farm. Now I rent a piece of land and grow different things on it. During 2011, all my savings went into saving my cattle. I bought fodder stalks and maize to feed the cattle. When my savings finished, I then sold my farm. I also sold my last sesame harvest. When all this finished, I then sold my two strong donkeys. At the end of the dry season I was very happy thinking that even though it cost me a lot, I saved my cattle as the gu rains were around the corner.

Then there were no rains in the gu. We had moved around and we did anything we could to save them, but in the end the cattle started dying, first one, then a few, then more. I remember one night I slaughtered fourteen cows and then eight the next night. When we saw that a cow was about to die, we slaughtered it so that we could sell the skin with which we could buy food for the children.

When all the cows died, we had nothing left to live on because we had sold all our assets and used up all our savings to save our cattle. So I, along with fifty other families, all Reer Hassan, wanted to go to somewhere where we could find help. We went towards Mogadishu, and at Kilometer 50 we were stopped by Al-Shabaab telling us that it was shame to go to Mogadishu for help since it was occupied by infidels. We stayed in that camp for four months. The first two months before Ramadan (July 2011) we were given nothing and we lost eight children (between the fifty families). But at the start of Ramadan we were given plenty of food.

Then we were moved back to where we [came] from. They [Al-Shabaab] brought us vehicles and transported us back to where we were from. There was nothing we could do in our area since we had no cattle or farm or anything, so I moved to Qorioley town after two months. Members of my clan in Qorioley supported me for a short period and then a son of my cousin who lives in the UK started supporting us. He supported me and three other families who lost everything for six months. He sent US $50 each family. We started farming, and within six months we had our first harvest and then we became self-sufficient. We are still poor, but thanks to God we can manage.

Those who had camels did much better than those, like me, who had cows.[16] Also those who had more people in town had better support, and this also meant that they had more people abroad.

Those who had cattle or small farms were the ones who suffered most. Many Garre and almost all of the Jiddo had cattle and suffered disproportionately in this crisis. The Jareer also suffered because they had small farms and no savings. They worked as laborers, but with almost all of their population in the same position they could not get work.[17]

The Jiddo were particularly disadvantaged because they were all in the same position. The Reer Aw Hassan, for example, had many camel herders who were in a position to help the minority who lost their cattle. But almost all of the Jiddo have lost their cattle, so they couldn't help each other. The majority of the Hawadle had bigger farms and could save most of their cattle.

The Garre had more grain stored from the previous harvests and many of them have moved their cows to faraway places and saved many of their cattle. The Jareer fled the area quickly when they saw the rains had failed. They just packed up and went to Mogadishu, while the Jiddo and us, we waited, trying to save the last cow until we had no more energy, let alone savings. You could say that we were just looking at our cows die, not realizing that this crisis was going to be a long one.

Saving the Livestock

This respondent explains the efforts that went into trying to save his cattle, the main family asset, an effort that was ultimately futile but that was repeated throughout southern Somalia. People sacrificed a lot to get their cattle through to the *gu* rains, which then never came. This informant points out how the cattle-dependent clans, such as the Jiddo, were disastrously hit in 2011, and how some clans such as the Garre and Reer Aw Hassan, who also have camels within the household or within the clan, were protected and could help fellow clan members. This interviewee also provides insights into the process by which remittances sometimes work where access to such financial support might come to assist the recovery of families, rather than to mitigate the impact of a worsening crisis. Those that did not have much livestock to keep them in their rural areas—particularly the Jareer—moved away more quickly.

The Juba Valley

The following interviews were conducted in the Juba Valley (Middle and Lower Juba Regions)—an area that was not the epicentre of the famine, but was very hard hit nonetheless.

7. A Biyomaal Woman from Jamaame District in Lower Juba

Our food [comes] from farming and milk from cattle. In the spring, we grow maize and beans. This is basically our food throughout the year. In the autumn, we grow sesame, which we sell so that we have cash with which we can buy other things we need such as sugar, other foods, and clothes. We also sell a few bulls every few years and use the money to buy more cattle if there is nothing pressing at the time.

In the difficult time we had we put our trust in God and did all that we could to survive. It was really a time of hardship where the few cattle we had were dying and we couldn't grow anything because there were no rains or floods. When people were moving to the refugee camps, we considered this very seriously but in the end decided that it would be bad for the health of our children and we might lose some of them in the disease outbreaks that always happen when people go to camps. So we decided to put our trust in God and stay put. My husband and our second eldest son moved the cattle around, moving from one place to another looking for pasture. In the end, most of them died. We had eight cows remaining by the end of the crisis. I and the rest of the children remained in the village. We used some money we had from the last harvest of sesame but food became very expensive and the money we had quickly ran out. My husband's cousin who had a shop in the area allowed us to take food on credit. He also called some distant relatives they had abroad and they sent money twice. I didn't receive money directly as it was sent to my husband's cousin. Each time he deducted some money for the debt, kept some for us, and gave us a small amount for the things we need. Normally we leave our money with him anyway, for safekeeping. So it was this good man that kept us alive in the drought.

Personal networks and access to credit.

This brief narrative highlights the importance of having an urban or business connection, and it also illustrates the social power and reach of the extended family in Somali society, where distant relatives often play a critical role. It also points to the increasingly high cost of food at the time across all of Somalia.

8. A Biyomaal-Jareer Woman from Jamaame District in Lower Juba

I am Jareer (Biyomaal), they say we are Biyomaal but I really see myself as Jareer only. We have a farm and keep livestock. We normally grow maize in our farm. Rains and the river flooding are important for our farm. In drought time, the rains failed and the river was almost empty. There was a little rain so we sowed some seeds. No more rains came and the stalks started to dry up. Most of the people then started to move to the refugee camps in Kenya. Some walked all the way to Mogadishu and some went to Kismaayo but most of the people went to Kenya. Only those who had strong belief and trust in God remained and thanks to God not many people died of hunger. A few died of weakness and diseases but not many died of hunger. Thanks to God, I have not lost any of my children. They have all survived and are with me now. On the other hand, those who fled to Kenya lost many of their children on the way.

Before the crisis, we had twenty-five sheep and goats. My husband took the goats and sheep to faraway places to save them from dying. In the end, all perished except for seven of them. This meant the job of saving our six children was left to me. I first went to Jamaame town where I ground maize for people. They paid me money. I then moved to Kismaayo, where I moved in with a woman I knew. She took me around to show me all the places where I could find cheap food. Then she showed me many families I could work for. I was washing clothes, cleaning houses, clearing frontcourts, and doing many other jobs. The woman has really helped me out by showing me around, finding me accommodation and jobs, and in the end saying: "Here you are: I showed you around and now it is up to you to make sure that you and your children survive!"

We did survive and I was actually doing well for a while. Then the fights started in Kismaayo again so I moved back to my place since the rains have started again and my husband was back at our village.[18]

Minorities, Movement, and Labor as Coping Strategies

This "minority" woman distinguishes the high mortality rates between those who left, where many died on the way to find help, and those who remained. She also points to the proximity of Dadaab in Kenya. The importance of mobility and splitting up the family comes across clearly here, with her husband moving away to try to keep the animals alive while she was able to find work in different towns and was apparently able to mobilize an old contact to do so. Other interviews point to the importance of larger-scale commercial farms as well as charcoal production in the Lower and Middle Juba Regions.

Journey to the Border and on to the Refugee Camps

9. A Rahanweyn-Gelidle Man Interviewed in Dadaab

I was a rain-fed farmer, and when two rains failed and there was increased insecurity from Al-Shabaab I felt unsafe for my family. I also had some boys who could be convinced by Al-Shabaab and I feared they might join them. Many of their age in Sakow have joined Al-Shabaab while many died in the fights. My three sons are now in school (in Dadaab).

I arrived [in Dadaab] one month before the Ramadan of 2011, coming from Sakow District. From Sakow we used vehicle transport but when we arrived in Dhobley we had no money. We were stranded there for three weeks. We sent the weak members of the family, like young children and their mother, by vehicle, and my three sons and I footed from Dhobley to Dadaab. We spent three days on the way. When we arrived, for one month we were only getting food from other refugees but when we got our card we started receiving food too. I have two wives and I moved with most of the children, but one wife and some children are left taking care of the farm. Nobody in our family died on the way, but when we arrived here in the camp we lost a child of two years.

We came to Dadaab because when you are in Sakow you don't easily get information about Dollo (Ethiopia). Dadaab has been a refugee camp for more than twenty-three years now. There were people from Sakow and even from our village who have been here for several years. We had their information. For Mogadishu, we were also running away from Al-Shabaab.

There are many challenges [to staying in Dadaab] including insecurity from the local community militias. The life is very difficult but good water services and free education for our children is why we are tolerating all the problems we have here. We only receive what we are given, but don't ask, because we fear for our lives from the host community and their clan members in the refugee camp. Even the staff members of the humanitarian agency are from the local community.

Yes, we all go back to do some farming or labor work, whichever is possible, to get some money to send for the family here. That is the only way to survive if you don't have business or someone to send you money. So that is common, especially for the Rahanweyn refugees.

Reasons for Moving, Maintaining links, and the Control of Aid

This revealing interview shows the fear that many parents have of their sons being recruited by Al-Shabaab, and how this factors into people's decisions about movement. The strength of social networks, even within a camp setting, is important, with assistance coming from earlier arrivals. The camps also offer opportunities not available at home, such as education, and although it is not mentioned, Dadaab is seen as a gateway to the rest of Kenya and the West. The issue of "gatekeepers" and control of the camps and their resources is also indicated, as it was earlier for Mogadishu; control of resources also lies within the staffing of aid agencies.[19] Finally, Dadaab is clearly also part of the well-established cross-border trade and seasonal migration between Kenya and Somalia.

Mosques as Humanitarian Actors

10. Interview with a Senior Somali Sheikh (religious leader) based in Kenya

The crisis happened in our neighborhood. We heard what was happening from the media and from the people. We then went to Dadaab, in July 2011, to see the affected people for ourselves and from there we sent an appeal through the media as we were accompanied by crews from several TV stations. We have raised the issue in the mosques and talked about it a lot. We created a committee to manage the money. I was a member of this committee. We held fundraising functions at this mosque and other mosques in Nairobi and Mombasa.

We bought food with the money raised. We negotiated with the food storeowners to get goods discounted. Transport companies and truck owners have also offered us free transport. The money transfer companies (the hawalas) have made all transfers for this purpose from anywhere in the world free. They also donated large sums of cash.

We have known Dadaab refugee camps for a long time and we were well connected to them. We had people in the refugee camps that we trusted so we used them to distribute the aid. They gave each household a card and gave them rations of food. These men worked also with the UN agencies in the refugee camps so they were allowed to use the UN stores and distribution centres.

The first people who responded to the needs of the new arrivals were the refugees who were already in there. They shared with them the little food they had and gave them some clothes. We asked the food store owners to package food in rations of 5 to 10 kilograms of rice, flour, and sugar, and also provided tea and cooking oil. The new arrivals were very much malnourished, and the weakest—the children and elderly—were on the verge of dying, so we purchased dates and nutritious powdered milk as rich foods for quick recovery. Then came Arab and Muslim NGOs who have gone down the same path we have gone through and used the same methods we have used. They came with money, bought food from the same stores, and distributed them to the refugees. Some of them moved into the camps and made their own camps there. The Turkish organizations were the best. They made their camp in the middle of the refugee camps. The UN and other international NGOs then arrived. By this time, the refugees were much better and well nourished. Most of the Arab and Turkish NGOs then left.

We realized that many people were dying before reaching Kenya so we started to send help to the areas people were coming from and to the IDP camps in southern Somalia, in Kismaayo, Bardere, Beledweyne, Baidoa, Elasha Biyaha, etc. We were sending money to people we trusted so that they could buy food locally and distribute it to the IDPs. The total money they brought was about US $700,000, of which $300,000–$400,000 was spent on refugees in Kenya and the rest in Somalia.[20]

We obtained about US $3 million in cash as well as food and other [in-kind] support such as free transportation and money transfers, in two months. In Somalia, we faced problems in Al-Shabaab-controlled areas. In Kenya's Dadaab refugee camps (Ifo and Dhagahley), members of the local clans administer the area and they tried to take a share of the aid using "the system" sometimes, and bandits in other times. They looted lots of aid. They came into the camps and intimidated those who were administering the aid distribution and looted some food. We had to use the police. We also asked the UN agencies to support us to protect the aid. Also in the local administration there are some people who are not from the local clan so we used them also to stop this looting.

The Humanitarian Compact Between Religious, Business, and Diaspora Networks

Somali religious leaders, their mosques, and their networks in Kenya were prominent in the "early" response to the famine although, as indicated, it was "early" only in relation to the arrival of distressed and dying people in Dadaab, and it was focused initially on Dadaab in Kenya, rather than in Somalia. However, these people and networks received money from throughout the Somali world, including the global and regional Somali diaspora, as well as other parts of Somalia. They also merged with the business community to raise money and deliver assistance. These religious networks would also have been able to tap into and influence resources from the Middle East. This interview also reconfirms the difficulties with and diversion of aid on the Kenyan side of the border.

Dollo-Ado in Ethiopia

11. A Rahanweyn-Lawai Woman in Dollo-Ado Refugee Camp, in Ethiopia

We had five cows and thirty-two goats before the drought. We were doing intensive farming, growing sorghum, maize, sesame, and cowpeas. Sesame growing started only three seasons before the drought. It was bringing in a lot of money but we later regretted this decision because we initially got money but lost it easily because there was no feedstock for livestock from the sesame. I do believe it was because of sesame growing by the people and Al-Shabaab pressure that made the drought as bad as it was. We had no access to any remittance. All those who had access to remittance are still there in their villages.

Al-Shabaab also introduced farm taxation, which has never been imposed before, even during the colonial period. We used to pay at the planting and harvesting times and the harvest zakat is again separate. They don't give the zakat to the poor people.

We kept a huge amount of sorghum stock because we sold two cows and bought sorghum. This was in December 2010. We tried hard to feed the three remaining cows and the goats. We pushed them to April 2011, but my husband said these cows will die so don't waste the food for the children on them. In May 2011, all the cows and half of the goats died. Because there were many relatives in the village, my husband asked me to help those who didn't have sorghum with what we had. He gave all the goats we had to those who had nothing. By the end of May 2011, we had finished our sorghum stock too. We shared our sorghum stock with those who had nothing. We called some relatives in Mogadishu to help us with something, which they did, and we used it to buy food on the way to Dollo.

[My husband] called all the elders and told them we need to go to another place to survive. Otherwise the drought would kill all the people too. The family head of these eleven families including my husband decided to move us to Dollo. We migrated from Ufurow District. We moved by foot from Ufurow to Dollo. We lost three children on the way between the eleven families moving together. We arrived in Dollo the month before the Ramadan of the drought year (June 2011). We spent fifteen days on the way. We used donkey carts to carry the weak children, water, and food.

We chose Dollo because it was nearer to us than Dadaab and Mogadishu, and it is more secure than Dadaab, Baidoa, and Mogadishu. Also, Al-Shabaab were controlling the way to Baidoa, and Mogadishu. They were the only ones who had resources and they were giving it to themselves and supporters so that everyone joins them on the basis of resources. We heard Dollo was good and that is why we came here.

In Dollo, we arrived and were received at Wabarka, where we registered and stayed two days, then moved to the transit point at Yubow. Here it was very bad because almost everybody fell sick. From the eleven families that came together we lost two children, including one of my daughters. We were then moved here, to Heloweyn camp. We are doing well. Initially, we were given good food but now we have problems with food because it is lacking important ingredients like milk, meat, and vegetables. However, we got education, medical, and water services for our children, which we never had in Ufurow.

Secure in Ethiopia

This interview indicates the pressure to share increasingly scant resources and then how the decision to move might be taken on a communal basis. Many respondents reported that Dollo was safer, but also that decisions to move were part of pre-existing information networks; those who went to Dollo having been set up with the withdrawal of Ethiopian troops and their Somali allies from Somalia in 2009. Of particular note is the human cost of moving itself, a significant journey, as well as the high mortality rate in the transit camps, a fact confirmed in official reports.[21] Access to basic services—education, health, and water—is clearly also an attraction, and the role of Al-Shabaab is again made clear.

A View from the Diaspora

12. A Hawiye-Murasade Man from the UK

The drought started at the end of 2010. We started receiving calls for help and alarming news from families in that area. Al-Shabaab were in control of the area as they are now and were not allowing any food aid. At the time, NGOs were still allowed to operate in the area, so they did some water trucking and that really helped, as food aid was not allowed by Al-Shabaab, and the NGOs were distributing some cash. Then as the drought was getting worse, Al-Shabaab banned all aid organizations and the NGOs had to stop working. It was at this time that sheep and goats [small ruminants] started to die, followed by cattle, and in the end camels started dying. I know families who had 110 small ruminants who were left with only ten.

As the drought progressed, those who were left destitute started flocking into the nearest settlements. The village had about 500 families, but 500 destitute families arrived at the village in a short time. The settled families did the best they could. Most of the families took in at least one family. On top of that they were collecting money and supplies for the others who were not taken by any family. As this was not enough, people started dying. Actually, many people started dying before they moved to the village. For three months, more than three people were dying daily in the village. When the village couldn't cope anymore and deaths couldn't be halted, they called for help from the clan members in Mogadishu. The village is remote and there was no media coverage or interest.

The clan members in Mogadishu responded quickly with cash and food. The food was bought in Mogadishu market and it bore the signs of WFP, so Al-Shabaab rejected it and it couldn't be distributed while people were dying. They also asked for the money to be handed to them so they could distribute it themselves. The clan refused to agree to this. There was a standoff for a while but in the end the elders of the clan put pressure on the clan members who were in the leadership of Al-Shabaab. Al-Shabaab yielded and allowed the cash and any food that didn't bear the signs of WFP or any other organization to be distributed freely. The clan members in Mogadishu responded well. I know one man who donated US $200,000 in one go. Many others were similar in generosity. The members in Mogadishu also contacted the diaspora members of the clan who in three months collected and sent more than US $1 million. The death rate started reducing and the deaths stopped altogether before the rains started.

When the rains started, the remaining cash was used to buy livestock for the people who lost their animals, as rains would have meant nothing for them without their livestock. People in the area also donated animals for this purpose. For example, my mother gave away ten sheep or goats to relatives. There was a lot of death in this area, but it was not reported.

At first, when people were calling me, I thought it was the usual calls that I used to receive as people always tell us stories to get money. Then we realized there was a problem. It took time to mobilize people. It also took time to persuade Al-Shabaab to let us help our people. All this contributed to the delay. It is also the case that many nomads put all their efforts into saving their animals and did not have much time to solicit money from relatives until their children were too weak. Some of them also were proud people who didn't want to ask for handouts. All these factors contributed to the delay. However, in the end, the family got their act together and halted the death rates before the deyr rains.

13. A Murasade Man in Central Somalia

My family consists of me, my wife, and seven children. I had 100 goats and sheep, a single male camel used for getting water for the family, and a rain-fed farm in which I grew beans and watermelons. Before the drought I was self-sufficient and had a peaceful life. I used to take my farm's products to a nearby village and exchange them with sugar and other items we needed. The drought changed my life dramatically. My sheep and goats started dying during the jilaal and by the gu I lost all of them. I decided to sell the single camel I had, but couldn't find any buyers as the drought affected everyone in the area. After a long search I found a buyer in the end who paid very little money for my camel.

While I was looking for a buyer, I lost two daughters, Fatima and Maka. I believe that they died of malnutrition. I decided to move the family to the village. I walked to the village and two days later I arrived with my remaining two children and my wife. We went to my paternal auntie's house. My auntie saw that the children were in a bad condition and she quickly gathered the family. The family decided that the children would be divided between three families: two families would take two each and one family would take one, and I and my wife would have to support ourselves.

I had some money remaining from the camel I sold but it was not enough so I started to work as a laborer fetching water and bringing water and selling it to support myself and my wife. I continued in this situation until the end of the drought. At the end of the drought I was one of those who were given some livestock by the clan to help us re-start our lives. I am now back on my farm with my family reunited. I have some sheep and goats, and a male camel. I am back in my old ordinary life, self-sufficient and regularly contribute to the wellbeing of the clan.

Hardships Even with Diaspora and Business Support

The Hawiye-Murasade are one of the major clans/sub-clans in Somalia. In contrast to the Rahanweyn and the Jareer, they, like many of the other major clans and sub-clans, have a level of wealth and diversification through their business and diaspora populations, which means they have alternative options in times of drought. As this interview demonstrates, however, even having such options is no guarantee that a crisis can be completely averted. But it can be mitigated and recovered from quickly. These socio-political hierarchies and histories in Somali society are well known in academic circles, though they are not well utilized by humanitarian actors or studied in-depth in terms of understanding vulnerabilities and resilience. The challenges faced with Al-Shabaab were felt at the clan level.

A Final View from a Major Private Company

14. The Director of a Major Somali National Private Company, Based in Mogadishu

We have centres in all districts and most of the bigger villages in South Central Somalia. Our staff in all these places had been following reports of what was happening in their districts. Every centre was reporting to me, and any community issue was followed up and we see what it is possible to do.

When the deyr 2010–11 failed, almost all our centres in Bay, Bakool, Gedo, Middle Juba, Lower Juba, and the Shabelles reported a critical need for water. In March 2011, we had a managerial meeting here in Mogadishu. Before we had the meeting there were staff contributing and doing water trucking at their respective district levels. This was what made us feel that things were serious. At the meeting it was decided five of us would go to Bakool (Wajid and Hudur), Bay (Baidoa, Dinsor, Burhakaba, and Qansaxdheere), Gedo (Bardera), the Jubas (Sakow and Buale), and the Shabelles (Qorioley and Aw Degle). We came back to Mogadishu after twelve days. We had the mandate to start water trucking in all these places and to do food distribution where possible, but Al-Shabaab refused us and we came back without doing anything. We were worried very much. They [Al-Shabaab] wanted 30 percent of the money allocated to do trucking or food.

By April and May 2011, things continued to deteriorate in all the districts we had visited and people started moving out to refugee camps or IDP camps. We would have stopped the movements if we had been allowed to assist people by March 2011. When people started moving out en masse by May 2011, and Al-Shabaab could not stop it or control it anymore, we started helping the people in all the places we visited. We also started helping people where they were displaced, especially Baidoa, Kilometer 50, Mogadishu, and Afgooye. In Mogadishu, we targeted mainly Badbaado camp, which was the main camp for Bay Region IDPs. In Kilometer 50 we spent more than $600,000 on food only. In this place [K50] almost half of the people taken there died, especially children. We assisted them to be moved to Badbaado and we followed them with the assistance. You know it is not easy to contain the situation once people are displaced.

We provided water and food as well as cash. In K50 and Badbado we were giving 25 kilograms of rice, 25 kilograms of wheat flour, 3 liters of oil, and 200,000 Somali shillings for milk, vegetables, and meat. We started mid-May and continued until January 2012. We have used more than US $1.8 million. Our focus was Bay (Dinsor and Qansaxdheere) where the main "halaag" [disaster] happened, Bakool, Lower Shabelle, Lower Juba, and Middle Juba populations. We were paying attention to Dinsor, Qansaxdheere, Qorioley, and Baidoa because these were the worst affected.

We faced different challenges including Al-Shabaab refusing to let the people in their village be helped at an early stage, no government participation in emergency response, but they also put many road blocks to loot the assistance. If you work in an Al-Shabaab area, the government will say you support Al-Shabaab and the same if you work in the government area. This puts our staff in a bad situation of security.

Yes, in terms of learning, we need to reduce duplication of beneficiaries but for us it is "sadaka"[22]—so as long as the person is needy and we give it to him/her, we have no problem. No, we don't want to work with government because they are very corrupt and this is our own money that we are giving as "sadaka" or charity, so we please Allah and get his rewards.

A Proactive Somali Business

This narrative illustrates the actual and potential social role that many Somali businesses play in the country, in the absence of publicly managed responses to disasters. The respondent clearly had a good overview of the evolving disaster, drawing on his field offices and staff, and the company appeared ready to start helping people relatively early in the crisis, but was constrained by Al-Shabaab. Ultimately, the company did provide significant resources to the humanitarian response. Many other Somali companies responded in a similar way.

Summary

While only a small selection of all the interviews conducted for this study, these narratives illustrate the complexity and diversity of Somali society, and the implications for people's differing ability to withstand the repeated and varied shocks they experience. This diversity reflects local ecology, and economic and demographic factors, as well as historical patterns of inequality in Somali society. Many of these are poorly understood by outsiders and not well addressed by Somalis themselves. They also illustrate more positive aspects of the Somali economy and society where social solidarity and connections at the individual, family, and clan as well as business and religious levels can and were mobilized to a great extent to help support people outside of the reach of the more formal humanitarian response.

These narratives began with the worst affected areas. This was within Bay region, among the Rahanweyn—highlighting particularly the districts and resident sub-clans of Qansaxdheere and Dinsor; and in Lower Shabelle—

highlighting the experience of the Jareer and Jiddo in Qorioley, Kurtanwarey, and Sablale. However, while these were two of the major focal points of the famine, the impact of the crisis at the time was widespread, and malnutrition and increased mortality were occurring in many other places, particularly as people traveled to areas where aid was arriving—Baidoa, Mogadishu, and the refugee camps in Kenya and Ethiopia. These locations offered many opportunities for profiteering, especially Mogadishu.

In addition to providing new insights and nuance into the social geography of the famine, these narratives inevitably raise new questions that require further understanding, as well as generating demands from humanitarian practitioners about if and how to incorporate such an analysis into humanitarian policy and programming. This is discussed further in Chapter 6.

6

DIVERSIFICATION, FLEXIBILITY, AND SOCIAL CONNECTEDNESS

UNDERSTANDING THE NARRATIVES

Introduction

As many of the narratives in Chapter 5 illustrate, local communities outside the areas where humanitarian assistance was available were left more or less on their own to cope with the worsening circumstances in the first half of 2011. While the experiences of the interviewees in Chapter 5 varied by location, clan, gender, and livelihood group, this chapter seeks to identify and further develop a number of common themes in their narratives. It begins with a brief discussion of Somali clans and an explanation of why such identities and characteristics are important for understanding the famine. Following this socio-political introduction is a discussion of specific livelihood changes that preceded the famine and contributed to increased vulnerability. This leads to a deeper interpretation of the way in which different groups coped with the worsening crisis in 2010–11. Finally, the chapter revisits the sensitive topic of the way in which social structure facilitates both inclusion and exclusion, including an analysis of the role of "gatekeepers" and Al-Shabaab.

Somali Clans and Clan Structure

Somalia is often referred to as a clan-based society, although some scholars contest the significance of clan. The Somali clan is described as a "segmented lineage" structure, which is continually sub-divided through the generations but claims a "total Somali genealogy."[1] Rather than being a fixed system, it is noted for its flexibility and relativism.[2] Following this argument, Virginia Luling describes the Somali genealogy as a "sophisticated construct" with many contested relationships.[3] She goes on to explain that while clanism rarely explains conflict, it does provide a critical framework through which politics plays out.

Five major clan families are commonly ascribed to all ethnic Somali: the Isaaq, Darod, Dir, Hawiye, and Rahanweyn.[4] Each of these clan families contains sub-clans, sub-sub-clans, and so on. Broadly speaking, these clans are associated with a particular territory, with the Isaaq predominantly located— and dominant in—the northwest (Somaliland); the Majerteen of the Darod, found—and dominant in—the northeast (Puntland); the Hawiye associated with Mogadishu and central Somalia; and the Dir in the far northwest and scattered elsewhere. These clans consider themselves the "noble," nomadic clans and were glorified as part of the state-building agenda in the 1970s and 1980s. The Rahanweyn have been marginalized historically and described as second-class citizens.[5] They are agro-pastoral in terms of livelihood and are the dominant group in the inter-riverine areas of Bay and Bakool Regions, but also the inter-riverine areas of other neighbouring areas. Within the Rahanweyn, there is a wide variation on the agriculture–livestock spectrum (livestock are relatively more important for some and vice versa). The Rahanweyn are also significant, as the dialect they speak—Af-Maay—is different from standard Somali or Maxatiir, and they have social and cultural differences from the major clans.

While the Rahanweyn are identified for their marginalized position, there are other hierarchies within Somali society, with the Somali Bantu occupying an even more "inferior" position—and referred to as third-class citizens.[6] Although they are often referred to by the general name of "Somali Bantu," they are in fact a heterogeneous group composed of indigenous Bantu populations as well as former imported slaves.[7] Bantu populations are particularly associated with riverine farming, living as small landowners and landless laborers, but also live within different Rahanweyn clans in the rain-fed interior.

"Tribalism" (clanism) was officially banned during the Siad Barre regime, although this ban was ineffective, and indeed the glorification of pastoral identity became part of the state-building process, reflecting the dominant position of the northern Somali pastoral clans in national politics.[8] This northern, pastoral bias in Somali politics and identity is an important and contested aspect of Somalia's politics today.

Clan identities and social networks provide a useful means for understanding notions of resilience and vulnerability. For example, Interview 13 in Chapter 5 refers to the Murasade of the Hawiye, suggesting they are relatively wealthy and diversified at the level of the clan, with significant business and diaspora communities. This description of diversification applies to many sub-clans within the "noble" clan families. Judith Gardner and Judy El Bushra, referring to the 1970s and 1980s, provide a snapshot of the diversification that was taking place within some elements of Somali society prior to the collapse of the state:

> For example, it would not have been surprising to find that an extended family includes: a son who lives as a nomadic herder in the rural area taking care of the extended family livestock; a daughter who is also a pastoralist, living with her husband in the rural area; another son at university in the capital training to be an engineer; a son working in a Gulf country who sends back money regularly to his relatives in Somalia; a daughter who trained as a teacher and is married to an army lieutenant; another son who runs a business in town using his brother's foreign currency to buy imported goods; an unmarried daughter who is a bank clerk; and a grandson studying computer sciences in the US. Within this web of livelihoods income or resources in-kind are transferred or negotiated between family members so as to support and maintain the whole.[9]

Following the collapse of the state, the emphasis within the diaspora shifted to Europe and North America, but the structure continued to be organized to share resources within extended families and sub-clans, diversified in space and occupation—and diversified, therefore, in terms of the risks to which they were exposed as well as the strategies upon which they could rely. The Rahanweyn and Bantu were largely excluded from processes of urbanization, education, and government employment, and therefore, to opportunities for working abroad during the 1970s and 1980s.

Though local exceptions and nuances abound, in general this degree of diversification distinguishes the "noble" clans from the Rahanweyn and the Bantu. The latter two, while having some business and diaspora communities, and therefore some degree of diversification, have a much smaller proportion of their populations outside the rural economy.[10] Within the Rahanweyn there are differences in this regard. In Narrative 1 in Chapter 5, a man from the Rahanweyn-Leysan reflects on one of the most diversified clans of the Rahanweyn. He notes that his clan will not allow people to die while they have something.

Many respondents described the Jiddo as having been particularly badly affected by the 2011 famine. Their predicament illustrates the convergence of geography, identity, and livelihood. The Jiddo are primarily cattle pastoralists, found at the lower end of the Shabelle River (Qorioley, Kurtunwaarrey, and Sablale Districts). They were considered relatively wealthy, having large numbers of cattle. However, in 2011, the unprecedented drying up of the Shabelle River in its lower reaches meant that water and pasture diminished and the Jiddo lost vast numbers of their cattle. In analytical terms, their wealth became a huge liability, largely because the river dried up (an extremely rare occurrence).

Livelihood Changes

Broadly speaking, as the Jiddo example suggests, there is a convergence between geography, clan, and livelihood system in Somalia. Indeed, much contemporary analysis of Somalia excludes any mention of clan on the assumption that descriptions of livelihood groups adequately capture clan dynamics. However, in the years prior to 2011, several significant changes were taking place within existing livelihood systems, some of which cast both wealth and vulnerability in new and unrecognized terms—in particular, changes in cash crops and cattle ownership.

One of the points repeatedly raised by respondents in areas closest to the epicentre of the famine—in certain districts of Bay Region, especially Dinsor and Qansaxdheere—was the importance of sesame cultivation in the dynamics of 2011. Many respondents reported that they had switched to growing greater amounts of sesame and invested the increased returns in cattle. This in turn contributed to greater vulnerability, as cattle are the livestock least able to withstand severe drought. The efforts people invested to save their cattle turned out to be a significant factor in the severity of the famine itself. Unpacking this dynamic, however, is a complex task.

Sesame has been grown for many years in southern Somalia, but has essentially been confined to the riverine (irrigated) areas of the Juba and Shabelle Valleys. Sesame oil is produced and consumed locally and is also exported. In rain-fed areas, the introduction of sesame is a more recent phenomenon. Available information on the total area devoted to sesame production in the inter-riverine areas is incomplete and doesn't necessarily show major increases in sesame production. These areas had been under Al-Shabaab control for several years and accurate figures were therefore difficult to obtain. But numerous interviews with key informants and farmers in a variety of different locations suggested that increasing sesame production had been a broader trend and provided explanations as to why traders from Mogadishu have been encouraging increased cultivation and providing credit to do so; why the demand for sesame oil (and price) has been increasing in the Middle East, where it is used in one of the main staples; and why the demand for and price of sorghum has remained very low and consumption patterns may be shifting in Bay towards more imported cereal foods. It also helps to explain the heavy taxation imposed by Al-Shabaab.[11]

This shift increased people's vulnerability to drought. In the seasons immediately prior to the *deyr* failure of late 2010, sesame production and returns were reported to be good, and many people invested these returns in cattle. A number of respondents commented that they briefly became "rich" before the famine. Cattle are, however, the first livestock to die in a serious drought. Moreover, the epicentre of the famine was in densely populated districts, relatively speaking, where grazing land was limited. Many who invested in cattle were primarily farmers, and were forced to rely on sorghum residue—and even their grain stocks from the harvest—to feed their livestock, since open grazing was limited.

When the drought started to bite in late 2010, two problems arose: first, sorghum stocks were lower than they would normally have been as less sorghum (and more sesame) was being grown, and second, demand for the remaining sorghum stocks dramatically increased with the drought—from both people and cattle. Many people reported feeding their cattle the same food they were eating, as well as the grass from their own roofs. Not only did the cattle succumb to the drought conditions, wiping out the newfound wealth, but this whole phenomenon also left human populations with lower grains reserves, despite having just come through a relatively good agricultural year (2010).

What does this mean in terms of the trajectory of the famine? If sesame had not been introduced or expanded so rapidly—or the proceeds invested in cattle—two consecutive rain failures would still have represented a serious deterioration in the situation. But had there been fewer cattle to protect and more sorghum stocks, it is easy to speculate that the deterioration in human conditions might not have proceeded so rapidly. And had some of the money invested in cattle been held in cash in a *hawala* instead, those assets would not have been vulnerable to drought.

And, of course, people are constrained by their basic livelihoods. Although not a new finding, camel pastoralists were actually the least vulnerable because camels are drought resistant and able to move long distances in search of water and browse. The groups hardest hit by the 2011 famine were agro-pastoralists and farmers, whose basic assets defy mobility. Indeed, there is some evidence that they had recently adopted production strategies and assets that made them more vulnerable to successive drought, but had done so in part to adapt to a changing set of conditions. Competition for irrigated riverine farmland had been increasing—likewise because of lower vulnerability to drought. But in this case, when the Shabelle River ran dry in some of its lower reaches in 2011, it made a usually fairly resilient group acutely vulnerable.

A Typology of Coping

The term "coping" has come to mean many things. On the one hand, it means that while the situation is bad, people are getting by somehow (i.e., they are "coping" with the situation). On the other hand, coping can have a range of meanings, from relatively minor changes in behavior or consumption all the way to literally starvation and death—in other words it can mean any form of altered behavior that a person, household, or group might be forced into in order to deal with an absence of food, water, shelter, protection, or some other basic human need. In the classic description, "coping" meant relatively short-term means of dealing with a setback; "adapting" meant longer-term means of dealing with a permanently or semi-permanently changed context.[12] This corresponds to contemporary categories that analyze "resilience" in terms of different capacities—also at the individual, household, and community level. "Absorptive capacity" is all about being able to absorb a short-term setback and bounce back to some pre-existing level of both current consumption or livelihood status and capacity (roughly speaking, "coping" in earlier parlance). "Adaptive capacity" is about being able to deal with the consequences of longer-term changes, without compromising future livelihood status or capacity (obviously, "adapting" in earlier parlance). A drought, a price shock, an episode of displacement, or other shock is usually the context for discussing absorptive capacity; climate change is, of course, the most-frequently discussed example requiring adaptive capacity. A third capability, "transformative capacity," is about not just keeping up with contextual changes but being able to shape that context proactively. This one is rarely discussed in the context of Somalia.[13]

Analytically, the problem is that these are never discrete categories or separate events. The symptoms of climate change are ongoing in the Horn of Africa, even when certain cyclical events like the El Niño Southern Oscillation lead to intermittent shocks. As discussed in Chapter 4, the famine of 2011 came about as a result of the combination of several simultaneous shocks. And the extent to which these shocks become humanitarian crises is almost always determined by the political and institutional context, not just by the magnitude of the shocks themselves. It is therefore difficult to separate strategies on which Somali people rely much of the time in a context that is hazard-prone even at the best of times from those strategies that people were forced to resort to in the context of a famine—which is to say, at the worst of times.

The results of over 400 interviews with households in areas that experienced the famine or households that had left famine-affected areas for Dollo-Ado, Dadaab, or Mogadishu, show a typology of strategies that have been in place for a long time, but which in the event of an acute crisis might be intensified. These are depicted in Table 6.1. While many of the strategies noted in Table 6.1 are discrete, they could well be categorized more systematically. These could be classified as strategies of diversification (diversification of risk, of livelihoods, and income streams, or of assets, and the ability to protect assets); flexibility (mobility of animals; flexibility to move parts of households or whole households; opportunistic exploitation of credit, natural resources, or aid) and social connectedness.

How individual strategies play out; which is invoked first, second, or last; and the longer-term consequences of some of these strategies all vary by social group. Some clans, for example, have much stronger links to a diaspora (and most diaspora remittances go to family members or close relatives—and thus remittances are a very clan-denominated strategy). Evidence from field interviews showed different clan groups living in the same area, but with different assets and different external linkages, responding to the worsening crisis in very different ways. Clans also have different access to aid and to aid agencies, with some clans dominating the local-NGO business in different locations, or playing the role of gatekeeper within international agencies.

These categories (diversification, flexibility, and connectedness) have gender dimensions. Women's and men's roles in Somali society have been changing over the last twenty years, with women becoming more active as economic actors since the collapse of the state; women are able to cross clan lines—for economic or social reasons—where men might not be able to.[14] While women traditionally had less mobility, very few women respondents mentioned this issue in coping with the crisis of 2011. Indeed, several of the interviews in Chapter 5 show how women had to be mobile (flexible), drawing on social networks (connectedness) to find help and ways to manage the crisis. Somali society remains highly patriarchal but gender relations are changing and are more complex than is often suggested. Nevertheless, the role of women under

Table 6.1: Typology of Resilience and Coping in the Somali Famine

Category	Examples	Level	Application/ Severity
Diversification	• Diversify livelihoods and assets • Diversification of risk • Diversify against drought risk (riverine farming and/ or camels) • Have a foot in the urban economy	Individual/ household Some diversifica- tion within clan or larger group	Mostly applies in the longer term as a means of reducing risk, not as a means of coping with shocks
Flexibility	• Physical mobility with livestock • Labor mobility (employ- ment) • Exploit different opportu- nities (including humani- tarian aid) • Outmigration as a last resort	Household Community-level decisions about when to move?	
Social "connectedness"	• Forms of mutual support • Usual: remittances; unusual: diaspora or urban contacts, etc. • Having "someone to cry to"; three concentric circles model	"Second circle" community level/ clan level Partly business level	Diaspora remittances stepped up in famine: food, water trucking Third circle as "system failure"
Political power	• Access to/control over aid	Household Community	Gatekeepers from powerful clans in IDP settings
Crisis asset protection	• Sharing food with livestock • Buying water for livestock • Moving livestock in search of grazing and water	Household Community	Feeding cattle thatch from roofs during drought Timing of livestock sales Out-migration usually as a last resort
	• Leaving someone behind to protect land if migrating • Decision making about when to sell animals, when to move, etc.		

Category	Examples	Level	Application/ Severity
Asset sales or depletion	• Sale of livestock • Sale of other productive assets • Land pledging or mortgaging • Feeding livestock thatch grass from house roofs to keep animals alive	Household Community	
Rapid livelihood adaptation	• Renting farmland (esp. riverine) to protect animals (access water/fodder) • Sharing lactating animals— move with non-lactating animals • Natural resource extraction: firewood, charcoal, thatch grass • Search for casual wage employment	Household or inter-household Wage labor in community as form of social reciprocity albeit a form of exchange	Some of these are "normal" livelihoods for poor people, others are coping strategies in crisis.
Credit	• Use of savings/borrowing/ debt • Borrowing/purchase on credit as one form of social connectedness	Household Business	Social networks portrayed in positive light; can lead to long-term indebtedness
Consumption strategies	• Changing diets • Borrowing food or money • Rationing strategies • Going hungry		
Household and inter-household demographic strategies	• Family splitting—both consumption-minimization strategy and resource-acquisition maximization strategy • Opportunistic access to aid resources/household splitting • Labor-sharing	Household Inter-household/ community	

Data: Field Interviews 2012–14.

Al-Shabaab was often severely constrained,[15] and one of the constant problems women faced during the crisis was gender-based violence, especially in the IDP camps.[16]

In general, the strategies described in Table 6.1 are not unique to Somalia—they have in fact been observed in many risk-prone, low-income areas of the Horn of Africa and other regions. Perhaps the most unique category of strategies in the Somali context is that of social connectedness. Social connectedness, social networks, or "social capital" are part of societies and livelihoods everywhere. But even though labor migration and remittances are a widespread phenomenon, the Somali diaspora is practically synonymous with the notion of remittances that support family members or close relatives at home in Somalia. The role of remittances in reducing vulnerability has received lots of attention, and indeed a whole industry (the *hawala* system) has grown up around the transfer of money to even the most remote places inside Somalia. But evidence is only relatively thin about the actual impact of remittances on livelihoods or food security, even in the famine.[17] Moreover, the notion of social connectedness is only partially captured by the practice of foreign remittances. The bonds of social obligation are very strong within clans and sub-groups in Somali society, but often do not cross clan lines, and often even within clans or sub-clans, there are other differentiating factors.

During the famine, these bonds can best be summarized as three concentric circles of connectedness. The first circle relates to immediate kin; this is where much—but not all—of the regular remittance connections reside. If a household or individual had connections to someone in the diaspora or in urban employment in a sector that was relatively immune to the crisis (business, in particular), or had strongly diversified assets themselves, then such a household was likely to survive irrespective of what happened to their own livelihood. On the other hand, in the absence of such linkages, or if the linkages broke down because the remitting individual or household also faced the same crisis, then connectedness defaulted to the second circle. The first circle doesn't extend more broadly.

The second circle relates broadly to clan and community, which often but not always overlap. Nevertheless, the second circle is based on "face-to-face" relations. While not necessarily providing a regular, or necessarily even reliable, source of income in the face of worsening circumstances, people did share what they could from their own resources. The second circle seems to be the critical one. It would be described in contemporary terms as "community absorptive capacity" and describes how much of a shock the broader group can withstand without its resource pool collapsing. Thus one cannot accurately describe the "absorptive capacity" of a given household without reference to this second circle. Even the first circle, which is more evident, is difficult to describe accurately or "measure"; the second circle is almost impossible to measure, but appeared to be the critical factor in whether a household weathered the famine or not.

The second circle is about sharing resources: it could be about *zakat*; it could be the basis for extending credit (from a shopkeeper or a relative/clan mate) when a household is in a bind; or it could be a more collective sharing of money or other resources. Examples of all these are evident in the narratives in Chapter 5 and other interviews.[18] When assessing this second circle, it is important to understand who is in and who is out (even within a clan or lineage-based grouping), the kinds of resources that might "circulate," and the diversity of resources and linkages. This second circle was weakened by various factors in 2011. One was Al-Shabaab's claim of *zakat* for its own use (thus taking it out of the circle); another was that wealthier or better-connected people had already begun moving out of the community because of Al-Shabaab harassment or other related factors not specifically connected to conflict. This meant the second circle was weakened even before the crisis hit. When this second circle collapsed, it did so suddenly and with little else in the way of a safety net.

The third circle is much more distant, and comprises people that one might not know, perhaps friends of the family or distant relatives. It might also be "big people" with whom one can assert some claim of friendship or social connection, however faint. This circle does not function in "normal" circumstances, but was evident during the famine.

Analytically, each of these gets back to the question of mobility and diversification, as well as the assets that flow within each of the circles. If, within the first circle (immediate kin), someone outside the country was remitting money, the recipient household or individual was relatively immune to the impacts of the famine—and indeed may have even benefited from those impacts (buying other people's assets at low prices, for example). On the other hand, if everyone in the immediate first circle was in the same circumstances as the individual or household under consideration, it collapsed fairly quickly and on the same time frame. The second circle can usually help the individual or household weather an idiosyncratic shock, and—up to a point—can assist more-vulnerable households in a covariate shock such as those experienced in 2010–11. However, the resources that circulate in this circle are finite, and difficult to measure in any way except after the fact.

The collapse of this second circle largely defined the onset of famine conditions in 2011. And this collapse was sudden and not necessarily predictable. But this collapse is indicated by individuals or households beginning to assert claims in the third circle. Several respondents described beginning to get phone calls from people they didn't know but who claimed to know their father, or their extended family, or the organization for which they worked. This started happening in May or early June 2011 (six weeks before the formal declaration of famine) in the centre of the famine, in Bay Region.[19] If one were to propose an "emic" definition for the declaration of a famine in Somalia, this was probably it.

Responses of the Somali Government

The Transitional Federal Government was peripherally involved in the response to the famine but this was more dependent on the goodwill and initiative of certain individuals rather than policy, and some government employees were actively competing to influence the direction of aid or attempting to profit from it. A Disaster Management Agency within the TFG was formed in July/August 2011 in order to respond to the unfolding disaster. This was a late reaction, triggered by the wider media publicity and other humanitarian activities rather than from its own early warning analysis. This agency reportedly linked with the business community, the media and especially with the OIC and its members and Somali agencies that were receiving money from the diaspora. The agency was able to raise some limited financial support from OIC members to equip an office (not from the TFG's own resources), and claims to have been involved in assisting with the work of these mostly Somali-led institutions. The extent to which this involvement was significant and added value to the work of these agencies is doubtful and at best minimal. In other words, in the absence of this agency, it is likely that the same set of actors would have carried out much of the same work.

There was no guiding policy or coordination within government for the DMA until 2013—and in fact, different ministries were competing to be involved in the process of aid delivery during the 2011 response. Beyond this more intra-institutional competition, many other government officials or people acting on behalf of the government were actively involved in diverting aid to their own clan members or claiming it and selling it on the market.[20]

Gatekeepers

One of the most intractable problems presented by the displacement crisis in Somalia, which long pre-dated the 2011 famine and of course has continued since, is the treatment of displaced people at the hands of so-called "gatekeepers." Gatekeepers pervade the humanitarian system in Somalia. They are most famous as the "managers" of displaced camps—probably nowhere more so than in the IDP sites in Mogadishu or the Afgooye corridor. But "gatekeeper" more generally means anyone who controls access to goods and services or the flow of information or who can withhold any of these. They can be found in humanitarian organizations, local administration and government agencies, or in the private business sector—particularly service contractors for transportation or warehousing for the aid industry; and inevitably, gatekeepers are found among the displaced themselves.

Much of this harks back to issues related to the political economy of external aid in Chapter 3. In a context of weak governance or rule of law, where weapons are plentiful, where most humanitarian decision-makers are geographically remote from the provision of services, and where crosschecking is difficult, the role of "gatekeepers" of all kinds becomes more pronounced. The UN Monitoring Group report of 2010 identified various activities of "gatekeepers" in relation to the provision of humanitarian assistance:

> The war economy is also an impediment to humanitarian assistance efforts. Some humanitarian resources, notably food aid, have been diverted to military uses. A handful of Somali contractors for aid agencies have formed a cartel and become important powerbrokers—some of whom channel their profits—or the aid itself—directly to armed opposition groups.[21]

The report went on to identify three prominent Somali businessmen who dominated the delivery of food aid in Somalia on behalf of WFP, and who regularly diverted a large proportion for their own ends. One was married to the head of a local NGO responsible for receiving the food aid. All were closely affiliated with armed militias. As much as half of the food aid sent to Somalia was reportedly going astray—mostly due to the ability of a small handful of individuals to control and manipulate the whole system.[22] Some of these businessmen's linkages to militias or to Al-Shabaab, or their willingness to pay off local authorities including Al-Shabaab, were behind the US decision to end their support for WFP in South Central Somalia in 2009. Although that decision preceded the publication of the UN Monitoring Group report, by then the evidence was clear enough.

However, for much of the famine period, the focus on "gatekeepers" was on individuals who provided physical space for internally displaced people to settle, provided some modicum of security, and controlled both the access of humanitarian agencies to IDPs and the access of IDPs to aid. A respondent from an Islamic charity gave the following account:

> There are gatekeepers who control the camps and take the food away from the IDPs if you don't give them a share. They either created the camp or took over the camp after people gathered there. In Mogadishu basically you are trying to help IDPs who are more like hostages to criminals. Another problem was when people who are not IDPs present themselves as IDPs. The problem was not only that they were taking food that they don't deserve but most often they were replacing the people who had genuine need. So you go to a camp, count the people and then bring food to them. By the time you bring food a gatekeeper replaces them with his own people and collects food that was intended for the genuine IDPs.[23]

Given the brutality of some of these people, the term "black cats" had arisen earlier to describe them.[24] These individuals were described in a post-famine report as people who "search for and identify an empty plot of land and, through connections with influential personalities in the area, establish IDP sites," or "existing land owners who ... set up sites to attract IDPs and aid" or "individuals who are appointed to run the daily affairs of a site by the local leaders (most often the [district commissioner])."[25] Though gatekeepers were reported as providing the services noted above (a place to settle, some degree of protection, and some degree of access to services), the report also noted the general tendency of gatekeepers to tax a significant portion of the aid in return for these services, restrict IDP movement (either to other IDP sites or the return to their places of origin), and otherwise engage in coercion, rape, and other gender-based violence. "What started as an attempt by gatekeepers to assist fellow human beings who had fallen on difficult times, has evolved into a lucrative economic opportunity for individuals with equally limited avenues for making a living."[26] The report suggests that the role of gatekeepers was an example of the "private sector" stepping in to provide a service. A far more critical look at the role of gatekeepers in Mogadishu, issued at about the same time by Human Rights Watch, painted a much less positive picture.[27] They reported repeated instances of rape, beatings, ethnic discrimination, restriction of access to information and aid, restriction of movement, and violent reprisals when any of these abuses were protested. Militias closely affiliated with the camp managers (i.e., the "gatekeepers") carried out all these abuses.[28] And this process involved not only private individuals but also authorities in the local and national government. In 2010, Bradbury noted that food aid moving within Mogadishu was subject to "taxes" at check points run by militias in TFG-controlled areas.[29] Menkhaus notes that in 2011, "A political quarrel within the TFG over whether or not to concentrate the IDPs in a few large camps had nothing to do with efficiency and everything to do with a struggle to control the food aid flowing in, and then back out of, the camps."[30]

Given the remote management nature of engagement by humanitarian agencies, these practices had been going on for several years with only limited or anecdotal information about them—and indeed at face value, the gatekeepers operated through "IDP committees" that looked on the surface like mechanisms for participation rather than repression. But the gatekeeper phenomenon goes much deeper than just the management of IDP camps. Given humanitarian agencies' dependence on local agencies or on a handful of senior national staff in country, in some cases "gatekeepers" control the flow of information within agencies in ways that are difficult to crosscheck. This has led to a rise in third party monitoring, or even covert monitoring, within agencies or between international agencies and their local partners.[31]

Their links to militias (at least in Mogadishu, not Al-Shabaab) and to the stronger clans in Mogadishu (whereas the majority of the IDPs are from the more marginalized clans or groups) have made the problem of "black cats" and gatekeepers one of the most intractable to deal with—and one of the most egregious examples of social exclusion as a driving factor in the crisis. In the case of Mogadishu, the vast majority of IDPs are from the Rahanweyn clan or are Somali Bantu, but most of the "camp managers" are reportedly from Hawiye sub-clans. Menkhaus notes that, in 2011, humanitarian agencies for the most part just did not have the clout to negotiate better access or greater accountability and accepted some of the diversion as "the cost of doing business"[32]—except that of course the issue of diversion was also linked legally with counter-terrorism laws, making the whole issue not only very difficult to deal with on the ground but almost impossible to have an honest conversation about.

A report commissioned by a group of agencies suggested some ways forward on the gatekeeper issue, including less reliance on remote management; more engagement with gatekeepers; some recognition of "good gatekeepers"; and greater reliance on participatory, community-driven management of IDP camps, as well as capacity building with the fledgling humanitarian institutions of the new government. All of these are good recommendations, but they fail to acknowledge some of the entrenched power of the less savory gatekeepers. The Human Rights Watch report calls for more human rights monitoring and for greater inclusion of concerns about gatekeepers in risk management and due diligence processes. Menkhaus is less optimistic about short-term solutions to the problem, noting that agencies had to negotiate with multiple actors to gain the limited access they had during the famine and that indeed negotiating with "black cats" and gatekeepers—and the militias to which they were linked—was as important to access to famine-affected populations as negotiations with Al-Shabaab or other armed actors. All had their own reasons for blocking or manipulating access:

> None of the most powerful actors in the Somali drama—Al-Shabaab, the TFG, the UN, the US, and Ethiopia—facilitated this [negotiated access] effort. ... [and] even if the international community had fully mobilized as soon as early warnings were issued in late 2010, it is not clear that that would have made a difference. Ultimately the problem was one of access, not resource mobilization, and the impediments to access were numerous and daunting.[33]

Summary: Coping, Resilience, Inclusion, and Exclusion

Understanding the capacity for Somali households and communities to cope with crises on the scale of 2011 requires several considerations beyond standard analysis of livelihoods and food security or early warning information. While many of the coping mechanisms noted here, such as livelihoods or asset diversification, appear to be fairly standard for dealing with chronic vulnerability in many places, the specifics of Somalia are also related to mobility, flexibility, and especially to social connectedness. This study has incorporated a close examination of clan and social identity into its analysis. This has provided insights into the level of diversification at the larger group level, that is, within extended families and sub-clans.

Diversification—away from the rural economy—had implications for vulnerability in 2011. The clans at the centre of the famine were among the most rural and least diversified in Somalia. Long-term diversification is itself a function of power and access to resources and networks. Ironically, these groups had been undergoing a process of livelihood change in the years leading up to the famine which may have been temporarily beneficial, but ultimately made some of them more vulnerable—particularly to the severe drought that struck in late 2010 and early 2011—because it did not involve diversifying their risks. Groups that were more flexible—either in terms of exploiting the mobility of their assets, such as camel pastoralists, or in terms of extending connections in the urban economy—were relatively less vulnerable.

Ultimately, the difference between being able to cope in extreme circumstances and not being able to cope came down to the issue of social connectedness. Vast quantities of ink have been devoted to the question of "social capital" in the past two decades and many efforts have been made to measure it quantitatively. In Somalia, livelihood groups have often been invoked as a proxy for social connectedness or social identity. The crisis of 2011 has highlighted the complexity of Somali social networks. These are defined to a large degree by kinship and clan, but in extreme circumstances, can invoke relations beyond clan. The extent to which these can be mapped, not so much retrospectively as we have done here, but prospectively, in order to inform decision making and policy has implications for future vulnerability mapping and a deeper understanding of resilience in Somalia, and therefore it is an important component of preventing future famines.

7

THE RESPONSE OF THE (WESTERN) INTERNATIONAL "HUMANITARIAN COMMUNITY"

Introduction

This chapter briefly reviews the response to the famine by the Western, UN-led "international humanitarian system," as it was constituted in Somalia from the 1990s up to the time of the famine. Chapter 8 examines the response of agencies that largely operated outside that system. This chapter reviews the reasons for the late response, gaps in contingency planning, and the constraints caused by "remote management" of aid, and then summarizes the response to the famine, particularly in terms of addressing food and nutritional needs. It concludes by reviewing the meta-evaluations of the response.

The (Lack of) Early Response

While there may have been some controversy about the adequacy of the information in the aftermath of the crisis, there is little controversy about the delayed response. Christopher Hillbruner and Grainne Moloney suggest that the critical issue was not the quality of the information and analysis but rather poor response. They identify five reasons for this:[1]

- Donor aversion to inadvertently supporting Al-Shabaab and strong counter-terrorism policies—and competing political and humanitarian agendas (however, these constraints were not present in Ethiopia and Kenya, where the response was also late).

117

- Donor discomfort with planning based on probabilistic forecasts (although this was neither new nor different from previous crises in the Greater Horn of Africa).
- Poor advocacy by the UN and NGOs.
- Lack of contingency planning and response analysis given the absence of major food aid agencies that is in turn associated with poor leadership within the humanitarian system.
- The slow speed at which governments recognized the problem and declared states of emergency in neighboring Kenya and Ethiopia.

Three big issues with the response are suggested: limited capacity for needs assessment and contingency planning, institutional constraints, and counter-terrorism measures—all of which contributed to a high degree of risk aversion by both donors and agencies in 2011.

Limited Contingency Planning and Needs Assessment Capacity

By 2010, relatively few agencies were left with a presence on the ground in central and southern Somalia. Some individual agency evaluations clearly highlighted the lack of preparedness and contingency planning throughout the humanitarian system. Some agencies noted being "less able to trigger an appropriate and timely response in the challenging context of a slow-onset emergency than in sudden crises. Initiatives focused on preparedness, including emergency planning, are still underdeveloped ..."[2]—a surprising development given the predictable nature of crises in the Horn of Africa.

The Real-Time Evaluation of the response, organized by the Inter-Agency Standing Committee on Emergency Response (IASC), identified a "huge gap" in needs assessments following up on early warning in Somalia.[3] The FSNAU conducts semi-annual seasonal assessments, but while these highlight countrywide needs, they do not necessarily provide specific details about the level of need in any given location. This lack of location-specific needs assessment was further compounded by access problems because of Al-Shabaab's restrictions. However, it also highlights the difference between the functions of different early warning organizations and agencies implementing humanitarian programs on the ground.

Institutional Dynamics and the Wider Decision-making System

Many of the most important factors determining the success or failure of early warning and early response remain in the institutional and political contexts within which decisions are made.[4] Levine et al. argue that early warning signals must be linked to livelihoods analysis, with a predictive capacity, which in turn are linked to early interventions. They suggest that early warning messages are not always followed, and do not always provide the necessary information to enable an early response. They suggest that even where specific projects provided locally appropriate livelihood-based analyses to inform early response, no corresponding contingency planning resulted. Labeling this a "system failure," they call for a comprehensive level of analysis involving all relevant stakeholders, including government, scientists, NGOs, and rural populations.[5] A major humanitarian sector evaluation for Somalia, covering 2005–10, likewise indicated that needs assessments have been problematic in Somalia for years, suggesting a lack of joint assessment resulting in over-assessment in some areas and none in others.[6]

At the national level in Somalia, early warning capacities are not embedded in strong internal bureaucracies and decision-making processes. Ethiopia and Kenya have both received considerable international support and investment in this area over many years, within—and in partnership with—government structures. But in Somalia, this investment remains in multiple international (i.e., external) institutions. Political considerations—for example, whether the populations concerned are marginal, or if declaring a "famine" or other crisis has political risks—determine the willingness for early response.

In terms of donors, Bailey notes that "political risk preferences are the primary determinants of early action," and that the accountability frameworks and "incentives are skewed towards delay."[7] Decision-makers tend to focus on the downside, but early action often has considerable cost benefits where, in the case of the famine for example, a failure to act early contributes to the creation of extremely large displaced and refugee populations, which donor governments will continue to support at much greater cost for years to come.[8]

Counter-Terrorism

However, in the case of Somalia, behind all the institutional constraints lurked the question of counter-terrorism. Throughout the run-up to the famine in 2010 and 2011, major donor support to mitigate or prevent a crisis was very low, and indeed it was zero for South Central Somalia in the case of the US donor agency USAID.[9] In the case of Somalia, political risk preferences, donor geopolitical concerns, and domestic political concerns appear to have completely trumped humanitarian concerns, until the declaration of famine forced a response. Given the difficulty of operating in South Central Somalia and the likelihood of aid "leakage," the risk of aid inadvertently falling into the hands of Al-Shabaab was weighed against the potential humanitarian costs of the unfolding disaster, and until the famine declaration the United States and many donor governments judged the former to be the greater priority. However, Hillbruner and Moloney (2012) point out that the response was also late in Ethiopia and Kenya where the counter-terrorism objective was less important, so counter-terrorism constraints don't entirely explain the late response problem.

Long-time observers of the early warning/late response problem more generally note that, although the specifics were different, there was not a great deal of difference between what happened in 2011 compared to earlier "slow-onset" crises that also failed to elicit an early response. Information systems are now more sophisticated than ever—in fact, some long-time observers doubt that they need to be as sophisticated as they have become if their purpose is really just to raise the alarm.[10] What is needed is more political will: decision-makers are still not rewarded for taking bold or risky action. Or perhaps more accurately, they are rewarded for not doing so. Rather, they are applauded for getting on the bandwagon at the right time, not too early and not too late. In 2011, according to this system, that time would have been in the weeks prior to the declaration. But that was clearly way too late to prevent major loss of life and livelihoods. In many ways, the culture of risk aversion was more pervasive in 2011 than in the 1990s or early 2000s.

Risk Aversion

Another reason for the slow response—again highlighted after the fact—was a deep aversion to risk-taking on the part of both implementing agencies and donors.[11] Even many senior humanitarian leaders working in or on Somalia felt they didn't have the credibility to push the system too far too fast in 2011.[12] Incentives to respond are still not built in. This is the impetus behind the development of triggers and trigger indicators (see below). But to be effective, triggers must be forward-looking and require consequences. The real question is how to embed response analysis within a framework that includes early warning information, triggers, and an accountability mechanism that facilitates decision-making. Several donors are working on this, but so far, nobody has really solved it. Solving the straightforward technical issue is difficult enough. When political or security issues are involved—as they inevitably are—it is even more difficult. In 2011, early response would have meant negotiating with Al-Shabaab. Most donors were opposed to this, even though Al-Shabaab was clearly blocking humanitarian access. Only a handful of agencies were trying to engage Al-Shabaab; there was no coordinated approach by the UN. Throughout this period, each humanitarian agency had to negotiate its access to famine-affected or at-risk populations on an individual basis. Menkhaus notes that, "None of the most powerful actors in the Somali drama—Al-Shabaab, the TFG, the UN, the US, and Ethiopia—facilitated this effort. All, in varying degrees, were impediments to humanitarian access. The result was very limited space for aid agencies to operate ..."[13]

Several donor agencies commissioned formal "after action reviews," but most remain confidential documents. The UK government commissioned a formal, public review of its response to the crisis—the report of the Independent Commission on Aid Impact (ICAI).[14] Several recommendations from the ICAI report include working on triggers for engagement and "trigger indicators" and making available three-year humanitarian funding—enabling planning and response to encompass a longer time horizon. But the ICAI report reflects a broader pattern of learning and response within the humanitarian sector more generally: technical issues have been identified and addressed, but the overarching political issues remain.

Balanced against these are the barriers to launching a response, highlighted by Oxfam and Save the Children.[15] Based on the premise that accurate and clear early warning of the 2011 famine in Somalia was given, the report suggests that a late response was due to donors' reluctance to commit funds based on uncertain famine forecasts and the lack of media exposure necessary to raise other funding. Echoing the criticism of Glenzer in the Sahel in 2005, they suggest that both the donors and the media required the disaster to be fully underway before it got their attention. Some agencies tried to raise the alarm earlier, including bringing in the media; others had an internal debate about when raising the alarm would get the most traction in the media.[16]

The funding that the humanitarian community was requesting in 2011, as manifested in the Consolidated Appeal Process (CAP), was also no different from the previous three years, despite a well-publicized and rapidly worsening crisis. And the CAP appeal was funded by donors to about the same degree—around 50 percent of the request—as in earlier years (Table 7.1). Indeed, the CAP itself can be seen as a constraint to the early response to the crisis, the 2011 CAP having been written before the 2010 *deyr* (short) rains failed, at a time when things seemed to be going well in Somalia. Changing the CAP

Table 7.1: CAP Appeals for Somalia, 2008–11

Year	Amount (in millions)	Funded by mid-year (%)
2008	$641	32
2009	$849	50
2010	$689	56
2011	$529	47
2011*	$1,002	78**

Note: Appeals are made in October/November of the preceding year.
Mid-year funding figures are for June/July.
* Revised Appeal after famine declaration.
** November 2011.
Data: OCHA-Somalia.

appeal required extraordinary circumstances—circumstances that, as it happened, were not deemed to have materialized until the famine declaration in July. Other elements of risk aversion that multiple post-famine evaluations mentioned included the general insecurity, the risk of diversion, and the fear of the legal consequences and danger to organizational reputations if diverted aid ended up in the wrong hands.

Constraints to the Response

Contingency Planning and Response Analysis

Despite reasonably clear early warning regarding the worsening situation, the response was late, and little was clear about what should be done.[17] No one had planned adequately for this contingency even though most of the humanitarian community knew the likely odds of the situation worsening dramatically.[18] In the absence of WFP, food aid options were limited. Ideally, livestock numbers would have been systematically reduced through commercial destocking programs with pastoralists, drought resistant seed would have been distributed to riverine agricultural communities as well as agro-pastoralists, and household resilience would have been bolstered through cash or food transfers to prevent a slide into malnutrition, destitution, and mass migration. As it happened, almost none of these programs were actually implemented on anything like a scale that was large enough to address the rapidly worsening situation.[19]

When the famine was declared, a major push for a rapid response was made. But even then, what the response should be wasn't certain. Under other circumstances, a crisis of this magnitude, triggered at least in part by a major production shock—and also partly caused by rapidly rising food prices—would probably have elicited a major food aid response. Indeed, had food aid been an option in mid-2011, it would almost certainly have been the preferred response. In fact, the International Committee of the Red Cross (ICRC) was still able to operate in South Central Somalia, and did implement a sizable food aid operation from August to December. But even this operation was suspended and eventually closed down entirely by Al-Shabaab in January 2012.

In July of 2011, however, a food aid response was, for the most part, not possible. The major food aid actors were not present, and Al-Shabaab clearly would not welcome another agency seeking to attempt a food aid program in the country.[20] Although the needs were many, including water, health, and emergency shelter for people displaced by the drought or the fighting or both, the main need was for some form of transfer that enabled people to have adequate access to food. In the absence of a food aid response, the remaining options were for cash transfers or some kind of food voucher program that worked directly with traders. Cash distributions had been tried in Somalia before on a small scale, and shown to be an effective means of supporting at-risk populations.[21] But nothing had ever been tried on the scale that was required in mid-2011. There were major risks. The first was the ever-present risk of diversion. Admittedly, the risk of diversion was no greater for cash than for in-kind food aid—in fact, many argued that the risk was substantially lower.[22] But some donors were wary, as cash would be a much more valuable and fungible target, and therefore perhaps more attractive. The second worry was that cash transfers would stimulate demand but might not necessarily induce a supply-response. If this were to happen, standard analysis showed that the price of food would just go up, making populations more vulnerable, not less.[23] "The debate over appropriateness focused on the ability of markets to respond to increased demand without further inflation or supply breaks, and the high probability of diversion given similar and recent experience with in-kind aid."[24] But none of the options on the table in 2011 presented humanitarian decision-makers with no risk.

Subsequently, two rapid market analyses were conducted that attempted to rely on existing information to project what might happen if substantial amounts of cash were injected into South Central Somalia in response to the famine. FEWSNET/FSNAU conducted one and WFP the other.[25] The results of these studies were similar, but were interpreted in widely different ways. FSNAU had conducted a roundtable in March on the possibility of cash interventions,[26] and showed that in southern Somalia a major injection of cash had led to an increase in food prices in only two of eleven cases—and often resulted in lower prices because it induced a supply response. FSNAU was criticized at the time for engaging in response analysis when its job was early warning. FEWSNET and FSNAU issued a joint market analysis in September.[27] They noted that markets continued to function in southern Somalia, and—with a few noted exceptions—suggested that markets would respond to increased demand.[28] But traders needed guarantees that they wouldn't be undercut by a large food aid distribution if Al-Shabaab suddenly changed its mind about food aid. And they also needed help to find large quantities of the most appropriate foods as some countries had export bans at the time because of the global food price crisis.

WFP's report found that while local cereal markets were generally well integrated with global and regional markets, several factors were negatively affecting market functionality and integration, particularly in the Shabelle and Juba Valley and the sorghum belt (indeed, FSNAU/FEWSNET had noted poorly integrated markets in these areas). The main factors included domestic production failure, regional trade restrictions, increased insecurity, and a limited formal import network for maize and sorghum, generally considered much lower value than rice. It also suggested "demand-side interventions (e.g., cash and vouchers) that improve purchasing power."[29] But the report emphasized that without a sufficient supply of local cereals (sorghum and maize), scaling up cash transfers or vouchers could increase food price inflation (hence also suggesting something like the sale of food aid or another import assistance program).

In other words, although emphases differed, the two reports offered basically the same analysis and suggested largely the same set of interventions. But they were used in widely differing ways: WFP report was used by some to suggest that in-kind food aid had to be part of any intervention; the FEWSNET/FSNAU report was claimed by others to "prove" that no food availability shortfall existed in southern Somalia.[30] In the brief window after the declaration, when it appeared that Al-Shabaab might allow WFP back in, WFP made it clear that they would actually not promote cash interventions, as they would cause food price inflation—despite the evidence that FSNAU and FEWSNET had already made available.[31] Al-Shabaab quickly made it clear that WFP would actually not be welcome to re-enter South Central Somalia.

All this points to the extent to which organizational objectives and organizational "ethos" were much greater determinants of response options to the famine than were either the assessments of need or the analyses of the potential responses on food security or on the functioning of markets. If one clear lesson emerged from all this, it is the importance not only of good, objective analysis but of linking that analysis to good planning—and to have all of this in place before a full-scale emergency is in process. Ironically, the analysis existed—not only the early warning, but also of markets and other risks—but in 2011, little of this was linked to specific contingency plans. Contingency plans appeared to draw more on anecdote than good analysis, and in many cases, contingency planning simply wasn't done.[32]

Remote Management

Remote management has been defined as "the practice of withdrawing international (or other at-risk staff) while transferring increased programming responsibilities to local staff or local partner organizations."[33] The key point is that ultimate decision-making authority is transferred outside the area of operation. This is primarily "an adaptation to insecurity or denied access. As such, it constitutes a deviation from 'normal' programming practice."[34] The use of the term is pervasive in the discussion of humanitarian or development programming in Somalia. The practice had reached extreme levels in Somalia by the time of the famine, but it was by no means new, nor restricted to Somalia.

The move towards remote management was the culmination of two trends. One was the increasing risk of aid workers being killed or kidnapped or being subjected to other forms of violence. By 2009–11, Somalia had become one of the most dangerous places in the world for humanitarian aid workers.[35] The other was an increasing effort on the part of humanitarian actors to continue operating in highly fraught contexts rather than simply withdrawing—"an approach that focuses on 'how to stay' as opposed to 'when to leave.'"[36] Ever since the end of the UNOSOM era, the senior management of humanitarian operations in Somalia had gradually relocated to Nairobi, Kenya. Over the years, fewer and fewer senior managers of humanitarian operations were located in Somalia and, over time, few had any personal experience of working in Somalia. Greater levels of responsibility for on-the-ground operations were delegated to junior staff and increasingly outsourced to local partner organizations. The nature of partnerships with local organizations varied widely over the years—from enduring and successful partnerships (between the International Committee of the Red Cross and the Somalia Red Crescent Society, for example), to remotely managed operations that relied on local staff, not local partners (MSF), to a raft of arrangements that are sometimes dismissed as "shotgun weddings" or short-term partnerships hurriedly thrown together to meet donor deadlines.[37]

As international humanitarian agencies became more risk-averse in this changed operating environment, remote management was the only practical option, short of withdrawing altogether, as indeed some agencies had to do. The decision to resort to remote management developed slowly over time, from an interim measure during relatively brief periods of heightened insecurity to semi-permanent strategies in response to worsening long-term security and access. As a result, formal policy or guidance about remote management was scant, either within organizations or more generally within the humanitarian system until the time of the famine.[38] By then, the practice of remote management had reached extreme levels, with almost no international humanitarian staff anywhere in South Central Somalia, primarily but not solely because of the threat from Al-Shabaab. But the practice of remote management also outsourced risk: the risk of being killed or kidnapped was almost entirely transferred to local staff or the staff of partner organizations.[39] In a report issued after the famine, MSF noted some of the negative outcomes, including diminished control over humanitarian resources, declining quality of medical care, limited or no ability to expand or adapt programs in response to worsening conditions, compromised principles, and limited ability to speak out on behalf of crisis-affected populations—in addition to the increased risk to national staff. Yet in this case, MSF believed that being able to operate remotely helped to "save the day" in Somalia.[40]

All these adaptations were less a deliberate strategy, and more a response to deteriorating security. But this not only meant increasing physical distance between humanitarian decision-makers and the affected communities—the erstwhile clients of humanitarian agencies—but also a growing remoteness in psychological and emotional terms, reducing the sense of solidarity that had captured the humanitarian spirit in an earlier age.[41] In Somalia, it also became more difficult to see changes, to understand the subtleties of the dynamics behind a situation, and to find new, innovative solutions to problems as they arose. And it made adherence to some humanitarian principles more difficult too, given the level of out-sourcing to local organizations, which inevitably have stronger connections to some groups and clans locally, or may even be controlled by certain clans. Given the nature of who was most vulnerable in 2011, this turned out to be a major issue in some areas.[42] So while the practice of remote management made the provision of aid possible, it also seriously undermined some of the bases of humanitarian action. Rapid scale-up under these circumstances likely increased the risk of diversion because partner agencies with relatively fixed capacity were suddenly relied upon to deliver larger amounts of resources in a short space of time.[43]

All of these issues raised concern before and during the famine, but none of them more than the issue of diversion. Remote management has inevitably led to the focus on due diligence in partner vetting, and on risk management—with risks including the diversion of aid, lower program quality, the disjuncture between on-the-ground realities and strategic decision-making and accountability. But it has been the issue of aid diversion that has received the greatest attention during and since the famine. "Risk management" practically became synonymous with reducing the risk of aid diversion, particularly to Al-Shabaab-related entities, or in Al-Shabaab-controlled areas. Yet much of the diversion was taking place in Mogadishu or other TFG-controlled areas as well. This emphasized the trade-offs between remote management (for security) and risk management (to reduce diversion). Physical presence can obviously be a deterrent to aid diversion. But physical presence was difficult—and impossible in lots of cases.

In addition to sub-contracting arrangements with local partners, remote management in Somalia during and after the famine was characterized by greater emphasis on remote or third party monitoring, including covert monitoring; the increased use of "distance technologies" like call-centres or the use of cellphones for post-distribution monitoring; remote sensing; and even suggestions for the use of drones.[44] All this was important to demonstrate accountability to donors—particularly around the issue of aid diversion—but has done little to build trust among partners.[45] Efforts to improve operations under conditions of remote management have included emphasizing capacity building, improving relations between international and local organizations, relying more on community-driven processes, and, especially, improving data collection. These efforts led to the establishment of one of the more innovative approaches to monitoring developed during the famine through the Cash and Voucher Monitoring Group (CVMG).[46] The UN also established a Risk Management Unit that helped UN agencies assess risk, review partners, and improve monitoring and evaluation, but ultimately even this new body was subject to many of the same constraints as the agencies themselves.[47]

Many Somalia analysts have emphasized the importance of relationships built on trust between outside agencies and local actors—trust that takes time to build, and which can be relied upon in crises. Most of the distance technologies built before and during the famine did not engender this kind of

Figure 7.1: Total Funding for Response, 2011

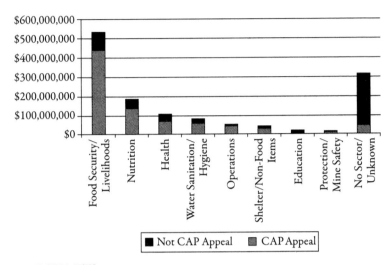

Data: OCHA/FTS.

trust but in fact seemed to presume the lack of trust. This factor is almost as important as the lack of security and lack of funding in the late response to the famine in 2011.[48] Indeed, one of the inevitable outcomes of increased due diligence is that many local agencies are no longer "approved" for partnership by donors, and it isn't entirely clear to such agencies what they must do to win approval. Many places under Al-Shabaab control continue to be "no-go" areas, even though they were the hardest hit during the famine. The result is that coverage is reduced in Al-Shabaab areas—making the impartiality of much of the humanitarian effort in Somalia questionable.

The Response

The international response to the famine, when it finally arrived, was "proportionate and appropriate" according to the Real Time Evaluation commissioned by the IASC.[49] The bulk of the response was to support increased access to food, but there were many sectors of intervention (Figure 7.1).

Four major elements of the response will be analyzed here: the unconditional cash and voucher response, conditional transfers, in-kind food assistance, and nutrition assistance. In theory, cash provided through unconditional transfers was money that recipients could use for anything, but by far the major objective of this kind of transfer in 2011 and early 2012 was to enable greater access to food. Conditional cash transfers were generally cash for work programs that included not only a payment to vulnerable households but which also endeavored to rebuild community infrastructure of various sorts. As Figure 7.1 makes clear, there were other sectors of response as well.[50]

Cash and Market-Based Programming

Since the end of the First World War, the predominant form of assistance to vulnerable people caught in crisis has been to send them in-kind food aid, and this has been a major part of US foreign policy since at least 1954.[51] Food aid played a limited but critical role in the response to the famine, but in the absence of WFP and with the antipathy of Al-Shabaab towards food aid, alternatives were clearly needed. A number of agencies had been advocating a greater role for cash responses in Somalia and they came together to form the Cash Based Response Working Group (CBRWG) in early 2011.[52] The group had evidence of the impact of cash transfer programming on a pilot basis in Somalia and argued that, given the lack of alternatives, the time had come to scale up cash transfer or voucher programs to enable people to access food via markets—a judgment backed up by the FSNAU market analysis.[53] Vouchers were redeemable for either specific goods or specific monetary values, for which pre-arranged values and redemption mechanisms had to be worked in advance, but many agencies believed they were less likely to be diverted than cash and less likely to be bartered or stolen than in-kind food aid.

A major agency was required to lead the response, and WFP was not in South Central Somalia, and not convinced that a market-based response would work anyway. In the end, UNICEF championed the idea, albeit somewhat belatedly. UNICEF was still present in Al-Shabaab-controlled areas at the time of the declaration and also led the nationwide nutrition programs, including in the famine-affected area, that staff feared would be swamped if nothing was done to address the food security problem. Eventually, seventeen agencies collaborated to implement a cash and voucher response in South Central Somalia coordinated by UNICEF and funded by a variety of donors (many of whom had neither scaled up a response to Somalia earlier in 2011 nor were particularly enthusiastic supporters of cash programming). From July 2011 to December 2012, about $110 million was devoted to unconditional cash and voucher programs.[54] FAO subsequently began a program of cash for work (CfW) in October 2011, with an additional budget of $45 million.[55] The combination of these two programs reached approximately 1.5 million famine-affected people in South Central Somalia, and constituted one of the biggest cash transfer programs in a single country in humanitarian history up to that time. Nevertheless, this program required an extraordinary effort to scale up quickly and, even so, only directly reached about half the famine-affected population.[56]

Unconditional Cash and Vouchers

One of the unique features of the unconditional cash transfer program was that it built in a third-party monitoring and evaluation component from the beginning, so reasonably good data was available on which to draw some conclusions about the unconditional response.[57] Several points from this evaluation are key here.[58]

Cash proved to be a rapidly scalable intervention in the context of Somalia, so even though it was not implemented until after the famine declaration, the cash transfer program quickly reached substantial numbers of vulnerable people. This was in part due to several key facets of the Somali economy. The first was the cellphone networks and long-functioning money transfer companies, or *hawala*, that were able to reach most of the country and that were mechanisms known and trusted by the population. For a fee, the *hawala* companies agreed to act as the conduit between agency and recipient, with agency staff cross-checking the list on the recipient end. The second was that Somali traders were able to reach practically everywhere in the country to supply markets, including Al-Shabaab-controlled territory. They were taxed by Al-Shabaab and all manner of other local authorities through whose jurisdictions they had to travel, but as long as the businesspeople involved were not directly contracted to a humanitarian agency (as they would be if they had been transporting food or other in-kind goods for the response), paying such taxes did not violate any laws. There was a concerted effort to work with traders to ensure a rapid market response.[59]

Even with these mechanisms, reaching the most severely famine-affected areas in Bay, Bakool, and Lower Shabelle regions, as well as parts of Middle and Lower Juba, was difficult. As much as half of all the cash transfer response went to Mogadishu and the surrounding areas, which no doubt drew displaced people into the exploitative environment that the city comprised for IDPs (large amounts of food aid could also be found in Mogadishu—the "aid magnet" phenomenon can't be blamed solely on the modality of cash). However, there is some evidence that IDPs who received cash benefits (as opposed to in-kind assistance—also widely available in Mogadishu) did remit some of those benefits back to relatives in their home areas on their own, also using the same *hawala* mechanism.[60] Households receiving cash transfers quickly recovered reasonably adequate food security status.[61] Despite fears that cash might be used for other things, the results clearly show that the biggest single use of cash was to purchase food, and the second biggest use was to pay off debts, most of which had been incurred to purchase food before the program was established, and restoring credit-worthiness was a clear prerequisite to any kind of longer-term livelihood recovery.[62]

The issue of food price inflation—which some had feared would be an unintended consequence of injecting large amounts of cash into an extremely resource-poor area prior to the program—did not ultimately emerge. This was at least partly because global food and fuel prices began to decline at about the same time as the famine was declared, and continued to decline for nearly a year thereafter. In addition, in some parts of Somalia—specifically the border areas and Mogadishu—there were significant imports of food aid. All this contributed to the drop in food prices generally, and prevented price inflation from becoming a factor in ongoing levels of food insecurity.[63]

Of the budget of $110 million dollars for the unconditional cash and vouchers response, some $92 million ended up in the hands of the final recipient—an average of 85 percent of the total budget. This in itself was an astonishing feat—and compares with something like about 35–40 percent of the total budget for in-kind food aid delivered under similar circumstances—given the high cost of transportation, storage, spoilage, and distribution of in-kind food.[64] Given the emphasis from donors on "value for money," this was a strong rationale for continued investment in cash programming, and in research and evaluation on the impact of cash and market-based programs.[65] Cash was therefore clearly an appropriate response under the circumstances; indeed, by 2012, most observers argued it was the most appropriate response.

Nevertheless, the use of unconditional cash did create some problems.

The first, already mentioned, wasn't so much with the modality of the transfer, as the fact that an inadequate amount of all types of assistance was reaching the most affected areas. So aid of all kinds, cash included, was implicated in the widespread migration to Mogadishu and surrounding areas, or to Kenya and Ethiopia. In areas where cash could be dispersed, a debate continued about the best way to target cash to recipients. The evaluation concluded that in the midst of an actual famine, household targeting was an expensive waste of valuable time, and that the emphasis should be on targeting geographic areas and then providing "blanket coverage"—meaning that all households in the areas selected would receive a transfer,[66] an idea that donors were unwilling to broach, given the worries about leakage to Al-Shabaab or other sanctioned entities.[67] Poor targeting practices limited some of the beneficial impact of cash transfers.[68] Nevertheless, agencies gained experience targeting at scale throughout the program, and new recommendations on targeting cash programs was one of the key areas of learning.

Second, with a relatively new programming modality, it wasn't clear where the coordination function lodged. The UN Cluster System is intended to coordinate responses in humanitarian emergencies. In Somalia, up to the time of the famine, the Food Assistance Cluster had been relatively moribund and devoted almost entirely to the issue of in-kind food aid.[69] To the extent that the cluster was involved in the discussion about cash in the first half of 2011, the leadership opposed cash programming.[70] Later in the year, a new leadership re-invigorated the cluster and over time took on some of the coordination, but by then several other groups had sprung up that were also playing coordination roles. As many as fifteen separate bodies were eventually engaged in coordinating cash interventions in one way or another.[71] Part of the issue was that cash or vouchers are modalities, not sectors. The cluster system is built around sectors. Over time, cash—and increasingly, vouchers—were used for a number of goods and services, some of which had little to do with food security per se.

And finally, of course, instances of diversion and fraud related to the cash transfer program occurred, and recipients were sometimes taxed on the amounts of the transfers. Much of the diversion had to do not just with armed groups like Al-Shabaab but also the staff of agencies.[72] While the amounts reported were small, it was a source of concern for the donors, who subsequently had their own forensic audits conducted.[73]

Cash for Work

Starting about the same time, The UN Food and Agriculture Organization (FAO) implemented a CfW program that in many ways was similar to the unconditional cash transfer program in that it aimed to improve famine-affected people's access to food and relied on market channels to make the food available. But it required people to work for the assistance. During the famine and immediate follow up period, this amounted to an additional $45 million worth of assistance.[74]

This program was somewhat more controversial, with some viewing the requirement for a labor contribution from recipient households in the middle of a famine as unnecessarily harsh. Critics pointed out that one of the factors that made some households vulnerable in the first place was a shortage of labor, and linking a labor requirement to assistance made this group doubly vulnerable. Also, in some cases, the projects being implemented simply couldn't find enough laborers because people were too weakened by the famine.[75] A two-week "unconditional wage" was initiated to enable recipients to regain some strength and nutritional status before work requirement began. In some cases, work requirements were reduced to account for the poor nutritional status of recipients. But these elements of the programs were often not implemented.[76]

However, this program involved the added element of public works—hence investment in community-owned infrastructure, such as the desilting of irrigation canals, or the construction of roads or markets. In short, the intention was not only to improve people's short-term ability to access adequate food by providing a cash wage for the work; it was also to rebuild some of the livelihood assets that had been lost or damaged by the conflict and the neglect of previous years. The CfW program was more complex to manage, because it involved both the transfer of money and the public works component. There was a limit to how much public work any one local organization could manage, thereby necessitating the use of many local partner agencies.[77]

The CfW program also included a rigorous monitoring component, including extensive qualitative impact assessments.[78] As with the unconditional cash transfers, the money was primarily used to buy food and pay off debts. Although some of the benefits of the public works program, such as the clearing of irrigation canals, accrued to better-off people in the communities, the actual cash transfer accrued to the more vulnerable target groups.[79]

A prolonged debate ensued between proponents of conditional and unconditional assistance and lasted long after the end of the famine.[80] But again, the debate was informed mostly on the basis of the organizational mandate and ethos of the lead agency: UNICEF was more worried about vulnerability; FAO put a greater emphasis on sustainability (or its "twin track" program of simultaneously addressing both immediate humanitarian need and longer-term development requirements).[81] In retrospect, targeting—not overall program strategy—should have determined who qualified for which kind of assistance; there was no "one-size-fits-all" solution to the debate. In practice, however, one or the other of these programs covered whole areas. In the future, the emphasis should be on diversification within programs. Ultimately, both FAO and UNICEF agreed on the need for better coordination on the ground—and indeed are part of a joint UN implementation strategy in the post-famine period.[82]

Nevertheless, when considering the famine in retrospect, the rapid scale-up of both the unconditional cash/voucher program and the cash-for-work program in extremely difficult circumstances must be seen as two of the few genuine success stories of the whole episode—ones which required a level of risk-taking and vision that was not generally present in the response in early 2011, or in other parts of the famine response.[83] One of the clear lessons from the whole episode is that cash responses can work on a large scale to provide relief from famine and acute food insecurity—if a few key conditions are met. Somalia in 2011 met those key conditions, and there is little doubt that the rapid rollout of a large-scale cash-transfer program helped to contain the crisis.

Food Aid

Food aid had long been the major response to any kind of crisis in Somalia, since any kind of crisis resulted in displacement from people's place of livelihoods and almost immediately threatened their access to adequate food.

Figure 7.2 depicts levels of food aid from 1999 to 2012 (with the earlier famine period of 1992–3 for comparative purposes). For much of the early 2000s, food aid played only a relatively minor role in supplementing commercial imports into Somalia, but after the takeover of the ICU government in 2006, food aid came to play a much larger role until it was cut off in 2010 (almost all the food aid in 2010 went to Somaliland or Puntland). From 2005 to 2009, Somalia was the fourth largest recipient of food aid in the world.[84] Figure 7.2 depicts very clearly the impact of the cuts in US food aid and the withdrawal of WFP from South Central Somalia. However, the story of food aid in Somalia during this period is not just one of humanitarian agencies providing access to adequate food—it also involves politicization, manipulation, diversion, and mismanagement.[85] By the middle of 2010, only one organization remained that had both access to South Central Somalia and the capacity to handle the logistics of food aid distribution on a large scale.

The ICRC had never left South Central Somalia, although, like many other international organizations, it had to manage most of its operations remotely, in this case working through the Somali Red Crescent Society in areas that it was unable to reach directly. The ICRC had maintained a separate identity from

Figure 7.2. Food Aid to Somalia (000 MT), Various Years

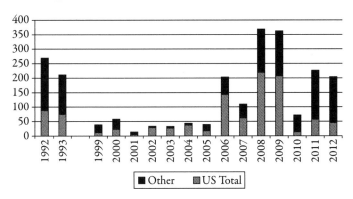

Data: WFP-FAIS.

much of the rest of the humanitarian community operating in South Central Somalia, and had negotiated access to some areas under the control of Al-Shabaab. The ICRC was not traditionally a large food aid agency in Somalia compared to CARE and WFP, but it retained its logistical capacity and had its own reasons for being skeptical about market-led responses in 2011.[86]

Between August and December 2011, ICRC distributed over 112,000 metric tons of food aid in South Central Somalia, including inside Al-Shabaab-controlled areas. This effort helped to address needs that were not met by the cash programs, in part because, at that time, the ICRC still had access to the most affected regions of Bay, Bakool, and Lower Shabelle (as well as other hard-hit areas under Al-Shabaab control).[87] In January 2012, Al-Shabaab forced ICRC food aid programs to close, ostensibly because some of the food aid was "outdated."[88] In fact, a number of agencies were expelled at this point because Al-Shabaab, having been forced out of Mogadishu and other lucrative markets, was losing its revenue bases and was trying to tax humanitarian agencies; refusal to pay up resulted in expulsion. But the loss of the ICRC food aid program was a major setback for the overall attempt to provide access to adequate food. Food assistance (both in-kind food and cash) recipient numbers dropped rapidly between November 2011 and February 2012 (see Figure 1.1). The expulsion of the ICRC was one of the reasons for this.

The World Food Programme was able to continue with food aid operations in accessible areas along the Kenya and Ethiopia borders and also scaled up in-kind food aid and the provision of prepared food in Mogadishu—so-called "wet feeding" programs. During the famine, the Organization of Islamic Cooperation (OIC) and Turkish agencies distributed at least 10,000 metric tons of food, principally in Mogadishu; in addition, Somali NGOs supported by Saudi Arabia and other Gulf states distributed at least 12,500 metric tons.[89] So food aid operations did continue, but mostly in Mogadishu or the border areas, and to some degree, they contributed to the aid magnet phenomenon.[90]

Given the shortfall of food in the market and the fear that a cash transfer program would lead to higher food prices, one idea was to sell food aid on the open market in Mogadishu at subsidized prices. This was proposed by USAID, and the intent was to reduce the prices of at least some commodities (and, presumably, enable traders to access food that could be transported to famine areas—although this was not specifically the objective). It took some time to find an agency willing to do this, but eventually the International Organization for Migration (IOM) agreed. But then the food had to be packaged in unmarked bags in order to circumvent Al-Shabaab objections, and thus couldn't be shipped from existing stocks in the region. In the end, the program took so long to gear up that the sale of this food in Mogadishu didn't start until February 2012, after the famine had officially been declared over (and by which time the price or availability of food on the Mogadishu market had largely ceased to be a major worry).[91]

Nutrition

Nutrition programs had been split among various different agencies in Somalia. Although many organizations were involved in one way or another in nutritional programs in Somalia, the supplementary feeding programs (aimed at controlling moderate acute malnutrition) had been the primary responsibility of WFP, whereas therapeutic feeding programs (aimed at severe acute malnutrition) had mostly fallen under UNICEF.[92] High levels of acute malnutrition had been observed in Somalia for a long time, even in the absence of particular shocks. And indeed, conflicting conclusions from some of the nutritional surveillance was one reason some analysts suggested that the information coming out of Somalia in early 2011 was confusing.[93] Nevertheless, the nutritional emergency was what drove the deteriorating conditions into a full-blown famine, and the evidence was clear for all to see.[94]

The scaling-up of nutrition programming was only possible when funds became available after the famine declaration. Blanket supplementary feeding programs as well as a cash distribution were proposed as attempts to fill the gap in food security assistance created in the absence of WFP's distribution of food aid. As a result of the stark increase in malnutrition and mortality, the majority of the nutrition response focused on preventing further deterioration of the nutrition status of vulnerable populations. This included scaling up targeted and blanket supplementary feeding programs for children under the age of five to help prevent acute malnutrition and these were sometimes linked to cash and voucher programs. Indeed, the threat of a massively worsening nutritional crisis was at least part of UNICEF's rationale for engaging in the large-scale cash response to protect access to food.

Several particular features of the nutrition programs were important. First, given the horrific conditions in which refugees were arriving in Dadaab and Dollo-Ado, "wet feeding" sites (i.e., places where people could get cooked food) were set up at reception points and attempts were made to provide for refugees and displaced people en route. But as noted in Chapter 4, these sites quickly became overwhelmed by the sheer number of arrivals. Likewise, in the aftermath of Al-Shabaab's pullout from Mogadishu, wet feeding centres and therapeutic feeding centres were rapidly expanded in the city as IDPs poured in from affected areas. More problematic was the extension of nutritional services in rural areas, particularly areas still under Al-Shabaab control. Nevertheless, over 600 sites were set up—mostly under the management of local agencies—to address severe and moderate malnutrition; the number rose to over 850 by late 2011.[95]

Between the mid-2000s and the time of the famine, the prevention and treatment of acute malnutrition had undergone a complete revolution, resulting in much greater emphasis on "ready-to-use" foods (RUFs) and on community-based programs that did not require both the malnourished child and a care giver to stay in a treatment centre. These approaches characterized the response in Somalia as well, although given the complexities of the crisis, managing community-based care proved difficult in some circumstances. Over the period of the famine, some 285,000 children were treated for acute malnutrition and an additional 120,000 were assisted with supplementary feeding programs. But close to half a million children were believed to be malnourished at the time of the declaration—a situation that continued to contribute to the infant and child mortality into 2012.[96]

Meta-Evaluations of the Response

The IASC[97] commissioned a major evaluation of the overall humanitarian response in South Central Somalia from 2005 to 2011, just as the crisis of

2011 was worsening—in fact much of the fieldwork for that evaluation was conducted during the height of the famine. The picture the IASC evaluation painted provides part of the context in which to understand the overall response during the famine itself. It notes, "The response in SCS [South Central Somalia] has often been reactive, utilizing supply-driven approaches that have most often focused on short-term humanitarian objectives. Comprehensive recovery responses have generally been sidelined and insufficiently prioritized, even during a situation when security was stable and access possible."[98] The report goes on to highlight the politicization of humanitarian aid, limited coordination, a heavy reliance on in-kind food aid in the years prior to 2010, short-term funding cycles, the perils of remote management, the high cost of basing the humanitarian effort for Somalia in Nairobi, and limited accountability to the most at-risk communities in Somalia. These themes would reappear in many of the evaluations of the famine response.

When reviewing the evaluations of individual programs during the famine—whether operated by UN agencies, international NGOs, or local organizations—the overall impression is one of positive outcomes. Evaluations noted that a specific project "showed the hallmarks of extremely well planned, partner-implemented responses,"[99] or "was known by the community as the one that averted massive displacement ... to refugee camps in Kenya,"[100] or was "particularly efficient as it managed to distribute large quantities of food at short notice ..." and so on.[101] These individual project evaluations have to be juxtaposed with other reporting done more at the overall sectoral or strategic level, and which are much more critical: poor geographic targeting; failure to retarget even a year into the program; attempts by authorities and militia to influence the targeting/registration process; taxation of the implementing NGO by local authorities; taxation of beneficiaries by local authorities and gatekeepers; taxation of traders and *hawala* agents by local authorities; double registration; errors of inclusion and exclusion—and of course the fact that all these programs were way too late to prevent widespread mortality on a scale unprecedented since 1992.[102]

The UN's evaluations were less biased and more honest, and WFP's own internal evaluation was quite critical. The report noted that up to the time of the declaration of the famine, WFP Somalia had not planned adequately for the contingencies that would ensure coverage in its absence in one of the region's most volatile and chronically vulnerable areas; had not adequately explored options for general food distributions; was inadequately accountable to donors and wholly unaccountable to at-risk populations; and "did not fully acknowledge and adjust to the political operating environment, nor their relationship with Al-Shabaab."[103] After the famine was declared, changes were made in a number of areas, most notably in improving the coordination of the Food Assistance Cluster.[104]

Other problems came to light in some of these evaluations. Agencies seriously misunderstood power relations around kinship and clan as well as between pastoralists and agro-pastoralists.[105] These power relations were crucial to understanding the dynamics of the crisis because the main victims in this famine were of the same social groups as the victims of the famine of 1991–2.[106] As people moved to aid concentration points, many of these same minority groups moved to areas controlled by powerful clan-based groups. In addition to targeting problems, instances of elite capture, diversion, and corruption were identified,[107] consistent with trends identified by the UN Monitoring Group.[108] This apparent inconsistency between individual-agency evaluations on the one hand, and larger-scale meta-evaluations and independent monitoring processes on the other, raises questions about the conditions under which in-depth analysis and critical assessments are possible in a context such as Somalia. An even greater discrepancy was evident between written evaluations and verbal interviews with humanitarian agency staff (see Chapter 9).

At the broadest level of humanitarian impact for 2011 and 2012, several meta-reviews and evaluations highlight the "life-saving" rather than "livelihood-saving" nature of the late response. Most individual agency reports and meta-evaluations agree that the humanitarian community was unequivocally late in addressing the most acute needs of people affected by the crisis.[109] Although donors were quick to react to the famine declaration and to pledge funds towards the crisis, actual delivery of aid on the ground came later; some organizations were not able to begin implementation until well in to 2012, when famine was officially declared to be over.[110] These evaluations focused almost entirely on the Western, UN-led, and OECD donor-funded response to the famine. But a variety of responses came from other agencies, groups, and communities. The next chapter examines these in greater detail.

8

THE SHIFTING INTERNATIONAL DYNAMICS
OF THE HUMANITARIAN RESPONSE

Introduction

One of the defining features of the response to the 2011 famine was the prominence of a group of humanitarian actors that had not traditionally been part of the mostly Western, UN-led humanitarian community in Somalia. These actors not only changed the perception of humanitarian engagement in Somalia but also brought in significant humanitarian resources. It is difficult to define this category of humanitarian actors because they are a heterogeneous group which has variously been referred to as "new," "emerging," or "non-traditional" actors—but which in fact is not really any of these.[1] In global terms, they include government agencies and various national agencies from a wide range of countries, including China, Brazil, India, Malaysia, Turkey, Saudi Arabia, and the Gulf states. They have all become increasingly active and/or visible in the provision of humanitarian aid.

This chapter focuses on a subset of these actors, all of whom were very active in the response to the Somalia famine. These include donors from Turkey, Saudi Arabia, and other Gulf states and their associated charitable agencies—in the case of Somalia, mostly agencies and donors associated with the OIC.[2] The academic literature on these agencies is limited, and there are only a small number of reports or other forms of "gray literature" which would help provide a better understanding of their activities in Somalia. Unlike other chapters in this book, which have drawn upon a large amount of literature and hundreds of interviews, we have drawn here on a smaller range of information. Interviews with these agencies, the staff who have worked for them, and those who still work closely with them were conducted in Mogadishu, Ankara and Istanbul, Doha and Kuwait, and within the UK.

A number of underlying questions informed these interviews: Given the highly politicized context at the time, particularly between Al-Shabaab and Western agencies, did the Muslim (and/or "non-Western") identity of these actors enable a humanitarian response that was distinct, complementary, or better able to access affected populations than their Western counterparts? If so, how, and to what effect? Are there lessons to be shared between the two sets of actors? To attempt to address these questions, a brief background to these actors is provided, followed by an account of their response and a discussion of identified themes.

Background

Over the previous decade, the global humanitarian aid contributions made by these "non-Western humanitarian actors" grew substantially, from about $35 million in 2000 to over $620 million in 2010.[3] Until recently, many of these donors (including China and India, neither of whom was particularly engaged in Somalia in 2011) were themselves recipients of international aid but began to play an emergent role in the humanitarian aid system as a result of their economic growth and increasing political influence. Mohamed Kroessin suggests that, according to official figures, Saudi Arabia was already the second-largest global donor, after the United States, at the time of his writing in 2007, providing $4 billion in foreign aid (developmental and humanitarian),[4] while in 2013 Turkey became the fourth-largest humanitarian donor in the world (although, by this stage, the vast majority of Turkish assistance was going to the Syrian refugee crisis).[5]

In a major study, the Berlin-based think tank, Global Public Policy Institute, had already pointed out that there was an "imbalance" in the international humanitarian system, which is largely controlled by a small circle of Western humanitarian donors who sit on the OECD Development Assistance Committee (OECD/DAC), whereas the recipients of international humanitarian aid are overwhelmingly in the global South.[6] They noted that the current international system tends to be dismissive of alternative approaches or traditions to humanitarian aid, and this has led to "uncoordinated donorship that may lead to duplications, gaps, and other inefficiencies in humanitarian response."[7] Kroessin names this distinction the "OECD–OIC dividing line" in his commentary on the lack of understanding and coordination between the OECD and the OIC, which serves as the coordinating mechanism for many of these donors and agencies.[8] In 2008, the OIC established the Islamic Conference Humanitarian Affairs Department with a clear mandate to coordinate OIC humanitarian work with all relevant international stakeholders.[9]

The Actors

Saudi Arabia is clearly a key actor within the humanitarian and development world, hosting the Islamic Development Bank and the OIC (founded in 1969 and 1973 respectively), and donating resources through these channels as well as through the United Nations. In 2008, for example, Saudi Arabia donated $338 million to WFP in response to the food price crisis at the time (the biggest single donation to WFP in its history).[10] Saudi Arabia is also host to various official Islamic relief organizations (al-Ighatha al-Islamiya), and more independent charities such as the World Association of Muslim Youth (WAMY).[11]

Turkish foreign aid has also expanded quite dramatically in recent years. The Turkish International Cooperation and Development Agency (TIKA) was formed in 1992 in response to needs in Turkish-speaking areas of the former Soviet Union. TIKA programming expanded rapidly in the Balkans during the war there in the 1990s. TIKA is focused on bilateral relationships, and is able to mobilize different arms of the Turkish government, including technical experts from different ministries, as part of its response, not a facet strongly associated with the Gulf donors.[12] Turkey also had a number of relief agencies and NGOs active in Somalia from 2011, including Kizilay (the Turkish Red Crescent Society), Humanitarian Relief Foundation (IHH), Kimse Yok Mu ("Is Anyone There?"), Doctors Worldwide, and Helping Hands. Several of these had had longer-term engagements with Somalia, but mostly not in a humanitarian mode.

Gulf countries such as the United Arab Emirates (UAE), Saudi Arabia, Qatar, and Kuwait have also become increasingly involved in humanitarian action globally and through various humanitarian platforms in the Persian Gulf region.[13] For some, such as Qatar and the UAE, supporting their national foundations and charities are seen as part of their foreign policy objectives.[14] In Qatar, the Qatar Foundation, the Qatar Red Crescent Society, and Qatar Charity are increasingly prominent in international circles. Kuwaiti agencies are less visible globally, but are well known within the OIC. Somalis and Somalia are also reported to have special status in Kuwait.[15]

The indigenous Somali Islamic charities are an extension of these international Islamic charities and NGOs. Two of the more prominent Somali organizations are Manhal and Zamzam Foundation, both of which have strong links to the Gulf but have also implemented projects for the United Nations, and the Zamzam Foundation has longstanding links with IHH from Turkey. Other Somali NGOs with strong links to the Gulf were also active in 2011.[16]

In addition to NGOs, many wealthy Gulf families have their own sizeable amounts of *zakat* wealth that can be mobilized at an individual's or family's discretion to respond to a needy cause. Although this practice was evident in Mogadishu (and Kenya) in 2011, as they operate on an entirely informal basis they were not part of the study.[17] The Red Crescent National Societies (NS) of Turkey and the Gulf states are an important set of actors, both as an extension of their governmental response, and for their size and experience. In Somalia in 2011, in addition to Kizilay, this included the Iranian National Society, the Qatar Red Crescent Society, and several others.[18]

The OIC is an important actor overseeing this group. As a coordination body, the OIC is the second-largest intergovernmental organization after the UN.[19] The OIC describes itself as the "collective voice of the Muslim world" and has a membership of fifty-seven states from four continents.[20] However, it is a governmental organization, differing from OCHA, a pure coordination body. The Humanitarian Forum, a UK-based platform established in 2005, works to improve understanding and exchange between Western and Islamic humanitarian actors,[21] and has been active with respect to Somalia, working to bring traditional humanitarian organizations and their counterparts from the Gulf, Turkey, and Somalia to discuss Somalia's needs.[22]

Characteristics

One of the underlying commonalities of the members of this group that were active in Somalia is Islamic identity and Islamic charity; this in turn is embodied (or represented) by the principle of *zakat*, obligatory charitable giving and one of the five pillars of Islam.[23] While this principle informs the policies of these actors, it does so to different degrees: at the individual level, many informants (and much of the literature) refer to the significance of this principle for their work; at an institutional level, this principle informs areas of work, particularly around education (secular and religious), health, support to orphans, construction of mosques, and distribution of food during the holy month of Ramadan; at the level of charitable funding, principles of Islamic charity and Islamic finance are inter-woven, with charitable funds originating from both private individuals and state-level funding mechanisms.[24]

While these principles of charity no doubt provide meaningful ethical and moral guidance for many, it would be naïve to suggest that the "political"—at the personal, institutional, or international level—is not also a dimension of this sector. One aspect of this "political" position is the role that NGOs and charities play in the evolution of civil society in different national (and trans-national) contexts, where they may, for example, represent different interest groups from local elites to popular, grass-roots movements. In the case of humanitarian assistance, little in-depth analysis has been done on the question of how resources are targeted or allocated and the potential biases in humanitarian distributions by Islamic charities and NGOs.[25]

Similarly, the varied political and cultural contexts of Turkey and the Gulf states are also relevant. As a democratic, secular state, Turkey is clearly distinct from the monarchical Gulf states.[26] Turkey has a large professional class and an active civil society, while many Gulf states draw on a large pool of imported labor (at professional and other levels), and others, such as Saudi Arabia and Kuwait, have a large indigenous professional class.[27] The staff structure and composition of staff between Turkey and the Gulf reflects this: Turkish NGOs are staffed and led by Turks in the field, while Gulf charities have a three-tiered system, with the executive staffed by "Khaleeji" (indigenous Arab nationals), other Arabs (typically Sudanese, Egyptians, and Palestinians) making up the remaining HQ staff, and field offices entirely staffed by host-country nationals.[28] These differences and characteristics have a variety of implications, including knowledge of local context, communication and decision-making channels, and motivations for reform or "professionalization."

The wider political context and foreign policy motivations of these donors are beyond the scope of this study; however, a number of points can be made. Various rivalries, competitions, and alliances exist among this set of actors, further complicated in recent years by the Syrian crisis and rise of the Islamic State in Iraq and Syria (ISIS). In recent years, Turkish foreign policy in Africa has become increasingly expansionary, and Turkey's involvement in Somalia is partly driven by this.[29] Some Turkish humanitarian agencies can be considered part of the "soft power" of the state—although some are strongly associated with opposition parties. The wealthy Gulf states have not invested in Africa to the same extent as Turkey (and China) have, and may have different motivations.[30] The ruling families and emirs are instrumental in determining some of the humanitarian directions of their "national" charities.[31] The Kuwaiti emir, for example, considers Somalia a special case and he encourages engagement. The growing prominence of a number of Qatari developmental and humanitarian agencies may reflect Qatari foreign policy considerations.[32]

Another implication of the national political context is the relative independence of NGOs and charities from their respective governments. Turkish NGOs demonstrate a more independent leaning where, for example, Andre Le Sage has described Islamic charities as often resembling "parastatal" organizations.[33] Red Crescent national societies form a distinct group or layer of humanitarian action, and are referred to in the Gulf as "invariably a conservative organization with close links to government."[34]

One of the underlying cultural factors in the Gulf is that of "*wasta*," which can be translated as "who you know," or "patronage." In the West, this is often associated with nepotism and has negative connotations. In the Gulf, the opposite is the case, and recruitment may be on the basis of the strength of "*wasta*."[35] Key informants who work at senior levels in Gulf charities, as well as key informants in Western aid organizations (UN and INGOs), suggest that such personal networks are of equal importance for all of these actors, whether Western or non-Western, despite differing labels. Within the humanitarian sector, this operating norm has implications for generating trust and building relationships. It also has implications for accessing funding and creates murky and fluid decision-making processes; one of the characteristics described of Gulf donors is their tendency to change direction unpredictably, in part depending on the strength of personal relationships: if people change, commitments to work may too. *Wasta* also worked during the Somalia famine by enabling Gulf-based actors to identify Somali partners to work with, once resources became available.[36]

Finally, the dominant narrative around any Muslim or Islamic charity or NGO (including many British Muslim NGOs) in the last ten to fifteen years has concerned the subject of accountability and counter-terrorism. These are not just concerns for these actors alone, as counter-terrorism legislation has had profound implications for Western agencies more generally; however, a sense of unfair treatment or "guilty until proven innocent" pervades many Muslim agencies with regard to counter-terrorism concerns.[37] Since September 11, 2001, many Islamic charities have lost funding and/or have been forced to work through the UN or Western NGOs in order to manage counter-terrorism-related constraints.[38] Again, the concerns around this vary among these actors but were not explored in detail.

The 2011 Humanitarian Response in Somalia

Although the response was heterogeneous, several themes can be identified that characterize the effort in mobilization and humanitarian response across these different actors. Drawing on the limited available documentation and interviews, this section reviews the response in terms of the broad categories of agencies.

Turkish Donors and Agencies

Since 2011, Turkey has achieved a particularly prominent place in Somalia, and in the imagination of Somalis, as a result of its engagement in response to the famine. Turkey had many reasons for its large-scale engagement with Somalia in 2011. Turkey has engaged increasingly with Sub-Saharan Africa, opening some twenty-two embassies in Africa in the last ten years.[39] Beyond foreign policy and humanitarian objectives, Turkish business interests were looking to penetrate the Somali market, to promote trade, and to engage in reconstruction and economic development. The introduction of regular Turkish Airlines flights from Istanbul to Mogadishu was an important component of this strategy. Somalia offered a strategic entry point to the Horn of Africa, and the famine provided both the opportunity and a certain humanitarian rationale for this strategy. Between 2011 and 2012, Turkey's official development assistance doubled.

Two important catalysts for Turkey's humanitarian response were the global images of starving children during the month of Ramadan, and the arrival of Prime Minister Erdogan of Turkey (with a large official entourage and family members) in Mogadishu in early August 2011. In Turkey, the fact that the famine declaration and the prime minister's visit took place during the holy month of Ramadan was critical to the levels of donations received. Most agencies acknowledge that the response would not have been so generous in other months. One agency described "people overflowing into the street" and lining up to make voluntary contributions for Somalia. Islamic solidarity is implicit in this.[40]

Another Turkish agency representative said their budget for Somalia increased fiftyfold in August 2011 (the month of Ramadan) even though the agency had been in Somalia since 1997. Each of the major Turkish NGOs ran its own fund-raising drive in Turkey, and together raised $150–200 million specifically for Somalia (some of which was spent on immediate famine relief, but much of which was spent on longer-term initiatives after the famine was over).[41] Erdogan's arrival was highly significant for shifting the perception of southern Somalia, and Mogadishu in particular, from a place that was hardly possible to work in to one that was in fact accessible. Erdogan was the first non-African political leader to visit Somalia in over twenty years.

In an August 2011 OIC meeting, the Turkish government pledged $280 million in overall aid, with the country providing $77.7 million in official humanitarian assistance to Somalia in 2011.[42] The official aid went overwhelmingly to the TFG—then-president Sheikh Sharif has long-standing ties to Turkey. As mentioned previously, Turkish NGOs (including Kizilay) raised additional funds totaling around $150–200 million for Somalia.

The actual humanitarian response was relatively straightforward with lots of food aid (almost no cash transfers or market-based programs) and medical aid. Longer-term projects were quickly planned, but along a fairly standard line of "projects": wells, hospitals, schools, and so on. Turkey also took over the management of a camp (Rajo) from the UAE Red Crescent. Turkish aid was predominantly distributed in Mogadishu (see discussion below). Most of the Turkish NGOs were new to Somalia and came with their Turkish staff. Turkish agencies also worked directly with local partners. TIKA and IHH worked with the Zamzam Foundation.[43]

Agencies From the Gulf States

At the same August 2011 OIC meeting, overall pledges for Somalia came to $350 million, with Saudi Arabia contributing $60 million, Qatar donating $6.8 million, the Islamic Charitable Organizations giving $290,000 in cash, and the UAE collecting $50 million through aid telethons.[44] The combined total funding contributed by these donors represented some 30 percent of all the aid committed for the famine response in Somalia in 2011–12. These were pledges and it has not been possible to verify actual disbursements.

Some of this money was distributed through the OIC and directly to Turkish and Gulf agencies while some went through the UN. With a permanent office in Mogadishu, Saudi Arabia has provided humanitarian aid to Somalia through international, regional, and bilateral agencies.[45] When the famine was declared in July 2011, Saudi Arabia pledged $50 million to support WFP in emergency humanitarian assistance for Somali refugees and an additional $10 million for the WHO for vaccinations and medical supplies.

As with the Turkish mobilization, media images of the famine were catalysts for generating and releasing funds, especially during Ramadan, and reflected a sense of Muslim solidarity. While this outpouring of public sympathy and support was significant, it is important to stress that this was not an early response. In fact, many Somali staff of Islamic charities on the ground used the expression *"Qaylo dhaan"*—"distress signal"—to explain how they were calling for attention from their headquarters and donors prior to the declaration of, and publicity around, the famine, but did not receive much additional funding until the media images went global.

National campaigns took place and national coordination platforms were established in some countries. In August, the Saudi National Campaign for the Relief of the Somali People was launched "for the people of Somalia suffering from drought and famine" with prominent national leaders making personal contributions. In Qatar, the Qatar Red Crescent, Sheikh Eid Charity, Qatar Charity, RAF Foundation, and Al Asmakh Charity formed the Qatar Relief Alliance (QRA), a funding and coordination platform which, to date, has only collaborated on the response in Somalia and the Philippines and predominantly in fundraising. A Qatar Solidarity Day with the people of Somalia and the Philippines was also organized by the QRA in late November 2011.[46] Many member countries of the OIC also became involved. Malaysia provides just one example: a national platform and several Malaysian NGOs became involved in Somalia.[47]

The OIC

The OIC played an active role in providing and coordinating assistance in 2011 and beyond. The OIC office was established in Mogadishu in March 2011. An OIC Relief Alliance, consisting of thirty-two NGOs, mostly from Muslim countries, was established with a mandate to coordinate humanitarian activities (agreed in July 2011 at a meeting held in Istanbul). A number of respondents reported that the OIC did a better job in Somalia than in many other crises but, as a governmental body, it has limited authority over NGOs. The OIC also reflects internal tensions within the Islamic world. Oxfam estimates that the OIC's coordinated activities of Arabic and Muslim NGOs reached over 1.4 million people between April and October 2011.[48]

The head of the OIC's Mogadishu office has stated that one of its aims is to fill the gaps left by the UN system, namely its inability to access certain areas.[49] Under the purview of the Relief Alliance, the OIC designated five organizations—Turkish Red Crescent Society, Federation of Arab Doctors, Qatar Red Crescent, Islamic Relief, and Department of Humanitarian Affairs of the OIC—to lead activities in five broad areas: management of camps, health services, food and emergency needs, media and documentation, and mobilization of resources, respectively. The OIC has signed memoranda of understanding (MOUs) with both WFP and OCHA to better coordinate food aid distribution in the Afgooye corridor near Mogadishu and other humanitarian activities.[50] In an effort to coordinate more effectively with other international organizations working in the Horn, OIC is also in the process of setting up a liaison office in Nairobi.[51]

The response of Muslim countries may also have been stimulated by regional rivalries and alliances, particularly at the donor level. The Sheikh Sharif government had ties to the Muslim Brotherhood in Egypt, which has close links to both the Turkish and Qatari governments. These associations may have also stimulated competitive responses by the UAE and Saudi Arabia. The fact that popular unrest related to the Arab Spring was at its height in mid-2011 should also be taken into account. Charitable actions abroad supported by domestic populations may have been useful for generating or reinforcing domestic legitimacy (as they do in the West). Thus it is difficult to generalize: some of these agencies have close links to the state, others do not.

Somali Islamic Charities and Somali Mosques

Manhal and Zamzam Foundation, as well as other local Somali NGOs, were very active in the famine response, receiving funds from many different sources in the Gulf and partnering with both Arab and Turkish agencies. Some of these organizations also implemented projects for UN agencies.[52]

Senior Somali religious leaders from Nairobi who visited the Dadaab refugee camp in late July, immediately after the famine began to receive widespread media attention, claimed that their links to the Gulf contributed to the mobilization of resources there. They also claimed they were among the first to provide relief in Dadaab itself (after the declaration), collecting funds within days (particularly from the Somali diaspora) and working with private traders and their own mosque and school networks in the camps to organize distributions.[53]

Emerging Themes

A number of themes emerge concerning the activities of these actors, including: sectors of intervention and the role of food aid; capacity; access; dealing with gatekeepers; dealing with Al-Shabaab, and perhaps an emergent—but alternative—set of principles.

Sectors of Intervention: Food and Medical Aid

During the famine, the response was mostly in the sectors of in-kind food assistance and medical aid. A striking feature of the food aid program was the composition of the food aid basket, as well as the scale and modality of distribution, particularly in Mogadishu. A well-respected member of staff for a Western NGO, working on the ground at the time, observed:

> After the declaration of emergency, when the Arab and Turkish response came, we became like a small local NGO in comparison to the size of their response. They were distributing shiploads of food a day while we were distributing truck loads. We were dwarfed by their response. They didn't care who got the food. They just gave it to everyone. Also the quality of the food they were distributing was good so people preferred them.[54]

On the one hand, this highlights the scale of the operation in Mogadishu, yet it also highlights the haphazard manner in which distributions were carried out—a common complaint from Western agencies.[55]

The composition of food items was quite different from the typical Western food aid basket, being made up of varying combinations of wheat flour, rice, cooking oil, powdered milk, and sugar, as well as many other high-value commodities such as tinned fish, meats, and dates (even cheese). Several informants reported that many animals (particularly camels) were being bought and slaughtered in Mogadishu and the meat distributed by these agencies as well.

These accounts reflect a concern expressed at the time by Western donors and agencies about whether planeloads and shiploads of food from the Gulf reached their intended beneficiaries or, given the high value of many of the items (including items such as jam and cheese), whether much of the aid was instead being sold on the open market.[56] Some observers pointed out that food aid was distributed inconsistently and unequally cross IDP camps, leading to potential strife within IDP communities.[57] Our field research certainly confirms much of this, though how much this represents the overall response in volume and time is unclear. However, these same criticisms plagued traditional humanitarian actors' activities a decade or two earlier.[58] And while the response also reflects a degree of spontaneity that is perhaps understandable and even justifiable—in terms of the wider benefit—in the immediate response to a famine, this spontaneity is not in itself a characteristic that the actors espouse publicly. It is also at odds with the careful management of development projects that Le Sage noted of Islamic charities in Somalia.[59] This may be a distinction between emergency and developmental approaches and may be mainly a result of the massive scaling up that took place in mid-2011.

The quotation above gives an impression of an abundance of unconditionally available food, at least for some time, with a high market value, which was largely confined to Mogadishu and the early weeks of the response, provided from Turkish and Gulf sources. While the Turkish agencies expressed little concern about the large amounts of (their) food aid on the market, respondents from the Gulf agencies, pointing to its wider utility in lowering prices and increasing supply, appeared to be less sympathetic to seeing this happening with their resources.

The means by which food and other commodities were distributed varied. Some aid was in the form of one-off distributions, rather than programmed into regular aid packages organized by geography or targeting criteria. Some of the "mercy ships" that arrived from the Gulf can be described in this way. There were many accounts of one-off distributions taking place in the IDP camps; they gave little sense that these were part of any more systematic programming, and alleged that they sometimes involved a lot of duplication. However, in other cases, whole IDP camps were taken over and managed more systematically: the UAE Red Crescent handed over control of the Rajo IDP camp to the Turkish Kizilay, for example, and the camp had its own bakeries supplying bread.[60]

The relatively high value of much of the distributed food meant that some of it could be monetized, and observers suggested that the released money was sent to support family members in rural areas. But in many ways, this highlights the inappropriateness of in-kind food, and the inefficiency of providing in-kind assistance. These were issues that WFP and Western food aid agencies were grappling with as recently as 2008.[61] A number of observers suggested that the nutritional content of some distributed foodstuffs was low and that donors were naïve about their cultural appropriateness, reflecting the donors' lack of technical knowledge.

Medium- to Longer-Term Work

Many agencies began to think about and planning medium- and longer-term work, particularly as they were Mogadishu residents and the city was flooded with IDPs, and many had started implementing resettlement programs by the end of 2011. These settlements can be significant in scope—likened to "model villages" with a school, a clinic, water facilities, and even "dormitories" for children to stay in. But they can also be limited in scale (to one or two villages, for example).

Turkish engagement included a full range of public works: beyond the immediate response to the famine, projects under TIKA's purview in Somalia include water development, health, and the rehabilitation of Mogadishu airport and government buildings. Turkish NGOs were also present in Somalia, where they mainly provided emergency food aid and medical care during the famine, but stayed on through the post-famine period to provide a variety of ongoing medical, water, and rehabilitation programs, as well as building mosques and schools.

Capacity and Systems

Many respondents from this group of actors commented on their lack of planning and "systems," including monitoring, evaluation, and impact assessments. The Turkish have an expression of a national trait: *kervan yolda düzülür* (or, "the caravan is organized on the road"), which emphasizes getting on with the job and worrying about the details later. The Somali staff of many of the Islamic charities made a similar point, contrasting their (and their Gulf donor's) "passion" for responding to people's plight, but acknowledging their lack of formal processes in comparison to those of Western organizations, and recognizing the importance of such systems but also being critical of the overly bureaucratic processes of Western agencies.

However, this may be more of a problem when scaling up quickly than in the core work of many of these charities. Le Sage praised the work of many of the same charities in 2004, but he was commenting on their core, developmental work. In this he stressed the importance they gave to local knowledge, trust-based networks, and the participation of local communities in their work, saying that Islamic charities will walk away from projects if they are seen to be failing.[62] One of the Gulf charities that Le Sage referred to was active in 2011 and emphasized that it was not a relief organization but had to become so very quickly and ended up being one of the largest agencies to respond. To do so, it sub-contracted over eighty local NGOs to assist. One of these sub-contractors, interviewed for this study, was critical of its larger partner for its lack of planning, costing, and systems, and its reliance on a moral–religious obligation to get the work done. This partner reported that it lost money on the arrangement and other sub-contractors experienced the same and pulled out.[63] Many of these sub-contracted "NGOs" were formed by small groups of people opportunistically coming together specifically to assist and/or gain employment during the famine. This example indicates the exceptional conditions in 2011, meaning that established ways of working were not capable of scaling up rapidly enough to meet the demand. Another international charity from the Gulf, present in Somalia for many years prior to the famine, reported that it was overwhelmed by the resources it received and claimed it would not respond at that scale again.[64] For specialist international charities and NGOs that did arrive in Somalia for the first time, the pattern was slightly different—some of the Turkish actors, for example, were unfamiliar with the context and were preyed upon by "gatekeepers." Nevertheless, a lack of "systems" does characterize this group.

Coordination

Clearly, in a volatile context such as Mogadishu, in the midst of a famine, while rushing to provide assistance, the ability to coordinate has limits. That said, and over time, the OIC is credited by many with doing a good job in Somalia, particularly in comparison to its effectiveness in many other contexts (lack of coordination is a common finding in many other, non-OIC, humanitarian contexts). The OIC had an international staff member in Mogadishu and received support from the Humanitarian Forum in London.[65] The OIC also established sectoral leadership to different agencies.

Nonetheless, many problems of coordination did exist within the OIC forum, as well as with the UN. Duplication—making double or triple distributions to some camps while missing others—was a more common problem. Turkish agencies claimed there was little coordination between themselves (as Turkish NGOs) or through TIKA. Some observers suggested that Turkish (and the Gulf Cooperation Council (GCC)) agencies felt excluded from the UN-led humanitarian system, but few agency staff said this directly. Many tried to collaborate with the UN-led system, but in the end decided that to be effective, they had to go it alone. The UN was too cautious, too bureaucratic, and too stuck behind concrete blast walls. Also, many UN coordination meetings took place in Nairobi, where the Turkish and Gulf agencies had little presence. The Gulf/Islamic charities we interviewed did not refer specifically to coordination with OCHA, but emphasized the limitations of OIC coordination.[66]

The UN-led system is more powerful and more experienced, and some Muslim or Middle Eastern NGOs expressed a fear of being "swallowed up" and of being unable to interact on an equal footing.[67] Longstanding perceptions on the ground in Somalia suggest that UN agencies had compromised their neutrality. UN officials expressed concern that the OIC and other non-Western actors had created a parallel coordination structure. One of the OIC's aims was to fill the gaps left by traditional actors, namely the UN, given the inaccessibility of many areas in Somalia owing to security concerns. Many members of the OIC attended UN-led cluster meetings at the field level, but parallel coordination structures between the OIC and OCHA made it difficult for either to gain a full picture of the humanitarian activities on the ground, especially in areas outside Mogadishu.[68]

Another example of the problems in coordination was the response within the Red Crescent movement. All of the national societies from other countries are supposed to work through the incumbent national society—the Somalia Red Crescent Society, in this case. In practice, this was not entirely effective: the SRCS commented that they did play a coordination role but that participation from other Red Crescent Societies was uneven and some preferred to go their own way.

As an intergovernmental body, the OIC, as well as many participating agencies, allied with the TFG to some extent. Many agencies were not very familiar with the local political context and the political dynamics between the TFG and Al-Shabaab, both of which were competing for legitimacy during this time. This had obvious implications for the way many of the agencies were perceived by Al-Shabaab, their Islamic credentials notwithstanding.

Access

The hope of both non-Western and more traditional humanitarian actors was that the Islamic agencies would have greater access to areas under Al-Shabaab's control (and therefore the epicentre of the famine).[69] In fact, the ability of these organizations to access Al-Shabaab-controlled territory was mixed at best and not nearly as great as had been hoped. Much of the initial relief was provided to IDPs in Mogadishu, since needs were evident and resources arrived in the capital by ship and plane and thus were in close proximity to needs. Many agencies did report distributions in other regions of southern Somalia, areas largely under Al-Shabaab control, but this soon proved difficult even for Islamic agencies, and many withdrew to Mogadishu. Others were expelled by Al-Shabaab, and a handful that had negotiated access with Al-Shabaab felt obliged to withdraw when they began to be accused of "helping terrorists" in the European press.[70] Again, hard data on distribution is difficult to obtain, but respondents estimated that between two-thirds and 90 percent of all Turkish aid to South Central Somalia in 2011 and early 2012 ended up staying in Mogadishu. Similar figures are evident in the limited data on end use. In the absence of accurate figures, similar estimates may be made for resources from the Gulf.[71]

Some respondents suggested that the TFG was discouraging non-Somalis (including Arabs) from entering Al-Shabaab areas. This raises a question about the propaganda "war" being played out between Al-Shabaab and the TFG at the time. For the Al-Shabaab leadership, who were initially reluctant to admit to the severity of the crisis, the scale of the famine was clearly a public relations disaster (in the previous year, they had claimed that their "ordained" rule had resulted in good rains and a bumper harvest). Given these dynamics, it is not clear to what extent Turkish and Gulf agencies adopted a deliberate approach of impartiality. Needless to say, all humanitarian agencies— "Western" and "non-Western" alike—were having difficulty remaining impartial, with the exception of ICRC and MSF.

Counter-terrorism legislation also played a role in limiting access. Respondents suggested that some prominent international Islamic charities are under scrutiny in their own countries, and suspect that this is at the behest of the United States. This is ironic, in one sense, because US humanitarian policymakers were actively involved in encouraging non-Western actors to engage in Somalia in 2011 precisely because they might be better able to access Al-Shabaab-controlled areas.[72] In general, the influence of counter-terrorism measures is known to have reduced the amount of funding British and Islamic charities received.[73] And, as noted above, there were more subtle influences as well, such as media accounts accusing Islamic, Middle-Eastern, and Turkish agencies of "supporting terrorists" if they were working in Al-Shabaab areas.

Dealing with Local Authorities and "Gatekeepers"

Mogadishu and South Central Somalia in general were all extremely difficult places in which to operate in 2011—in particular due to the constant attempts to divert or loot assistance intended for famine-affected groups. This was no different for Turkish and Middle Eastern agencies, which were subject to exactly the same problems as other agencies on the ground: lack of security in TFG-held areas, and the corruption and predatory activities of TFG officials, roving militias, and other "gatekeepers." To some extent, these agencies were able to use their Islamic identity (and the fact that they had not been part of the politicization and political economy of aid in Somalia previously) to increase their access and effectiveness.

One respondent, a Somali citizen working for one of these agencies, sets the scene:

> On the government side there was total lack of security. There were many arguments about whether we could distribute food or not, because we might do more

harm in distributing. People were safe in their camps but when we took food to them there was always bullets flying around and someone might get injured or killed. We thought about this long and hard. One day we took 1,000 baskets of food to Abdiaziz district of Mogadishu to distribute. We put the food on the ground. It was good food; each basket contains seven different foods. Soldiers came in and started firing at the crowd. We all ran away. The soldiers and the people looted the food. We didn't distribute any of that food. We had to change the distribution post. This is the only time that we lost all the food and we couldn't distribute any. There were lots of risks.[74]

The clear implication was that the arrival of the soldiers was associated with the efforts of powerful people to steal the food, and that their arrival on the scene was not coincidental. While this description might apply to anyone working in Mogadishu, the following quote provides insight into if and how agencies attempted to manage this environment:

These [gatekeepers] were often individuals taking over an area where IDPs had gathered and making it their own camp. The [gatekeepers] would then tax aid given to people. Initially, they would request that an agency deals with them directly. If not, and police or authorities were used, they would tax the people later. One way to get around it was to go to the camps at night, distribute cards to the IDPs and say where the food can be collected. The problem remains today, with gatekeepers keeping IDPs present by, for example, not allowing them to take their belongings away. It is their business.[75]

These quotes highlight a number of issues. First, the influence of gatekeepers was a constraint for all agencies. Second, there was pressure to accommodate gatekeepers while also adopting strategies to bypass them, for example by distributing cards at night with instructions detailing where food could be collected. Others admitted that the Mogadishu district commissioners were simply given some 10 percent of the ration cards to "keep them on their side," and sometimes another 5 percent went to the local police or security forces, to ensure security and prevent disruptions at distributions. The respondent commented that these practices were "so prevalent and widespread that it became the norm in Mogadishu."[76]

Overall, Islamic charities were trying to control distributions and minimize losses to gatekeepers in much the same way as the Western humanitarian agencies were, but their Islamic credentials did not grant them any special ability to bypass gatekeepers or other local influences altogether.

While these examples came from Somali and Islamic charities that had a long history and were well embedded in Somalia, other newly arrived actors without a pre-existing understanding of the context were more vulnerable to outright capture by various actors. Some Turkish agencies fell into this category. For example, some within the TFG criticized the tendency of Turkish organizations and diplomats to work directly with the president, bypassing both the government and civil society, and being captured by the president's clan interests as a result. This was recognized as a problem by Turkish informants but is thought to have improved over time.[77] At the end of 2013, Turkey stopped providing direct budgetary support to Somalia—reportedly worth around $4.5 million per month and often provided in cash.[78]

Dealing with Al-Shabaab

Working in Al-Shabaab areas was highly problematic for all actors in Somalia. A respondent working for one of the Islamic agencies noted that:

> Different groups controlled different parts of the country. There was Al-Shabaab and the government. In Al-Shabaab areas, there was so much control and lack of freedoms that we couldn't do our job properly. But if you didn't fall foul of these rules ... there were no other gatekeepers and you could distribute your food without any problems. I was imprisoned in a container for two nights in September 2011 because I distributed food in "wrong" areas.[79]

Another agency reported that its relief goods were redirected to areas other than the ones they had targeted, and there was little they could do. Agencies did not explain on what basis they worked in Al-Shabaab areas, but made it clear that once an agreement had been made, it was possible to work. Obtaining such agreements was very difficult and usually involved agreeing to fees and taxes (just as Western agencies did). Only one agency claimed they stuck to their principles (of refusing to pay these fees) until they were banned themselves. Many informants suggest that there was virtually no alternative to paying these fees to Al-Shabaab in order to distribute assistance in areas they controlled.[80]

In summary, while many of these agencies did distribute relief in Al-Shabaab areas, they all faced considerable difficulties in making such arrangements. The limited available evidence suggests that an Islamic identity did lead to improved access to Al-Shabaab-controlled areas, but this was short-lived, and as early as October 2011 these agencies were subject to most if not all of the same constraints in Al-Shabaab areas as Western agencies. Thereafter, many simply withdrew to Mogadishu. It is also not clear what role impartiality or perceptions of impartiality played in this dynamic. Western agencies were clearly perceived as less than impartial, but given their relations with the TFG, many Islamic agencies seemed to be equally partisan.

Risk, Proximity, and Solidarity

One sentiment expressed by many of the staff members of these agencies (and their Somali partners) was that they were "better for the people," and were more in tune with their needs. They were able to work more closely with the people in the affected areas and had to take more risks to do so. A number of Somali staff interviewed from this group were arrested and held by Al-Shabaab as a result of operating in areas under its control.[81] While recognizing some of the strengths of working for Western agencies—better salaries, training, and support—they noted that an Islamic organizational identity facilitated their proximity to people in some affected areas.[82] But this varied by area and agency.

The Turkish effort was also characterized by a willingness to take risks. Staff working for Turkish agencies claimed that "we don't know the meaning of risk," or "we are a bit crazy and a bit brave."[83] Several Turkish aid workers were killed in Somalia, and the Turkish embassy was attacked by Al-Shabaab—presumably because of Turkey's close links to the TFG. Whether officially secular or explicitly faith-based, a connection to Islamic values was a common factor informing the work of almost all of these agencies. Much of their effort emphasized peace-building as much as humanitarian assistance.

But this whole humanitarian effort was also informed by a spirit of voluntary action, which had both positive and negative sides. Staff from one subcontracting local NGO noted that when they complained that their salaries didn't cover their basic living expenses,

> They told us that we were all volunteers and working for the sake of God. Their argument was basically that the loss was our contribution to the operation. I believe this was just a cover for their failure to prepare and plan well. I was working day and night for free. That was fine with me as I volunteered to do this job. However, running whole operations on this basis was not sustainable and many smaller organizations pulled out because of this problem.[84]

Some of these characteristics might be described in terms of (more classical) humanitarian principles. Although few respondents used the term "impartiality," the emphasis on meeting needs and prioritizing needy people came through strongly. There was a strong implicit criticism of Western agencies' claims of impartiality. On the other hand, there was an awareness that with such a major focus on Mogadishu, much of the aid from non-Western actors could hardly claim to be impartial either.

Impact and Learning

As noted, there is little information detailing the impact of these organizations on the famine response. The available reports only outline the basics of any activities undertaken. Little documentation was obtained (or even claimed) in relation to monitoring, evaluation, or impact assessments. There was, however, a significant difference in relation to learning. The Turkish agencies we interviewed were open about this and explained that they are still learning and recognize some operational shortcomings. A "learning culture" clearly takes time to build in the very operationally oriented world of humanitarian action, and there is a good deal of variability within OIC agencies just as there is in Western agencies. A learning culture is also dependent on organizational openness and a willingness to learn from past mistakes.

Towards Greater Cooperation?

This discussion has raised as many questions as observations. Yet a number of themes can be identified. In terms of access and impact, the non-Western and Islamic agencies had a considerable presence and effect in Mogadishu, particularly in the first weeks and months of the famine response, and raised a considerable amount of money through both private contributions and official allocations. A relatively small proportion of their overall assistance reached regions outside Mogadishu directly (through aid agencies) or indirectly (through the monetization of aid, which was then sent back to rural families). There is, however, little hard data on this point.

These actors faced many of the same challenges of insecurity, gatekeepers, and interference by local authorities (TFG and Al-Shabaab) that Western agencies faced. There is no clear evidence suggesting that these organizations as a group were systematically better able to manage or bypass these factors, particularly in the light of the rapid and huge scale-up that was required. Rather, it appears that these agencies were overwhelmed by the resources available and scale of the response required, and trade-offs and accommodations were made in order to gain access to local populations. While other research does suggest that Islamic charities often have well-established local networks and an in-depth knowledge of the local context, applying these in an insecure and large-scale emergency response is a somewhat different matter from the circumstances observed in earlier analyses.

There is, however, an interesting trade-off between modalities based on trust and a spirit of volunteerism and those based on established and experienced systems and processes. It could be argued that the most well-informed Western organizations combine these qualities, but many Western agencies are deeply trapped in security and counter-terrorism concerns, operate by remote-management, and are often led by staff who are not familiar with the context. Turkish, Middle Eastern, and Islamic agencies, while largely stuck in Mogadishu, were at least on the ground and could observe these constraints directly. On the other hand, there is little doubt that some of these agencies could benefit from improvements in programmatic areas—improvements that are rapidly being implemented in other humanitarian responses, including Syria.

The visible presence of Turkish and other Islamic charities on the ground was in stark contrast to Western donors and agencies that operated remotely from Nairobi. However, with a few notable exceptions, Turkish aid mostly focused on IDP populations in Mogadishu, suggesting that the advantage of an Islamic identity in accessing Al-Shabaab-controlled areas was often more perceived rather than actual. And questions also arose about impartiality given these organizations' relationship with the TFG.

There are still major political, cultural, technical, and linguistic differences between the OECD and OIC actors, both at the donor and agency level, and certainly at the field level. Western agencies seem to have made little investment in understanding the role and experiences of Islamic, Middle Eastern, or Turkish actors in Somalia, despite their long presence in the country. Nevertheless, it is clear that both groups have much to offer—and learn from—each other. This theme will be revisited in Chapter 10.

9

2012–14 AND THE AFTERMATH OF THE FAMINE

Introduction

The famine was declared over in February 2012. The indicators of humanitarian wellbeing had improved significantly: mortality had declined to near baseline levels in late 2011, and the prevalence of malnutrition and a variety of indicators of food security had all improved notably. Within the humanitarian community, the discussion quickly turned to post-famine recovery, but especially to the notion of "resilience," and the question of what could enable vulnerable communities in Somalia to overcome recurrent cycles of crisis.

Against this post-famine background in South Central Somalia, groundbreaking political developments soon followed that gave rise to a sense of resurgent optimism about Somalia. In February 2012, the combined armed forces of AMISOM and Kenya finally drove Al-Shabaab out of Kismayo, depriving it of key revenues accruing from the control of Kismayo port; Al-Shabaab was subsequently driven out of key strongholds in Baidoa and the Afgooye corridor. The shifting security situation forced Al-Shabaab to change tactics and foreshadowed a longer-term trend of AMISOM—and subsequently the Somali National Army—pushing Al-Shabaab out of many of the larger urban areas it had controlled.

This chapter traces the developments in Somalia after the famine. These include, first, the political transition to a representative government, but also the policy pivot to "resilience" as the focus of humanitarian action and external engagement with Somalia more generally (still within the overall international strategy of supporting state-building and countering terrorism). Second, the chapter addresses the question of what was—or should have been—learned from the 2011 famine, including both the technical shortcomings in the response and the political changes required to prevent the recurrence of famine in Somalia. It then presents partial evidence of the extent to which these lessons are actually being implemented. We put forward our own analysis of the critical points of learning from the famine and what needs to be done to institutionalize this learning. Chapter 10 highlights some of the constraints to this institutionalization.

Somalia in Transition: 2012 to 2014

By August 2012, a long-anticipated transition from the TFG to a more genuinely inclusive national government had taken place, leading to dramatic changes in the way Somalia was governed. The "road map" to the transition included a lengthy process of negotiation among four principal parties: the TFG itself, the administration of the Galmudug region, the semi-autonomous region of Puntland, and the Ahlu Sunna wal Jama'a movement. The transition culminated in clan elders from areas controlled by these authorities selecting some 825 delegates to attend a constituent assembly to elect a national parliament, and subsequently a new president.[1] Although similar processes had failed twice previously to lead to an actual political transition in Somalia, the election of a Somali Federal Government (SFG) seemed to succeed, with the unexpected election of Hassan Sheikh Mohamud as president, who replaced Sheikh Sharif in the first successful presidential election by a representative body since 1967.[2]

The combined effect of the political transition and the apparent decline in the reach of Al-Shabaab led to a "groundswell of optimism," and some observers even drew comparisons to the Arab Spring. In 2013, long-time Somalia observer Matt Bryden noted that "after more than twenty years of conflict, crisis and statelessness, and twelve years of ineffectual transitional authorities, the Somali Federal Government ... has been welcomed as Somalia's first 'post-transition' government."[3] The "six-pillar" strategy of the new government included the ambitious goals of political stabilization, economic recovery after years of conflict and crisis, construction of a more enduring peace, delivery of services, improvement of relations with the international community, and encouraging internal national unity within Somalia.

The United States officially recognized the new government of Somalia in early 2013, and other governments soon followed suit. Delighted by the prospect of a new and different Somalia, donors quickly chipped in to support the new government, pledging more than a billion dollars at conferences in London, Yokohama, and Brussels in early to mid-2013.[4] Enthusiasm and support for the new government was evident in the return of many Somalis who had remained in the diaspora for a long time, and a surge of investment of foreign and diaspora money, particularly in Mogadishu.[5] How far beyond Mogadishu this "bubble" extended was open to question.

However, many of the same constraints that had prevented earlier attempts at transition continued to undermine efforts by the new government in Mogadishu. First, clan interests and those of several Islamic factions continued to hold disproportional sway over the new government. One faction was the "Damul Jadiid" group or the "new blood" that had been part of the Islamic Courts Union government in the mid-2000s, and which had strong links to the Muslim Brotherhood in Egypt (a long-standing opposition movement in Egypt, which briefly ruled the country in 2012–13).

Second, several regional initiatives threatened to undermine any newfound sense of national identity or unity. The most important of these was the so-called "Jubaland initiative." Even before the SFG was elected in Mogadishu, efforts were underway to establish a semi-autonomous region in the Juba Valley, including the regions of Lower and Middle Juba and Gedo. At the instigation of several governments in the region, the regional body, the Inter-Governmental Authority on Development (IGAD), brokered the process. The objective of the initiative was to establish a regional authority with the status of a federal member state (like Puntland), but the security and economic interests of both Kenya and Ethiopia were also important factors in their involvement in the Jubaland initiative.[6]

Third, even though it was clearly being slowly overpowered militarily by AMISOM and the Somalia National Army, Al-Shabaab was also undergoing a political metamorphosis. The famine was described as a major propaganda defeat for Al-Shabaab.[7] Numerous reports noted that the famine and Al-Shabaab's "clumsy response" had caused significant damage to the group's "already questionable reputation for good governance."[8] As a result of its unsustainable agricultural policies, extractive taxation policies, restrictions on movement, and direct expulsion of humanitarian agencies, many observers blamed Al-Shabaab for the devastating effects of the famine, though other analysts noted that many other parties were also partly responsible.[9] While Al-Shabaab's "anti-WFP discourse" was easier to accept during times of relatively good food security, support for the group dwindled as food insecurity worsened.[10] Growing increasingly discontented with the group's handling of the deteriorating situation, the public's protests in areas that Al-Shabaab controlled reflected the group's "deteriorating relations" with its populace.[11] Some went so far as to say that the famine lost Al-Shabaab its political currency— but they continue to rule much of South Central Somalia.[12]

The 2013 edition of Stig Jarle Hansen's book on Al-Shabaab says very little about the famine, and in that sense, puts the humanitarian crisis in the context of a much larger, existential crisis that Al-Shabaab faced at the time.[13] But Hansen concurs with Jackson and Aynte in suggesting that more space existed for negotiation with Al-Shabaab over humanitarian access than was sometimes thought.[14] Both these works provide some insights about operating in very tightly controlled humanitarian space in a complex emergency and in the context of the "global war on terrorism."

Al-Shabaab's affiliation with Al-Qaeda was strengthened by the experience of 2011, and the number of foreign jihadists in Somalia was believed to have increased.[15] In 2013, Al-Shabaab organized an attack on Mogadishu's main court complex in April, bombed the Turkish embassy compound in Mogadishu in July, and, most dramatically, attacked the Westgate shopping mall in the affluent Westlands neighborhood of Nairobi, Kenya, killing some sixty people in retaliation for Kenya's involvement in the conflict in Somalia.[16] One of Al-Shabaab's leaders, Sheikh Hassan Dahir Aweys, was ousted in an internal power struggle in June 2013 and was taken into custody by the Somali National Army.[17] This was symptomatic of the internal dynamics in Al-Shabaab at the time—a long power struggle between different factions was coming to a head, ultimately resulting in the recognition of Ahmed Abdi Godane as its uncontested leader. Godane himself was subsequently killed by a US drone-missile strike during an offensive in September 2014. All of these factors served to make Al-Shabaab more—not less—dangerous both internally and internationally, even as the territory it controlled continued to shrink.

By mid-2014, the sheen was fading from some of the hopes of 2012 and 2013, with the Center for Strategic and International Studies declaring that:

> just two years after [President Hassan Sheikh] Mohamud's taking office, the outlook appears bleak. Al-Shabaab, though weakened, is far from defeated and continues to carry out regular attacks; the process of writing a new, permanent constitution has reached deadlock; and the federalism process has proven a source of conflict. The violence surrounding the emergence of the Interim Juba Administration (IJA) in May 2013 was replicated in Baidoa in March 2014, when competing factions tried to establish federal member states in Southern Somalia.

Moreover, corruption continues unabated and political infighting has weakened the government ...[18]

This situation was compounded by a worsening of the humanitarian situation in mid-2014, with some organizations suggesting a parallel with 2010–11.[19] Those fears proved to be overstated, but there was no doubt that after two relatively good years, several areas of Somalia were suffering a deteriorating food security situation.[20] In this context, questions were being raised about both what had been learned from the experience of 2011–12, and what—if anything—was being done differently as a result.

The Rise of the "Resilience Agenda"

While the 2011 famine in Somalia has had many longer-term policy impacts, the one that clearly stands out is the pivot away from repeated attempts to address chronic problems through limited-duration humanitarian programs, and towards addressing what has universally come to be labeled "resilience." Cycles of crisis and recovery—often triggered by drought—have been part of life in the Greater Horn of Africa for as long as humans have inhabited the region; but, since at least the 1970s, a series of recurrent drought crises—sometimes related to predictable events such as the El Niño Southern Oscillation, sometimes not—were inevitably complicated by political and market factors and by underlying crises of environmental degradation and livelihoods. The recovery time between crises seemed to be growing shorter and shorter, to the point that some areas seemed to be in almost perpetual crisis.

In the aftermath of the 2011–12 famine, this observation led donors, agencies, the UN, and the Somali Federal Government to call for improvements to be made in the resilience of communities regularly affected by crisis. The concept of resilience references earlier efforts to reduce vulnerability, but its proponents argue that resilience is a new and separate phenomenon, and one that holds the key for overcoming the cycle of recurrent crises and attendant humanitarian responses.[21] The policy discourse on resilience has dominated the discussion about international engagement not only with Somalia and drought-prone areas of the Greater Horn of Africa but also in the Sahel and other areas caught in protracted or repetitive crisis. Indeed, by 2013 or 2014, all the main donor agencies had developed strategies for promoting resilience in the Greater Horn of Africa and elsewhere.[22]

Although the impetus for the discussion about resilience grew out of the 2011 crisis, a number of elements of the theme are not new. The concept of resilience comes from ecology, where it is used to refer to the ability of an ecosystem to absorb and recover from shocks and stresses.[23] A variety of definitions for "resilience" exist, but most focus on the ability to withstand shocks and adapt to change without a decrease in either short-term wellbeing or longer-term ability to recover and improve—whether the unit of analysis is an individual, a household, a community, or, at a slightly different level, an institution. The definition offered by a DFID policy paper comes as close as any to summarizing the debate: resilience is "the ability of countries, communities and households to manage change, by maintaining or transforming living standards in the face of shocks or stresses—such as earthquakes, drought or violent conflict—without compromising their long-term prospects."[24]

Attempts to build resilience define policies and programs that support an ability to "bounce back" or recover rapidly from a shock or stressor and to reduce vulnerability to the next shock. This implies an emphasis on both current and future time frames and on both "current status" and "future capability." Much of the learning about past crises stresses the trade-off between these two: "consumption smoothing" implies compromising future capacity to ensure current consumption; "asset smoothing" implies some current sacrifice in order to protect future capacity.[25]

Resilience Strategies

As the notion of resilience has gained currency, governments in the Greater Horn of Africa and a variety of agencies have developed programmatic and policy frameworks to promote resilience, and they bear some resemblance to each other. In Kenya, the "Ending Drought Emergencies" strategy that emerged out of the 2011 drought has two aims: first, to make all sectors more "drought-proof"; that is, to strengthen people's resilience to drought. Second, it seeks to improve the monitoring of drought and especially the needs emerging from drought to ensure early action to mitigate the impact of drought, under the purview of the National Drought Management Authority (NDMA), set up in 2012.[26] In Ethiopia, the response to the 2011 drought seemed to confirm that the strategy, already in place, of relying on the Productive Safety Net System worked well when a scaled-up response to a particularly bad drought shock was needed. An NDMA policy had been put in place in 2010, with the overall objective of reducing the risk and impact of disasters through the establishment of a compressive disaster risk management system within the context of sustainable development—a shift in emphasis from "disaster response" to "disaster risk management." In the Ethiopia policy, risk financing is the major mechanism of early response, triggered by indicators that track major hazards such as reduced rainfall but also measure livelihood outcomes such as food security or health status.[27]

In Somalia, even as the response to the famine continued, the three major operational UN Agencies (the Food and Agriculture Organization, the World Food Programme, and UNICEF) devised a joint strategy for building resilience. It was developed in coordination with governments in Somaliland and Puntland and with the new government in Mogadishu after it was formed in 2012. The key tenets of the strategy include strengthening productive sectors to enhance household income, enhancing basic services to protect human capital, and promoting safety nets to sustain the basic needs of chronically at-risk or destitute populations.[28]

In the Somalia strategy, the enabling environment includes improved knowledge management, a policy and regulatory framework for effective service delivery in each sector, and local governance and local institutional development for playing crosscutting and supporting roles. Like the Ethiopian policy, this strategy represents a shift from crisis response to crisis prevention. Though led by the UN, the intent is to implement it in conjunction with regional governments and the new Somali Federal Government. By 2014, the strategy had begun to be implemented in areas of Somaliland and Puntland, as well as Gedo Region in South Central Somalia. Various NGO consortia have emerged to address the resilience agenda as well. Major donors have called for proposals that include programming time frames of up to three years. For the most part, by 2014, these programs were only just getting under way, and few if any had been evaluated. However, according to some observers, if the humanitarian and development community is really trying to address the issue of building resilience, it must tackle much more serious constraints than just those noted above—including the sticky issues of clan, land and natural resource access, power, governance, basic service provision, and corruption—that aid organizations have traditionally tried to avoid because of the political implications.[29]

Critics have argued that, even if the concept of resilience was sufficiently well defined to be universally applicable and implemented, an unrealistic perspective of what is possible in the aftermath of a crisis can lead to poor response—actually making vulnerable communities worse off.[30] However, in the aftermath of the worst humanitarian crisis in the Greater Horn of Africa in two decades, there was a clear impetus to try to address both current suffering and underlying vulnerability, and the notion of "resilience" was the touchstone on which much of the effort was based. The question of how much difference this was making in the lives of people in the famine-affected areas of South Central Somalia remained something of an unanswered question—even by 2014. And there was evidence that while "learning" was one thing, incorporation of learning into policy and practice might be another.

Learning from the Famine of 2011–12

So what can be learned from the response of humanitarian agencies that had been working in or on Somalia for several decades? Clearly, much was learned from the experience of 2011–12. The obvious secondary question arising, however, was whether that learning was reflected in policy and practice in the post-famine period—particularly with regard to the issue of resilience and how a repeat of the famine could be prevented. Addressing these questions raises some issues about how much was learned from the terrible events of 2011 and whether that learning has led to different ways of working that will prevent the recurrence of similar events.

Five critical issues arise from the analysis here that should be taken into consideration with regard to the question of building resilience: information and early warning; the lack of early response; questions around risk management; specific interventions compared to the overall response; and the tendency to focus on technical issues at the expense of the political and institutional context and the constraints such contexts entail. This section addresses these questions, and then assesses the extent to which they have or have not been incorporated into current policy and programs. By examining program proposals developed for humanitarian and resilience interventions in Somalia in 2013–14, we sought evidence of the extent to which these "lessons learned" were being incorporated into programs and policies in the post-famine period. This analysis was, at best, a limited proxy for the question "What Was Learned?" However, the results of the analysis give some interesting insights into the kind of learning that was being prioritized.[31]

Early Warning and Information

Although the analysis has shown that the problem of the late response was not because of a lack of information, several technical issues related to information should be raised. First, seasonal assessments are not the same as needs assessments. The former—typical of FSNAU's major assessments—provide an overview but do not (and cannot) provide specifics about programming at the local level. They need to be complemented by contingency planning and assessment at the local level, as highlighted above. Second, users of information must be able to understand the difference between classification (such as the Integrated Phase Classification or IPC) and early warning. This is the difference between making statements about the recent past and making statements about the near-term future (a point we explore in more detail in Chapter 10 under famine theory). Confusion over these different kinds of information—and the degrees of certainty that can be expected from each of them (particularly in conflicts where access is a constraint)—led to the conclusion that information was inadequate in 2011, and that much more information is needed to avert future famines. In fact, better understanding of existing information—tied to the way in which information is used—is the core of the problem.

A third early warning issue relates to regional information sharing. Agencies in Ethiopia claimed that they did not know what was going on in Somalia in 2011 and were surprised by the continuing numbers of refugees arriving and by their condition. On the other hand, agencies working in Somalia claimed that they lacked information about the devastating conditions in which Somali refugees were arriving in Ethiopia. Yet evidence shows that the information clearly was available. Regional information sharing—and accountability for sharing it—is likewise an issue that requires further attention. By 2014, it was not clear that this issue had been adequately addressed. In other regions, such as the Sahel, a regional humanitarian coordinator has been appointed, but similar roles have yet to be established in the Horn of Africa.[32]

A final point about information relates to both the "non-Western" actors and to local communities. Whatever else might be said about the responses of local communities and their diasporas, and the non-Western humanitarian actors, neither group was particularly well tuned to formal early warning information in 2011. Greater engagement with early warning and information systems more generally is part of the professionalization that Turkish and Middle Eastern actors are now seeking to build. The challenge for formal early warning systems, crucial for timely action and accountability, is to build in more (two-way) communication with affected communities.

The analysis of the 2013–14 proposals found much more emphasis on the analysis of natural hazards and physical landscape than on analysis of the political situation. Political hazards are often not even described, much less analyzed. The proposals didn't particularly address any of the issues raised here, since they are rather more systemic in nature, and not something that an individual program proposal would necessarily address. Local early warning information or mitigation strategies were commonly mentioned in proposals, but early warning systems or programs that used local social networks were the least-commonly mentioned innovation resulting from learning.

Early Responses

Possible solutions to the problems of late response have been proposed since the famine. These include several key points outlined above: developing "triggers" and embedding "trigger indicators" in the early warning and decision-making process to ensure the linkage of early warning to action (and to reduce the element of human dithering); developing "no regrets" responses that incorporate early action of a type that will be a good investment even if no major crisis subsequently develops (to reduce the fear of initiating a large-scale response before the extent of a crisis is clear);[33] and "crisis modifiers" or set-aside funds within longer-term programs intended to give program managers more flexibility to react quickly to changing situations on the ground to initiate rapid mitigation programs. Some programs in Somalia now incorporate these elements—although, as noted above, many still do not.

Longer-term work is focusing on "scalable" social safety nets, linking the provision of emergency assistance to already existing services, or delinking service provision in crises from one-off humanitarian responses. In East Africa, this is built mostly on experience from Ethiopia and Kenya, where such systems functioned reasonably well in 2011.[34] Strengthening social protection is an objective in Somalia, but much less exists to build on there. Somalia has little national capacity to manage safety nets (a key ingredient to success in Ethiopia and Kenya) and counter-terrorism restrictions have resulted in the bulk of this work being implemented somewhere other than the places most affected by the famine.

About half of the 2013–14 proposals addressed the notion of "crisis modifiers": contingency funds in long-term programs that can be mobilized rapidly in the short term to mitigate the onset of a crisis; or "no regrets" programming—programs that could be introduced to mitigate the onset of a crisis, which would have beneficial impacts even if a severe crisis did not eventually result. At least one donor took a somewhat different approach to the same issue: instead of having a flexible line item in an ongoing program, a separate fund was established that can be accessed to respond to an emerging crisis. The notion of scalable safety nets was mentioned in almost half the proposals. Proposals gave evidence of developing safety nets and incorporating them into ongoing programs but, for the most part, the means to build in the capacity to expand rapidly during or in the lead-up to a crisis was not made clear. In other countries in the region, these are government-led programs; in Somalia, they are largely implemented by external agencies.

The issue of "trigger indicators" came up in almost half the proposals reviewed, but it was often not clear that these really referred to forward-looking indicators, or could trigger early response programs in a timely way. Only a tiny handful of proposals suggested an integrated approach to early warning, trigger indicators, and early response mechanisms—a surprising finding, given the evaluation of the 2011 crisis and the immediate post-famine discussion in 2012.[35]

During the famine, Somali businesses and Islamic charities in the country initiated limited early responses. Water trucking appeared to be the most common early response. In addition, at least one private company reported that it was ready to respond with limited emergency relief two to three months before the declaration of the famine. One of the more notable and early responders, the Baidoa Business Group (composed of religious leaders, local leaders, business communities, and the diaspora), helped IDPs with food and other commodities from mid-May. Somali households and local communities were of course responding throughout the course of the crisis at the local level and by drawing on remittances from their kin in other parts of the country, in neighboring countries, or in the wider diaspora. The catalyst for a sea change in the scale of the response, however, came with the declaration of the famine, and the media coverage that came with it.

Risk Management

Somalia remains something of a special case, partly because of the history and legacy of aid in the country, and in part because of terrorism and counter-terrorism concerns.[36] The area of learning most evident in current programming is risk management—especially reducing the risks of aid diversion. This raises an unanswered question: exactly who bears the risks when interventions are made in difficult places such as Somalia? Although aid diversion was widespread in the period prior to the famine, from 2013 onwards the biggest risk to humanitarian agencies in Somalia after staff security was clearly perceived to be accusations of fraud or diversion, either by staff or by partners. Fraud can occur through local partners' or through agencies' own staff: "measures to counter fraud/diversion," and "partner accountability" were by far the two most frequently cited post-famine innovations in the program proposals we reviewed. By 2014, the risks associated with remote management had become intolerable to most donors, and as a result, many agencies had moved out of the highest-risk areas. Other agencies' proposals simply downplayed the element of remote management or suggested that it would only be relied on temporarily. This indirectly leads to one of the unintended impacts of "learning" from the famine, which was, in effect, to stay away from the areas that were the hardest hit by the famine. Most of these proposals simply avoid any mention of working in Al-Shabaab-controlled areas or propose working in a token district or two, with the main body of activities elsewhere (Somaliland or Puntland)—areas less in need, according to FSNAU at the time.[37]

During the famine, these risks were outsourced down a line that began with donors, passed through international agencies (UN or NGO), and often wound up with a local organization operating on the ground. Ongoing legal and reputational risks constrained any fundamental alteration of these dynamics, and in the ability to prevent, mitigate, and respond to the threat of famine in a timely way.[38] While changes have been made, and the risks of aid diversion have probably been reduced, it remains unclear whether this has improved the overall capacity to prevent or address famine.

Specific Interventions Compared to the Overall Response

The most innovative response to the Somalia famine of 2011–12 was the rapid implementation of a large-scale cash transfer program. It was also late— not scaling up until after the declaration and after a relatively heated debate about the appropriateness of cash or market-based responses. In early 2011, strong opposition to cash interventions came from certain quarters based on the fear of further food price inflation, or aid diversion. Nevertheless, this complex and new kind of programming—with which agencies mostly had only limited experience—was quickly brought to scale between August and October of 2011 and helped to bring some of the worst impacts of the famine under control.[39] Contrary to the fears of some critics, injecting large amounts of cash into a resource-constrained environment did not lead to food price inflation. One major factor in this was that the lead agencies worked closely with traders in Mogadishu to ensure a supply response.[40] The other was the attempt to assess markets and their ability to respond to demand. This was part of a relatively new field of "response analysis"—the consideration of alternative program modalities in light not only of market impacts but also recipient preference, non-market risks, gender and intra-household effects, and other factors.[41] The evidence shows that the cash was mostly used to buy food or pay off debts incurred earlier—debts that were incurred mostly to buy food. Cash and voucher programs were not immune to some of the problems that had accompanied in-kind assistance, but cash and vouchers were scaled up much more quickly than would have been possible with a food program,[42] offered greater choice to the end recipient, and transferred a much higher proportion of the aid budget to the final recipient.[43] Food aid did play a role in the response—with major ICRC food distributions in the famine-affected areas and efforts of a number of agencies in border areas and in Mogadishu. And major efforts were made in other sectoral areas.

Nevertheless, one of the inescapable observations from the review of impact assessments is that the evaluations of individual projects or programs generally paint a positive picture about the appropriateness of the intervention and its impact, and about learning from the crisis. Yet virtually all the meta-evaluations of the overall response to the famine paint a picture of ignored early warning, risk-averse actors, late responses, politicized priorities, and a major loss of human life and destruction of livelihoods. The seemingly irrational conclusion is that lots of good individual interventions added up to a botched overall response. Several factors explain this: first, the authors of individual project evaluations were consultants hired by the agency that had implemented the project or program, so may have had strong incentives to portray the intervention in a positive light, whereas the authors of the Real-Time Evaluations and other meta-analyses were responsible to other authorities and may have had more leeway to be critical.[44] Second, most of the individual evaluations were conducted on programs that didn't even begin until after the famine was declared, so they simply ignored questions about timeliness. In effect, individual evaluations took the beginning of a given intervention—not the beginning of the crisis—as the baseline against which improvements were evaluated. Third, many of the respondents we interviewed had a sense that while they (or their agency) had learned from the experience and worked hard to improve their own programming, they did not think that other agencies had done so, and certainly not the humanitarian community as a whole.[45] This externalization of the problem suggests the limited extent to which humanitarian actors as a community of practice have really come to terms with the impact of the overall response, or what was learned from the experience. Much of the learning remains atomized at the level of the individual agency, or even individual staff member. This is one factor contributing to the sense of "malaise" described in Chapter 10.

Some other, genuinely needed innovations at the system level (i.e., not at the level of individual programs) have certainly been based on learning from this crisis. These include humanitarian funding on a three-year time-horizon, now promoted by several of the major donors working in Somalia. In addition, a three-year UN Consolidated Appeals Process is putting UN humanitarian programming on a three-year planning basis. This is welcome news to the agencies operating in Somalia and the communities they serve. And there is a recognition that smaller investments in prevention and resilience will result in much larger savings in humanitarian response in the next crisis, and regional evidence exists to support this assertion.[46] However, the impact of this in Somalia has yet to be measured. By 2014, a number of key informants suggested that although longer-term funding was available, it was not really leading to a longer-term perspective in application (i.e., implementing agencies were not taking advantage of it).[47] The extent to which learning is translated into alternative approaches still boils down to individual personalities and leadership, and has not yet been institutionalized.[48]

Chapter 6 highlighted the observation that the resilience of Somali communities revolves around diversification (particularly diversification of risk), flexibility or mobility, and social connectedness. Notions of diversification are finding their way into programming—though may be more focused on diversification of assets and income streams rather than risk per se—but the notions of flexibility and social connectedness are more difficult to build in to programs or policy. Nevertheless, the evidence here suggests that the bulk of the preventive and responsive actions—not only in the first half of 2011, but in the whole crisis—came from local actors: communities, social networks, the local business community, and even local authorities. The main point of learning here would be the necessity of understanding Somali systems and not undermining strategies of flexibility and connectedness.[49]

Technical Versus Political Constraints to External Response

While progress has been made in addressing many of these technical issues, some of the biggest constraints in 2011 were to be found in the political realm. Virtually everyone agrees that the security and counter-terrorism agenda trumped the humanitarian imperative in 2011, and would do so again under similar circumstances. The general consensus emerging from the research was that, while there was ultimately a political cost to pay for the famine, the political cost of donor resources ending up in the hands of Al-Shabaab would have been much higher, particularly in the United States, but also in other Western donor countries. The "system" responded to these costs, and as a result, insufficient external assistance was devoted to the crisis until it was declared a famine. If future humanitarian emergencies are to be managed better—and future famines prevented—this issue must be resolved beyond doing a simple (and completely out-of-context) political cost–benefit calculation. Several key points deserve to be highlighted.

First, there are real choices here—choices that put the lives of hundreds of thousands of human beings at risk in 2011. A full discussion of the choices around counter-terrorism restrictions has yet to take place. A 2013 report by the UN Office for the Coordination of Humanitarian Affairs and the Norwegian Refugee Council concludes:

> In Somalia, the restrictions placed upon humanitarian actions through sanctions and counter-terrorism measures are considered by many in the humanitarian community to have compounded the already difficult operating environment in the Al-Shabaab controlled areas ... While it is impossible to determine the extent to which the abrupt decrease in aid (or indeed other consequences of counter-terrorism measures) contributed to the famine that followed in mid-2011, some relationship cannot be discounted. Certainly the severity of the food crisis and the publicity around it prompted a reversal of donor policy.[50]

This reflects a broadly held view—but one rarely put on the table—that counter-terrorism measures directly undermined humanitarian action.[51] Second, while trade-offs are inevitably made, the view that humanitarian action somehow undermines counter-terrorism objectives is not supported by any evidence. Recent research has challenged the assumption that access and assistance cannot be negotiated with groups like Al-Shabaab.[52] Field interviews noted that, in many circumstances, it was possible to negotiate access with local Al-Shabaab authorities, and even to hold them accountable for stolen or diverted goods.[53] Although Al-Shabaab routinely taxed, harassed, and expelled humanitarian agencies, dialogue with Al-Shabaab and similar groups still proved to be possible, and it is imperative if future famines are to be prevented. And the only recourse to humanitarian agencies is concerted collective action against taxation by non-state actors. The fact that a major humanitarian operation eventually got up and running in areas controlled or influenced by Al-Shabaab without any apparent contribution to the erosion of counter-terrorism goals suggests that this discussion is not about an either/or trade-off. But this only works if negotiated access is coordinated and if humanitarian agencies are broadly perceived to be independent of political and security agendas.[54] The constraints of counter-terrorism laws are likely to become greater in the future, and humanitarian actors of all kinds need to learn to negotiate the protection of human life and dignity in the face of both terrorist groups themselves and counter-terrorism legislation:

From one viewpoint, counter-terrorism laws and regulations could be said to represent just one more in a long line of specific examples of the enduring and entrenched dilemmas central to the humanitarian project, especially how to act in accordance with the humanitarian principles of independence and neutrality in complex conflicts that involve terrorist groups. Yet from another viewpoint, these laws and regulations may require humanitarian organizations to face new, if no less fundamental, choices about whether to accept government funding for life-saving operations, especially if—as seems possible—donor governments' concerns about the vulnerability of the aid sector to abuse by terrorist groups continue to grow.[55]

Fear of counter-terrorism sanctions is a factor affecting non-Western actors as well—in some ways even more so, given the Islamic identity of many of them and the "guilty until proven innocent" attitudes about Islamic agencies noted in Chapter 8. Some of these actors were able to work in areas controlled by Al-Shabaab but reported that it was still difficult, even after access had been negotiated. Accusations of "assisting terrorists," particularly in Western newspapers, forced some of these agencies to pull back from Al-Shabaab areas. No single agency or party, acting alone, can achieve much progress. Making progress on collective action in fraught contexts such as South Central Somalia will require a frank, all-parties discussion, and to date the incentives against an honest collective discussion remain higher than the imperatives towards engaging in it—a topic we take up in Chapter 10.

10

PREVENTING FAMINE

AN UNFINISHED AGENDA?

Introduction

The threat of famine in Somalia remains: while the specific series of events that took place in 2010–11 is unlikely to be repeated, limited progress has been made in the effort to prevent future famines. This book began by reiterating what we already knew about the famine: its multiple causes, its main impacts, that it was foreseen but not very well mitigated, the role of Al-Shabaab, and the conflict with the TFG and AMISOM. The fear that aid could and would fall into the hands of Al-Shabaab was one of the major reasons for the delayed attempts by Western agencies to mitigate the crisis. Much of the response, particularly in the first half of 2011 and especially in Al-Shabaab-controlled territory, came not from the international humanitarian community, but from Somali communities themselves—people's own social networks, the local business community, the diaspora and, in some cases, Al-Shabaab. But little of this was recorded, and most of it took place in areas unreachable by outsiders and, as such, this response was poorly understood and supported. Chapters 5 and 6 addressed these issues.

Various factors led a number of actors from countries in the Middle East, from Turkey, and through Islamic support networks, to engage in the famine response. Likewise, much of this response was not well documented and took place outside the long-standing Western humanitarian response to Somalia. Chapter 8 addressed these issues. The international humanitarian response mechanisms did respond—albeit belatedly—and helped to contain the crisis. This was discussed in Chapter 7 and some of the learning from this was discussed in Chapter 9.

This final chapter addresses some of the other questions that emerged from the research. First, throughout the famine and post-famine period, nearly all parties—but particularly Western humanitarian agencies and staff—sensed that something is deeply wrong with the practice of humanitarian assistance and famine prevention. Second, for all the handwringing about the failure of external agencies, equally important constraints within Somali society both worsened the impact of the famine and made future prevention more difficult. Third, all of the analysis highlights the question of accountability: accountability for the causes and the constraints; accountability for the response failure; and accountability for learning. Yet the issue of accountability remains largely untouched. Addressing these questions, and incorporating all this into our understanding of famines, is critical to preventing a recurrence of the catastrophe.

A Malaise of Humanitarian Action in Somalia?

Throughout the course of the famine and the post-famine period, a deep sense of malaise was palpable in the Western, Nairobi-based international humanitarian assistance system for Somalia—phrased more than once as a view that the system is not "fit for purpose," or even, the system is "rotten."[1] Part of this phenomenon is simply the geographical and psychological distance between Nairobi and Somalia: during the actual famine, many humanitarian workers expressed frustration over their lack of knowledge about what was happening on the ground. Rarely has there been such a large emergency, with such overwhelming amounts of data and information, and yet such a dearth of any real sense of what was happening on the ground.[2]

This general sense of malaise could be broken into several inter-related categories of concern and a collective inability to address these concerns, including a deep sense of fragmentation, doubts about aid diversion and the legal threats this involved, the lack of impartiality and accountability, risk aversion in the face of all these, and nagging doubts about whether anything learned from the hard experience of 2011 would prevent the reoccurrence of famine in Somalia. Much of this malaise affected the Western humanitarian agencies and donors; the view from non-western actors was somewhat different; and part of the problem was systemic in that it affected all actors.

Fragmentation and Mistrust

By 2014, the humanitarian community working in Somalia was quite fragmented. Donors, UN agencies, and NGOs (international and Somali) had very different views on the constraints to humanitarian action. Much of the written documentation about the famine and the response from the humanitarian community that was in the public domain by 2014 was optimistic: while mistakes had been made in 2011, lessons had been learned and new systems had been put in place. Privately, however, many aid workers expressed a much more negative view: the aid system in Somalia corrupted both benefactors and beneficiaries; it was beholden to political agendas that had little to do with the humanitarian imperative of protecting human lives or livelihoods; and under current circumstances, little was being done—indeed, little could be done—to change things.[3]

Few agencies would divulge the results of internal reviews or audits on programs in Somalia, even under strictly confidential terms, for fear that admitting mistakes would lead to blame and stigmatization. In fact, to some extent, sharing any type of data or information has become more difficult.[4] The competitive structure of funding was discouraging information sharing. Funding for protecting the limited recovery gains in Somalia was faltering. The realities in the field simply could not be made to match with the rhetoric from headquarters of either donors or agencies. Agency staff turnover had been high and new people had to relearn the same lessons—often the hard way.

Aid Diversion

The diversion of aid had always been a problem in South Central Somalia,[5] and the more "remote" management became, the more widespread the problem was. Given the lack of access to places of operation, monitoring local partners and activities had been very difficult during the famine, and had not become any less fraught in the post-famine period. The rise in third-party and even covert monitoring had helped to increase accountability to donors in the short term, but was not building genuine trust among partners in the longer term, and the widespread perception was that it was probably undermining genuine trust.

Accounts of the diversion and the "elite capture" of aid[6] abounded in Nairobi, but no one could speak openly about either. Even seasoned aid workers would look around to see who might be listening before speaking frankly about the problem, or clasp their hands over their ears if someone else was being too frank, because they simply didn't want to know—knowing about diversion of aid was equivalent to being complicit in it. This led to a whole category of "Nairobi public secrets" (i.e., things that everyone knew, but no one could talk about without fear). This included the fear of being singled out for blame, sanctioned, or, worse, being charged with a crime. No aid worker was charged with any crime, but it escaped no one's notice that the few agencies that had dealt with the issue of diversion of aid "on their watch" in an open and honest manner found themselves not only sanctioned by (at least some) donors, but also unable to get information about what they had to do to clear their names and rebuild their reputation. And everyone knew that these problems potentially affected all agencies to some degree or another.

Impartiality and the Undermining of Humanitarian Principles

It had long been known in the humanitarian sector that providing assistance on the basis of humanitarian need could go wrong in two different ways. This is the so-called "targeting problem": how to ensure that assistance actually gets to the right people in crises. One way that things can go wrong is that not everyone who actually needs the assistance receives it—"under-coverage" in targeting language. The other way is that aid ends up in the hands of people who don't actually need it, or "leakage," as it is known.[7] Aid diversion and elite capture are extreme forms of "leakage." But when the management emphasis is on reducing "leakage," this inevitably increases "under-coverage." By 2014, the overall amount of assistance—and in particular the geographic targeting of that assistance—was being determined by risk criteria, not by humanitarian need. In the aftermath of the famine, little aid was made available in large areas in Somalia—irrespective of humanitarian need in those areas—undermining the core humanitarian principle of impartiality. A version of this phenomenon had, of course, been symptomatic of the late response to the 2011 crisis. This lack of impartiality added to the sense that activities being undertaken in the name of humanitarian aid were undermining the very basis on which humanitarian activities have long been undertaken.

Research in the post-famine period indicated that this undermining of the impartiality of humanitarian assistance was one factor that soured relations between Al-Shabaab and the humanitarian agencies as far back as 2008–9, leading Al-Shabaab to believe that agencies were among the forces arrayed against them.[8] Much of the funding in the post-famine era, particularly for "resilience" programming, was not going into Al-Shabaab-controlled areas for fear that it would be diverted or taxed in contravention of counter-terrorism laws. Yet this determination of the allocation of aid by risk and political criteria rather than need was in clear violation of humanitarian principles and the codes of conduct of both agencies and donors. No one was comfortable discussing this.

Risk and Risk Aversion

In humanitarian terms, 2014 was a bad year in Somalia, yet there was little enthusiasm for building on the lessons of 2011 by investing in early action. To some degree, safety net programs were being scaled up, but precious little existed upon which to build. The risks of working in Somalia had increased. Al-Shabaab still controlled much of South Central Somalia, but was under ever-increasing pressure from AMISOM, which had now officially been joined by Kenya and Ethiopia. This made any kind of humanitarian negotiation with Al-Shabaab more difficult, not less. By 2014, it was also clear that the risks of working in Somalia were not going to be jointly shared: for the most part, if a donor provided funds to an agency, the agency shouldered the risks.[9] This "outsourcing" of risk cascaded down institutional relationships from donor to international agency, and international agency to local NGO. While much of the risk to personal safety was outsourced to local agencies, much of the financial, legal, and reputational risks remained with the international agencies.

Agency staff felt they had little choice but to accept these conditions, but while there were strong incentives to prevent diversion, the disincentives to reporting it when it happens were equally strong. Many staff noted that if a case of aid diversion was discovered, then it was easier not to report it, as this would require additional effort, and would only get the agency in trouble.[10] If organizing monitoring visits to field locations during the famine had been difficult, it was becoming even more so in the post-famine period. There were frequent reports of partner agencies blocking field visits for "security reasons," but international agency staff were fairly certain that security concerns were a convenient rationale for simply keeping prying eyes at a distance. This in turn led to more covert monitoring and the uses of remote sensing to monitor programs, and more "due diligence" in partner vetting, but it also underlined the lack of trust and made risk-averse behavior more likely.

To be sure, agencies' risk-management practices had improved significantly.[11] In general, if diversion hadn't been completely stopped, it had at least been made more difficult. A UN Risk Management Unit had been established in 2012, and was helping to keep track of over $4 billion in UN funding. It provided help not in only vetting partners but also vendors and prospective staff. All these measures helped to build some good practices, institutional capacity and memory, and gave donors some confidence to keep some funds flowing in South Central Somalia, despite the risks. But it was also differentiating Somali agencies on the basis of criteria that weren't clear to the agencies themselves or their international partners—some being "treated as pets, others vilified."[12] And clearly the risk management procedures were often opaque to those they affected, and the overall emphasis was more about reducing the risk of diversion rather than systematically managing that risk—in other words, developing robust means of weighing the risk of diversion against other risks—in particular, the risk of renewed humanitarian crisis. This was all very demoralizing to the humanitarian sector.

The financial implications of an honest discussion (the possibility of sanctions by donors or reputational damage in the press) are a problem for humanitarian actors in many contexts; the potential legal complication stemming from counter-terrorism legislation is an additional factor in Somalia. Yet virtually everyone agrees that the only way to address the problem is by having an honest discussion, and getting all the actors on board for collective action to halt the problem; in the absence of that conversation, the problems would simply persist: none of the risks are likely to go away any time soon. But the financial, legal, and reputational risks make an honest discussion about operating in Somalia very difficult. This contributes to the assessment that "the system is rotten." The same perception was noted by Somalis in the country, by Somalis working in the aid system, and by the non-Western agencies.[13]

Numerous respondents noted that while donors were willing to take greater risks during the crisis, the "appetite for risk" had diminished significantly in the post-famine period. During the famine, there had been some willingness to prioritize getting assistance to people, even if it meant less control over who actually received the aid, but agencies who did so had to keep quiet about it,[14] and the appetite for taking such risks had diminished significantly by 2013–14.

Learning and Accountability

As noted above, much was learned in the crisis, but putting that learning into practice has proven more difficult than anticipated. "Learning and change" is more evident at head office level and on paper than in "real" field practice. Many respondents had begun to question how much was actually learned. With high staff turnover, institutional memory is low. Notably, few experienced hands in the humanitarian community thought that very much had fundamentally changed—individual agency officials believed that they were better prepared for another crisis in Somalia, but most expressed doubt about the ability of the system to "get it right" in another major crisis.[15] The problems of coordination, diversion, remote management, and access all remained, and the "gatekeeper" issue and the problems arising from political constraints had not really been dealt with either.

With regard to serious attempts to learn from the crisis, some agencies (donor or operational) undertook thorough After Action Reviews. But those who did were, for the most part, reluctant to share them, and the findings rarely found their way into the public domain. Hence agencies were still finding it difficult to deal honestly with mistakes a number of years after the famine, and, for the most part, levels of trust are such that people feel it is dangerous to share documentation that might admit mistakes. All this makes having an honest discussion about operating in Somalia with anyone besides very trusted colleagues extremely difficult and underlines the sense of a "damned if you do and damned if you don't" malaise in the system.

Much of this sense of pessimism emerges from a comparison between the changes made since 2011 and the older, pre-existing problems that remain. Multi-year funding is now in place, for example, that makes planning longer-term interventions in Somalia possible. But many respondents do not believe that the humanitarian community has taken advantage of this.[16] The resilience agenda now has more traction than it ever had before, but it isn't clear that the programming strategy (or the funding) has kept up with the rhetoric or that the new narrative is any more capable of resolving some of the old problems than was previously the case.

Non-Western Actors

The sense among the non-Western humanitarian actors in 2014 was rather different. They had become major players on the global humanitarian scene.[17] Though far from a homogenous group given their significant differences in ethos and operating procedures, these agencies share a number of common characteristics, including an Islamic identity and principles of charity, and a spirit of voluntary action that is notably absent in the more highly professionalized Western agencies. This in turn led to greater solidarity with people on the ground and a greater presence in Somalia in 2011, in contrast to the politicized and securitized Western aid system in Somalia, which has long been perceived by many in Somalia as neither neutral nor impartial.[18] Of course, Islamic and Middle Eastern agencies had political and economic interests behind their engagement as well—and indeed, while at least some of them had been relatively successful in managing the constraints that working in Somalia entails, in some cases they also fell victim to the same clan interests and other problems that Western agencies faced. Moreover, a degree of mistrust still exists between the Turkish, Middle Eastern, and Islamic agencies on the one hand and Western agencies on the other, despite the ample possibilities for greater partnership—and the fact that both groups have plenty to learn from each other.

Malaise at the Systemic Level

While much of the malaise described here is manifest at the level of individuals or agencies working in a specific context, much of this discussion resonates more broadly, and at the systemic level. Both state and non-state actors have manipulated humanitarian aid for their own political purposes in many contexts, including but not limited to Somalia.[19] In 2002, Fiona Terry immortalized the notion that humanitarian response is "condemned to repeat" its mistakes.[20] Various reviews suggest that the humanitarian system has grown by accretion rather than by strategy and is not able to cope with the increasing frequency and severity of crisis.[21] Understanding these issues deeply, in context, is the only way that the "system" can begin to be adapted to fit the demands made on it.

Calls for greater accountability of all actors for the consequences of their actions (or the lack thereof) have repeatedly been made.[22] These calls address the actions not only of humanitarian actors but also the nominal government of Somalia at the time (the TFG, and later the SFG) and the controlling authority in most of the famine-affected area (Al-Shabaab). With regard to humanitarian culpability, no group completely escapes blame: donor agencies, donor governments, or humanitarian agencies (be they UN or NGO). But none of the major UN agency staff in charge of the response in Somalia in 2011–12 have faced any form of sanction, despite various real time evaluations or reports noting the failure of contingency planning and the widespread failure of response in the first half of 2011.[23] Donors do not appear to have suffered any consequences, even though for the most part they were slow to respond in 2011. Some NGO staff feel they have been unfairly blamed for the failure of the response, though few have been sanctioned as individuals either.

However, at least in part because of the threat of repercussions, it is very difficult to have an honest conversation about learning that is in any way transformative of a system that clearly did not work very well in 2011. There is no doubt that a lot of valuable lessons were learned—often the hard way—about working by remote management in a complex operating environment characterized by multiple hazards to affected communities and multiple risks to humanitarian organizations. Having a discussion about learning is possible, so long as it is fairly generic and technical. But political issues are sensitive and talking about accountability at all is very difficult. Seeking a way out of this malaise is a topic we explore later in this chapter.

Internal Constraints

None of the analysis of external constraints in humanitarian prevention or response is an argument to excuse the internal causes within Somali society for their role in both instigating the famine and exacerbating its impact. And though research shows that greater engagement with Al-Shabaab may have enabled greater humanitarian access, this in no way excuses the actions of Al-Shabaab in exacerbating the crisis. Al-Shabaab not only failed to recognize the severity of the growing crisis until it overwhelmed them but many of their policies were directly to blame for making people more vulnerable to the combination of back-to-back failures of the rain and the global food price spike. Al-Shabaab was also a major obstacle to all actors who tried to assist, including humanitarian agencies, but also those private companies that attempted to provide relief, as well as clans that mobilized responses, the mosque-based networks, Islamic charities, diaspora groups, and agencies from Turkey and the Middle East.

Somalis' own social hierarchies and history of social exclusion provides an important dimension in understanding the events of 2011. Marginalized and minority groups such as the Rahanweyn and Somali Bantu continue to be looked down upon—and are often exploited economically—within Somali society.[24] The exploitation of the displaced Rahanweyn and Bantu in Mogadishu by members of more powerful clans was commonplace in 2011.[25] These factors are independent of the influence of Al-Shabaab. Menkhaus notes that the humanitarian community faced multiple constraints to responding adequately in 2011. He concludes, "Put another way, Al-Shabaab could be cleared out of much of south Somalia but that would not necessarily guarantee humanitarian access in the event of renewed famine."[26]

The more powerful clans of the Galagadud and Mudug Regions were able to mobilize assistance from their business communities and diaspora, and despite

Al-Shabaab's presence, the evidence suggests that this contributed to changing the trajectory of the evolving disaster in Central Somalia. The Rahanweyn and Bantu, in contrast to the Hawiye, are also among the most rural, sedentary, and least diversified groups in Somalia, and while resources were shared widely within their social networks, their options were more limited owing to their weaker political position. As the crisis deepened, resource flows through social networks and diaspora linkages increased overall, but only broke across clan divides once the media images took centre stage and an emotional reaction generated a wider Somali solidarity and resource mobilization process. The only exceptions to this clan-based flow of resources were the larger private companies that were prepared to assist early and anywhere.

Accountability

Throughout the post-famine period, calls were made for greater accountability—to donors because they demanded it, but more importantly to famine-affected people and communities. Experts are virtually unanimous that famines will continue to be a threat until real accountability to affected parties becomes a genuine part of famine prevention, not only on the part of humanitarian workers and agencies but also donors, the UN and, above all, national governments and controlling authorities, whether state or non-state actors.[27] However, by 2014 there was a weary sense that the donors are where the real power lies, and hence the party to whom all the real accountability accrues. Genuine accountability to affected communities is an uphill task even when communication is good and contact is frequent between agency and community; in Somalia, where contact is infrequent and mostly indirect, and where "gatekeepers" in many cases dominate the exchange, such accountability is much more difficult.

All of this raises deeper questions about accountability for famine: What leadership should be accountable, and to whom? Repeated calls have been made for greater accountability for acts of both commission and omission—addressing not only humanitarian actors but also the nominal government of Somalia at the time (the TFG) and the controlling authority in most of the famine-affected area (Al-Shabaab). No group completely escapes blame, but so far, no one has been sanctioned.

However, having an honest conversation about accountability is difficult. Somalia is a complex context where accountability is dispersed among a multitude of actors. In most contemporary analyses, the state has the first obligation to protect the rights, dignity—and access to food—of its population.[28] In the case of Somalia—perhaps the most complete case of state collapse in modern history—where does accountability lie? Given the diffusion of responsibility between internal and external actors, between state and non-state actors, and between humanitarian and political actors, who is responsible for such a catastrophic loss of lives? The IASC Real-Time Evaluation put the onus squarely on donors and the traditional international (UN-led) humanitarian system, noting that in the absence of a functional central state, the "failure of early action was as much a function of donor reluctance to fund as it was a failing of the UN-led humanitarian system."[29]

The accountability of leadership for strategic decisions has also been questioned at the individual organizational level. The evaluation of WFP Somalia, for example, blames some of the impact of the famine on the lack of "contingency planning for possible withdrawal, and insufficient consideration of the consequences of donor policy changes and the increased risks to vulnerable populations from the withdrawal of WFP food aid in southern Somalia in early 2010."[30] Many evaluations sidestep the issue of accountability, and it remains a very murky issue in relation to non-Western actors.

The issue of accountability is clear in many of the proposals reviewed from the 2013–14 period, but it is mostly about accountability for money, whether from local partner to international agency, or from agencies in general to donors. Other notions of accountability, such as accountability to the recipients of humanitarian assistance—so-called "downward" accountability—are still relatively rare. International standards now exist for the accountability of humanitarian actors (both donors and implementing agencies) to recipient communities, and the issue of accountability to crisis-affected populations underpins both the general and the Somalia-specific literature on how to prevent famines.[31] However, a wide gap remains between these perspectives and the realities on the ground, where the issue of "downward" accountability is hardly mentioned. All of the factors in these proposals tended to highlight the technical, programmatic learning from the famine, but hardly reflected any of the political issues that arose, and which should have also been learned from. This is another reflection of the malaise of Western humanitarian action in Somalia.

Taking a broad view of famine in today's globalized and interconnected world, Howe and Devereux point to the complex—and frequently negative—synergies between natural, economic, and political factors, and suggest a framework for collectively shared accountability.[32] They propose that, in the aftermath of famines, each stakeholder's role should be examined and some form of proportionate accountability be assigned to each. The question of accountability, of course, must also be raised not only of external actors but of Somalis themselves. One attempt to operationalize a Howe–Devereux "accountability matrix" highlighted the role of Al-Shabaab both in aggravating the circumstances that led to the famine and in blocking much of the response, but notes that this doesn't explain the lack of a robust response from the international community. The study notes that:

> the famine declaration galvanized a rapidly scaled up relief operation—not only in Somalia, despite continuing problems of insecurity and restricted access, but also in Ethiopia and Kenya, where no such challenges existed to explain the delayed response. This suggests that the famine could have been prevented. This fact alone means that some blame must be attached to the donor community and implementing agencies.[33]

Sue Lautze and her co-authors, reviewing the specific impact of the Somalia famine, locate responsibility in this case with humanitarian actors, and argue that an "accountable executive" should be appointed within each agency. The accountable executive would be responsible for demonstrating that all necessary actions have been taken to mobilize logistical, technical, political, and financial resources based on early warning information.[34] This responsibility should include recourse to removal from office if necessary. But in fact, even where specific failings are outlined in evaluations or reports as noted above, little has been done to hold any specific individuals to account.

The role of the Transitional Federal Government in response to the famine in any organized institutional sense was limited, and the question of what value it added to prevention, early warning, or response is mostly a moot point. The evidence instead highlights the neglect and profiteering from aid by individuals and networks speaking in the name of the TFG.[35] This discussion, however, raises much deeper issues of accountability within Somali society. In her book on "clan cleansing," Lidwien Kapteijns makes a powerful and controversial case for the "social reconstruction" required to address longstanding clan-based prejudices and hate narratives that continue to be reproduced in Somali society and politics. Her analysis focuses on narratives and associated violence between the major clans (in particular the Darod and the Hawiye), not the exclusion or predation by the major clans on the marginalized clans—the Rahanweyn and the Bantu.[36]

Given the roles of the state, the major clans, and the international humanitarian community, accountability to recipients of assistance has been particularly weak in the case of Somalia.[37] This ties the treatment of accountability back to Glenzer's argument that the entire system of early warning and famine response will only ever be able to achieve "partial success" until these systems are tied (i.e., accountable) to the needs of famine-affected people.[38]

A final point relates to an apparent trade-off between accountability and learning within the humanitarian community. While some in the humanitarian community were willing to explore these issues, discussions about learning (i.e., questions about what went wrong and what we learned from this experience) often ended abruptly when questions turned to accountability (questions about who was responsible for what went wrong). This was often the case even when talking about relatively minor mistakes. Only a handful of the bravest humanitarian workers were willing to talk about overall accountability for a famine or their role in it. Most blamed someone else. Pressing too hard on questions about accountability ran the risk of shutting down the discussion about learning. In theory, there is little doubt about the link between accountability and famine, but in practice—despite being the worst famine in over a decade—there is little evidence that the experience of Somalia in 2011–12 has led to advances in operationalizing accountability. It is still perceived as a blame game, with the object being the identification of some one person or agency to blame. In the case of Somalia, that is a grave misperception—an attempt to escape the collective failure that the famine represented. All of this, of course, significantly exacerbates the sense of "malaise."

Accountability and the Political Economy of Aid

Given the scale of the resources devoted to humanitarian response in huge disasters such as Somalia in 2011–12 (measured in the billions), it is worth asking about accountability from a different angle. At various points in this book we have referred to the legacy of aid in Somalia: the "beneficiaries" include not only the intended recipients but also a multitude of actors associated with humanitarian agencies. This includes many agencies themselves and the infrastructure that supports them, many private contractors, and the various "gatekeepers" within the system. Billions of dollars of aid have been spent on, or in the name of, Somalia since the 1970s. What has happened and continues to happen with all of this money? Many Somalis also ask such questions. How much is spent financing this infrastructure in comparison to how much reaches "needy" people in Somalia? (A significant proportion is spent in Nairobi, Kenya, rather than Somalia itself.) Finding out how much money has been pledged to a crisis is straightforward, but finding out exactly how it was spent is much more difficult and it is almost impossible to arrive at definitive conclusions about its impact. Other studies on Somalia have pointed out the many unforeseen consequences of aid inflows—including the capitalization of a new and different private sector in the 1990s,[39] or a cornering of the market of some of the supporting infrastructure.[40] These outcomes are not, of course, foreseen in policy and programmatic objectives.

This study has not specifically attempted to reconstruct the broader political economy of aid in response to the famine of 2011–12, but the scale of resources involved, the structural constraints, the continuities of issues identified, and the limited learning that has been institutionalized, are a source of concern to many people interviewed both inside and outside of the humanitarian aid enterprise, and surely raise uncomfortable moral questions as well as suggest some further lines of inquiry.

Seeking a Way Out of the "Malaise"

The first section in this chapter described the symptoms of a "malaise" of the formal humanitarian system. But much of this story describes a broader set of problems—incorporating both the external (humanitarian and political/security) environment and the internal (local) context. While this particular story describes Somalia, the symptoms could fit many contemporary political and humanitarian crises. Somalia in 2011 was perhaps an extreme case, but it was not an outlier as these issues have been observed in many crises.[41] The important issue, however, isn't just to describe the symptoms, or even to attribute causes to this malaise, but rather to suggest ways that the malaise might be overcome. These include understanding the different causes and different past attempts to address shortcomings of the humanitarian system from within. Ultimately, addressing the malaise will require some frank internal dialogue, but there are strong incentives against such dialogue.

Understanding the Causes of the Malaise

Some of the causes of the humanitarian malaise are structural—that is, they exist almost irrespective of context; others are more context-specific. Perhaps the first element in addressing the malaise is to understand which is which. Structural features of humanitarian action include the competitive structure of financing, the separation of "buyer" (donor) from "client" (recipient) and the principle (and impetus) of independence in the face of the obvious need for collective action.[42] UN agencies and international NGOs have become very large, complex organizations which struggle to find a balance between humanitarian capacity and ongoing development or poverty-reduction programming. Other elements are more Somalia-specific. They include understanding the limits of remote management, or more broadly, remote engagement; a cynicism towards global priorities ("a hundred thousand people have died in the Syrian civil war, and the world is up in arms about it—but nearly that many people die every year in Somalia and it is considered 'baseline mortality'");[43] and the realization that the gatekeeper issue isn't just something "out there" in Somalia—it is an in-house issue for nearly every agency (i.e., the agencies' own staff members, both national and international, have been implicated in the gatekeeper system). Some of these issues can't really be fundamentally changed, but if recognized and well understood, some of their corrosive effects can be mitigated.

The second element in addressing the malaise is to understand the difference between technical and political constraints. The analysis here suggests that much more emphasis has been put into analyzing and addressing technical constraints at the expense of understanding and addressing political constraints. To some degree, this concern is also broader than just Somalia. But this problem has to be addressed in context, on a case-by-case basis. The issues are too complex to be tackled at a global level. And the third element in addressing the malaise is about accountability—including accountability for learning.

An Honest Dialogue about Accountability and Risk

All of these elements reiterate the need for an honest discussion that involves all the key parties in order to address the "humanitarian malaise." The need for such a discussion may be global, but the discussion almost by definition has to be local—though the leadership for such a dialogue might have to be external. The first issues requiring attention are about the risks faced, the consequences of aid going astray, and the impact of legal restrictions in light of the humanitarian imperative and the widespread loss of life in 2011. These are not new topics, and they certainly aren't going away. An analysis of accountability and responsibility is needed. Nearly all parties agree that accountability for actions taken or not taken is a major factor in preventing famine. Yet the incentives against such a discussion—which may involve some admission of failure—are very difficult to overcome.

This dialogue should also include a clear analysis of the trade-offs between counter-terrorism objectives and humanitarian objectives. It is clear in retrospect that these are not either/or choices—that is, a major response to the famine did not appear to undermine the effort to contain Al-Shabaab.[44] But the fear that some aid would "leak" to Al-Shabaab definitely undermined any effort to mitigate the crisis, or to respond to it in a timely way. This fear affected more than just the Western humanitarian effort—it also had an impact on diaspora groups who were trying to help, because of constraints on the banking system as a result of counter-terrorism measures. A major bank in Minneapolis (a centre of the Somali diaspora in the United States) closed down its operations to Somalia at the height of the famine because of fears that it would run afoul of counter-terrorism measures.

This question goes far beyond the confines of Somalia. Questions about operating in areas controlled by armed non-state actors—sometimes formally labeled "terrorists," sometimes not—also affects the humanitarian response in Afghanistan, Sudan, Syria, Iraq, Yemen, Nigeria, and many parts of the Sahel, to name but a few contemporary humanitarian emergencies. While the specific nature of the risks and trade-offs may vary, the question is of paramount importance globally. But understanding these risks and trade-offs in context is crucial to being able to address the dilemma facing both humanitarians and the affected populations caught in these conflicts.

This discussion also needs to address the question of risk sharing. It is striking that this question was not addressed at all in the program proposals we reviewed.[45] Agencies believe they have to shoulder the risks (physical security, risk of financial loss, legal and reputational risks) almost on their own, with the security risks often outsourced to local partners. Several donors insisted that, by not requiring agencies to repay grants where money clearly went astray, they are in fact bearing the financial risk. Part of the problem is that none of this is clearly spelt out—sometimes donors did not require repayment; sometimes they did. No aid worker has ever been prosecuted for breaking counter-terrorism laws, but statutes are on the books that could lead to prosecution. And the reputational risks are not just in Somalia, as being charged with "helping terrorists" would be ruinous to an agency globally. Everyone laments the risk aversion that characterized the nature of the response in 2011, but there are very clear reasons for that risk aversion, and so far, little has been done to resolve this.

Simply having an honest dialogue, involving all the parties engaged in humanitarian response, would help to clarify and address some of these concerns. Such a discussion would have to be held under something akin to the Chatham House rule, and granting some kind of amnesty for the admission of past mistakes may well be necessary (certainly the threat—whether perceived or real—of criminal prosecution for incidents of aid diversion is the primary disincentive to holding such a discussion).

A Professionalized Humanitarianism?

Much has been made of the attempt to professionalize humanitarian action in the twenty-first century. Michael Barnett highlighted the origins of this trend nearly a decade ago.[46] Indeed, professionalization has been suggested as the best means of addressing some of the "malaise" of earlier humanitarian fiascoes.[47] Humanitarian action has long been criticized as naïve and based solely on "good intentions." Critics from Michael Maren and Linda Polman to Dambisa Moyo have blasted humanitarian assistance or Western aid more generally over the extent to which it can do more harm than good,[48] while several noted analysts have tried to demonstrate ways of preventing or at least mitigating this harm.[49] Much of the emphasis on the reform of humanitarian action has its roots in some of the failures during the post-cold war era—particularly the Rwanda genocide, the resulting refugee crisis in Zaire, and the protracted conflict in the Balkans. Out of those debacles grew initiatives like the Sphere Project on minimum standards for humanitarian response,[50] the Humanitarian Accountability Partnership and the Action Learning Network for Accountability and Performance,[51] and numerous subsequent efforts such as the Good Humanitarian Donorship Initiative.[52]

All of these were in place, and their standards, processes, and guidance were very much a part of humanitarian response by the time of the Somalia famine, as evidenced in both the content and the sheer volume of documentation on the response to the famine. The Sphere guidelines were in place and agencies routinely did their best to adhere to them. Good analysis was available, and good monitoring and evaluation resulted in well-documented programs. At face value, the technical quality of the response was high, and both humanitarian policy-makers and field workers were accountable to a more professional ethos and code of conduct. But despite meeting all the criteria of a more professionalized humanitarianism, the response in Somalia in 2011–12 was overwhelmingly assessed as having been too late, extremely risk averse, managed only from afar, and mostly unwilling or unable to challenge the political priorities of the donor countries that eventually funded the response. Of course, the trend towards a more professional and institutionalized response was not the cause of this, but by the same token, all these characteristics of a more professionalized humanitarianism were unable to prevent the delay, the remoteness, and the risk aversion—and have not only done little to prevent the "malaise" outlined above but offer little in terms of suggested ways out of the current "malaise."

A Dialogue among Humanitarian Actors

A comparison with the admittedly less highly professionalized but more hands-on approach of some of the non-Western humanitarian actors is instructive. There is much less documentation or evidence of the impact of the Turkish and Middle Eastern donors and agencies, and their response was no more rapid than that of Western agencies (although it should be noted that the Turkish and Middle Eastern agencies were much less linked in to the early warning and information systems). But the sense of aid worker solidarity with the affected community was stronger.[53] These actors were more willing to run risks to reach the affected populations—and in a few cases paid heavily for the risks they ran. None of these observations suggests direct causation, but a much deeper analysis of the links between professionalism, solidarity, and a humanitarianism inspired by a spirit of voluntary action (each, on its own terms, a good thing) is clearly needed. This suggests the need for a deeper conversation between the traditional, mostly Western, actors and the variety of other humanitarian actors, be they formal donors and agencies from Turkey, the Middle East, and other non-DAC countries, local NGOs or faith networks. This dialogue must be characterized by genuine mutual interest, not cooptation or the expectation that one group should control or "coordinate" the other.

Since the late 1990s, it has been fashionable in the Western humanitarian aid community to promote rights, and to dismiss charity as paternalistic and demeaning. Non-Western actors—particularly Islamic actors—put the issues of charity and of voluntary action squarely back in the centre of humanitarianism, at least in terms of intentions. Humanitarianism inspired by a spirit of voluntarism offers a somewhat different vision compared to the more professionalized humanitarianism of the West. The experience of Somalia in 2011 doesn't entirely vindicate either vision, and presenting this as an either/or choice would miss the point: nothing is forcing humanitarian actors to choose between a professional, but risk-averse and arms-length response on the one hand, and a more solidarity-based but less professionally informed response on the other. Context is extremely important in this case, but the evidence certainly does suggest that both groups have ideas and experiences that should be shared.

A Dialogue on Internal Constraints

Within Somali society itself, the family and clan remain the institutions that offer the most protection in times of crisis, including in times of famine. However, they also remain the major fracture that divides people. Accountability and protection of the most vulnerable in society, regardless of clan identity, is difficult to engender when political and economic competition and survival is so fierce. A dialogue on internal constraints should include all elements of society, including the major victims of the last two famines. The Arta political process was an interesting example to draw upon, led by Somalis, engaging society at large and utilizing a rich oral culture—poetry, plays and songs were commonly used.[54]

Part of the constraint to any such dialogue—be it among the traditional Western humanitarian actors, engaging non-Western actors, or engagement among Somali communities—is the question of who would be perceived as an honest broker, and who would have the convening power to invite all parties to engage. This might have once been a role of the UN, but the UN is clearly not able to fulfill this role any longer.

Beyond Dialogue

And finally, if the evidence suggests that the quality of the overall management of and response to a humanitarian emergency or famine depends heavily on quality of leadership, then it is only logical to emphasize the need to build the capacity of that leadership and to empower leaders to act in a crisis. Part of the problem with holding leaders accountable for the success or failure of a major humanitarian response is that it is not clear whether they have adequate authority to make decisions. This has been a priority of the "transformative agenda" of the Inter-Agency Standing Committee since 2011.[55] The impact of this initiative is not yet clear.

Famine Theory

Declaring a famine is basically declaring a failure, whether it is a government that does the declaring or, as was the case in 2011, the United Nations. This partly explains the problem of late responses. Incentives are built in to avoid admitting this level of failure unless and until the evidence is overwhelming. This observation alone should inform our view of famine. Nevertheless, several points about our understanding of famines should be revisited.

First, although different strands of famine theory emphasize different causal factors, actual famines almost inevitably have multiple causes. The analysis here notes at least three triggering factors (drought, conflict, and high food-price inflation); three underlying causes (the collapse of the state, a chronic livelihoods crisis, and extreme environmental degradation); and several complicating factors (the absence of major humanitarian actors such as WFP, the presence of armed non-state actors—formally designated as terrorist organizations—and concerted international action to contain or destroy them, the restrictions of counter-terrorism laws, limitations on movement, forced displacement, and shifting livelihood strategies based on market demand for cash crops, among others). All of this is aligned with complex emergency theory, but goes well beyond it. And of course these multiple factors clearly resulted in entitlement failure—but that is more of a result than a cause per se. There were clear elements of production failure, market failure, and response failure in Somalia, and the last of these is where the issue of accountability arises. All this implies a pragmatic—and perhaps deliberately eclectic—use of famine theory as an explanatory tool rather than as a hypothesis-testing exercise.

Second, users of information must learn better to distinguish between classification (as provided in the IPC maps and more generally by the seasonal assessments noted above) and early warning. Classification is definitive—but to achieve this certainty, it is a retrospective analysis. That is, it summarizes information about known conditions, generally using "trailing" indicators of wellbeing, particularly the prevalence of global acute malnutrition, and—in the case of actual famines—mortality rates. Early warning is prospective—and by definition, probabilistic. Early warning will never be 100 percent certain; to be useful, it must be tied to contingency planning with clear triggers based on "leading" indicators. In other words, information has to be tied to both current status and predictive indicators. Neither of these observations is by any means a new discovery, but the experience of Somalia in 2011 suggests that these differences are still not well understood by practitioners and policy-makers.

One of the discussions arising out of the 2011 experience in Somalia ran something like this: "Since it took the declaration of a famine to fully mobilize a response, doesn't it make sense to lower the threshold for declaring a famine to elicit an earlier response?"[56] But this idea is based on this misunderstanding of the difference between classification and early warning. To the extent that response is made contingent on certainty, it will always be late, even if the thresholds for declaring a famine are lowered. The issue isn't about setting a lower bar for declaration; the issue is about strengthening the link of early warning to action, and about improving accountability for that action by developing triggers and building accountability mechanisms into them.

The analysis in Chapters 5 and 6 suggested that much more room exists for local definitions or classifications, and indicators of early warning as understood by Somali communities. This is also not a new observation,[57] but only limited progress has been made in this area. Retrospectively, it is possible to ferret out the links of social connectedness, mobility, and diversification to the deteriorating conditions in Somalia in 2011, and to plot the course of the crisis in terms of a much more internal or "emic" logic. Observers had also noted, however, that some humanitarian actors likely put too much stock in the coping mechanisms of Somali communities and therefore underestimated how rapidly the situation was deteriorating in early 2011.[58]

A deeper analysis could have prevented these misunderstandings, but would it have made a difference in mobilizing a response? Comparing the Somali narratives of the famine in Chapter 5 with the humanitarian narrative as told by early warning and assessment information in Chapter 4 reveals remarkably similar stories. But the extent to which Somali social networks were quicker in responding to the worsening crisis suggests that perhaps the answer to this question is uncertain: some aspects of the local response—particularly with regard to water—started up fairly early; other elements, including mobilizing the diaspora to a different kind of intervention, took longer. But complementary information (both the "external," quantitative, and objective data of formal early warning systems—together with the internal, and perhaps more subjective data about experiences on the ground and means of coping with them) could make a stronger case for mitigative interventions. Accessing such information in a timely way in South Central Somalia remains a challenge. However, to date, relatively few attempts have been made to incorporate the more local definitions of famine into a broader, systematic famine analysis or discourse.[59]

But the issue of famine thresholds and early warning is not the only one. The real issue is linking evidence-based early warning to contingency planning and access issues (with other issues like whether proscribed groups control the affected area, counter-terrorism policy, donor constraints, and agency capabilities factored in) and with accountability mechanisms in place to ensure that actions are triggered. The research cited above suggests that opportunities to negotiate access with Al-Shabaab would have been greater, but overall, engagement with terrorist groups still has to be worked out in recognizable terms in famine theory. Nevertheless, groups that have been sanctioned as terrorist organizations increasingly control both territories and populations that are subject to humanitarian emergencies, so engaging with these controlling authorities will continue to be an important component of understanding and preventing famine. Likewise, insights about Somali resilience are important to incorporate into the overall understanding of famine. Understanding the sequence of events that led to the breakdown of social support networks is important not only to information systems aimed at tracking famine but also to interventions aimed at preventing and mitigating famine.

Finally, any attempt to come to grips with famine must deal not only with causal factors and the failure of accountable authorities to prevent famine but must also deal with internal, societal factors which, while they don't in and of themselves cause famine, certainly exacerbate its impact. In Somalia, this includes not only the obvious factors such as the policies and actions of Al-Shabaab and the predations of the "gatekeepers" but also more subtle mechanisms of social exclusion, access to and control over riverine land, and profiteering from aid.

Preventing Famine: A Still Unfinished Agenda?

Somalia in 2011 may look like a unique case: the combination of factors leading to the famine, the obstacles faced in prevention and response, the high death toll, the new modalities invoked to address the famine once it was declared, the intervention of many different kinds of humanitarian actors, and the post-famine malaise that affects many of these actors all sound like a story that hasn't been told before, and perhaps one that is compelling only in an idiosyncratic sort of way. It is true that this particular combination of events was unique, and may well not recur in the same form. But the underlying theme is that while this particular combination of causes and constraints may be idiosyncratic, the complexity of these factors is likely to recur, and unless a more globalized humanitarian community recognizes this and proactively takes steps to prepare for this kind of crisis, events of the magnitude of Somalia in 2011–12 are likely to recur. The threat of famine has not been vanquished. The horrible events of 2011 demonstrate graphically that the threat and actuality of famine are unfortunately very much still with us.

The roles of multiple humanitarian actors and even multiple humanitarian communities may make the issue of coordination more salient, but in fact should make addressing future crises a more manageable task, not a more difficult one. A larger, more diverse humanitarian community is an asset, not a liability, but the actors need to get to know each other better, to understand their different principles, their strengths, and their liabilities. The roles of local communities, first responders, and diasporas are not new topics, but are still misunderstood. Building the resilience of local communities to withstand shocks is important, but external actors will continue to be important—especially when the shocks are of the magnitude that hit Somalia in 2011.

Addressing the malaise of humanitarian action and the long history of aid is critical to the context of Somalia, but these are microcosms of bigger issues that face humanitarian action in many other contexts. Addressing accountability for crises—whether they reach the severity of a famine or not—is critical to future prevention, mitigation, and response efforts. If famines result from a "collective failure," then building a collective accountability mechanism is absolutely essential. Not only do technical constraints have to be addressed, the political constraints do too. And managing competing imperatives—that is, preventing and mitigating humanitarian emergencies in the context of political and security constraints, not simply "managing" the latter at the expense of the former—requires not only honest dialogue among humanitarian actors but with political and security actors as well. With courage and leadership, the humanitarian communities working in Somalia could address these issues—and perhaps yet salvage from the famine of 2011 an example from which the rest of the humanitarian community could learn. Another shock or crisis is very likely in the Horn of Africa, but with good learning, it need not be the humanitarian catastrophe that characterized 2011–12.

ANNEX

METHODOLOGICAL NOTE

The research on which this book is based was an eclectic mix of a number of different approaches and sources of information. At the heart of the research were three different approaches. The first was an extensive review of the existing documentation on the famine, the early warning and prediction, the assessments of the damage, the response, and the evaluations and reviews. We didn't keep a precise tally of everything that our team initially reviewed, but estimate it to be something over 500 documents in these various categories. One of the outputs for the donors that supported the study was a formal desk review that synthesized the findings of some 180 of the most relevant or important reports, evaluations, assessments, and in some cases, peer-reviewed journal articles and books into a deeper review. That review can be found at: http://fic.tufts.edu/publication-item/lessons-learned-from-the-somalia-famine-and-the-greater-horn-of-africa-crisis-2011–2012/

To put it mildly, much of the information that we reviewed was not convergent in terms of understanding different elements of the famine. Trying to resolve some of the divergence in interpretation was one of the objectives of the key informant interviews that we subsequently conducted. We knew from the start that a major missing element from the analysis of the famine was any comprehensive analysis of what had happened inside Somalia, in the epicentre of famine-affected areas, where for the most part neither humanitarian assistance nor journalists were allowed to go. Over the course of 2013–14, our field team was able to interview some 400 households and key informants to put together a picture of what happened in these areas, which primarily included towns and villages in the districts of Qorioley, Jamaame, Baidoa, Burhakaba, Dinsor, Qansaxdheere, Luuq and Ceel Buur; displaced populations in Galkaiyo, Baidoa and Mogadishu; and refugee populations in Dadaab, Kenya and Dollo-Ado, Ethiopia.

Some of this interviewing was in-person, in areas where the researchers could safely reach, and some of it was by telephone. Somalia, irrespective of whatever else one might want to say about it, has very good cellphone networks in much of the country, including rural areas. During the evaluation of the cash transfer program that several members of the research team had been involved with, telephone-based methods were perfected for identifying key informants through Somali social networks—so that when the interviewer eventually reached a key informant by cellphone, the latter knew who the former was, and had been introduced by a network of trusted intermediaries. This method was adapted further and used for this study, and proved to be a good method of being able to interview people in places where, because of Al-Shabaab restrictions or other reasons, the team was not able to go in person. But it also proved to be a very useful method for cross-checking findings even in places where the team was able to reach—triangulating findings and narratives as told to different researchers relying on different methods to reach different respondents in similar social categories.

Like all good qualitative research, this study sought to maximize the variation of respondents within the categories of interest to the research. As such, the team interviewed men and women in all areas (although, given social dynamics, admittedly more men than women), rural and urban informants (although this category is blurry as many informants interviewed in urban locations, including IDP and refugee settlements, were originally rural and referring to their rural livelihoods), typically by clan or socio-political categories as well. Religious leaders and business people were also reached in many locations. The identity of the two senior researchers, neither of whom was from "majority" clans, was an important component of reaching a diversity of actors, including many "marginalized" and "minority" populations. Within the scope of the study, riverine farming, agro-pastoral, pastoral, displaced and non-displaced, and urban populations were interviewed. It will be clear to readers with geographic knowledge of Somalia that while the list of social categories represents an attempt to be as comprehensive as possible, the number of geographic locations reached was only a small sample—but a sample deliberately selected to try to maximize the range and variation with regard to the experience of the famine. Likewise, sampling within each of these categories was limited, but aimed to maximize the variation within the obvious limits of conducting research in the fraught environment of South Central Somalia, much of which is still under the control of Al-Shabaab. Growing out of this effort are not only the Somali narratives of the famine that appear in Chapters 5 and 6, but also explanations that appear in a number of other chapters.

The second main element of interviewing was with key informants with the "humanitarian community" broadly defined: obviously, the front-line humanitarian aid workers, but also the managers, the decision-makers and analysts within the (mostly Western, Nairobi-based) humanitarian agencies, as well as donor agency officials, diplomatic and foreign policy officials from donor countries, government officials from affected countries in the Horn of Africa (including to a limited degree, Somalia itself), other external analysts who had in some way or another been involved in the analysis of the famine or the evaluation of the response or both. While the initial intent of these interviews had been to reduce the divergence in the analysis found in some of the documentation of the famine, in the end—as explained in Chapter 9 and other places—these interviews in many ways increased the sense of divergent explanations and understanding of the famine.

This key informant interviewing also involved a similar range of actors from the non-Western humanitarian actors—in Turkey, in some of the Gulf states, and Islamic networks based in Nairobi or the UK, and with many of these actors in Somalia itself. The findings from these interviews are found mainly in Chapter 8, but also inform the discussion in many other parts of the book. Altogether, some 175 key informants across all these categories were interviewed in 2013 and 2014. As noted above, several members of the team had been involved in the evaluation of the cash transfer program in 2012, and the findings from that study obviously to some degree informed the analysis here, as well as other, ongoing research that took place in the Horn of Africa during the period of the famine.[1]

Lastly, we tried wherever possible to access and reanalyze quantitative data sets on the famine from a variety of sources. In this we were only partially successful. Data and reports from the FEWSNET and the FSNAU are mostly already in the public domain, and were relatively easily accessed. Data from some of the evaluations undertaken were available, and financial data was available from both the OCHA Financial Tracking Service (FTS) and from development initiatives. In other cases, it proved to be extremely difficult to access data, and in many cases, actual data sets had to be laboriously reconstructed from figures found in monthly reporting bulletins or other sources even though it was clear that the original data sets existed. Much of this data—whether made easily available or reconstructed in the manner just described—is presented in Chapters 4 and 7. The reluctance to share data—even with researchers with appropriate credentials and introductions—is one symptom of the malaise and mistrust that characterizes a significant element of the contemporary humanitarian community working on Somalia that we describe in detail in Chapter 9. It dawned on us only slowly that, in being unable to gain direct access to quantitative data from a variety of sources, we were actually discovering a serious element of the qualitative analysis. Such were the twists and turns of trying to get to the bottom of the story of what actually happened in Somalia in 2010–12.

The whole research team met in Nairobi in mid-2014 to assess progress, review results, and begin to synthesize findings. A series of private meetings were subsequently held with key stakeholders from different constituencies to solicit feedback on initial conclusions and findings. These constituencies included donors, UN agencies, and non-governmental organizations, as well as a group of Somalia observers—experts who were not necessarily involved in the response to the famine but who knew Somalia well, and a group of senior Somalis—some of them from the humanitarian aid world, but many of them also key observers of trends and events in Somalia who were not necessarily implicated in the response to the famine. Other, smaller meetings of various sub-groupings of the study team met frequently throughout 2013 and 2014 to continue analysis of the research findings.

These meetings led to the holding of public presentations and a seminar with many of the key actors in Nairobi and Mogadishu in late 2014, where many of the actors met to hear our findings, debate their meanings, and consider the implications. Similar outreach sessions were subsequently held in Washington, New York, Boston, and London. Although we didn't keep attendance records from any of these meetings, our estimate is that some 350–400 individuals participated in these outreach meetings. The discussion and debate in these workshops constituted one final component of the "data" on which this analysis is based, and provided valuable crosschecking on our interpretation of evidence in the public domain and from our own data collection efforts.

NOTES

1. INTRODUCTION

1. FSNAU and FEWSNET, "Food Security and Nutrition Analysis Unit (Somalia), FEWSNET July 20, 2011 Press Release," Nairobi: Food Security and Nutrition Analysis Unit (Somalia), 2011. The FSNAU was careful not to put a precise number on the death toll because of doubts about population estimates.
2. UNDP, "Human Development Report: Somalia," Nairobi/New York: UN Development Programme, 2001.
3. T. Hagmann and M.V. Hoehne, "Failures of the State Failure Debate: Evidence from the Somali Territories," *Journal of International Development*, 21, 1 (2009), pp. 42–57.
4. K. Menkhaus, "Vicious Circles and Security-Development Nexus in Somalia," *Security and Development*, 4, 2 (2004), pp. 149–65. K. Menkhaus, "Somalia: They Created a Desert and Called it Peace(building)," *Review of African Political Economy*, 36, 120 (2009), pp. 223–33.
5. P. Little, *Somalia: Economy Without State*, Bloomington: Indiana University Press, 2003; Little, "Somalia: Economy Without State," *Review of African Political Economy*, 30, 97 (2003), p. 4.
6. L. Hammond and H. Vaughan-Lee, "Humanitarian Space in Somalia: A Scarce Commodity," London: Humanitarian Policy Group, 2012.
7. S.C.S. Elhawary, "Humanitarian Space: A Review of Trends and Issues," London: Overseas Development Institute, 2012.
8. FTS OCHA, http://fts.unocha.org
9. WFP, "Somalia: An Evaluation of WFP's Portfolio," Rome: World Food Programme, 2012, J. Darcy, P. Bonard, and S. Dini, "IASC Real Time Evaluation of the Humanitarian Response to the Horn of Africa Drought Crisis: Somalia 2011–2012," New York: IASC, 2012.
10. F. Checchi and W.C. Robinson, "Mortality among Populations of Southern and Central Somalia Affected by Severe Food Insecurity and Famine during 2010–2012," Rome/Washington, DC: FAO/FEWSNET, 2013.

11. C. Robinson, L. Zimmerman, and F. Checchi, "Internal and External Displacement among Populations of Southern and Central Somalia Affected by Severe Food Insecurity and Famine during 2010–2012," Washington, DC: FEWSNET, 2014.

12. Ibid. See also, Population Movement Tracking Unit, UNHCR (Jan. 2014) http://data.unhcr.org/horn-of-africa/Somalia.php

13. De Waal characterizes the Rahanweyn as second-class citizens and the Bantu as third-class citizens. See A. de Waal, *Famine Crimes: Politics and the Disaster Relief Industry*, Oxford: James Currey, 1997.

14. Checchi and Robinson, "Mortality among Populations of Southern and Central Somalia."

15. M. Bradbury, "Normalising the Crisis in Africa," *Disasters*, 22, 4 (1998), pp. 328–38.

16. M. Bryden, "Somalia Redux: Assessing the New Somali Federal Government," Center for Strategic and International Studies, 2013. See also UN Monitoring Group, "Report of the Monitoring Group on Somalia Pursuant to Security Council Resolution 1853 (2008)," New York: United Nations, 2010.

17. Associated Press, "Somali Militants Shut Down Red Cross Food Aid," London: 2012.

18. A version of Figure 1.1 was sketched out impressionistically by James Darcy et al. in the "Real Time Evaluation of the Humanitarian Response to the Horn of Africa Drought Crisis: Somalia 2011–2012." Figure 1.1 takes the same idea, but uses actual data to trace the trajectory of the crisis and the response.

19. None of these labels were very accurate or descriptive—a theme we explore in Chapter 8—but all were used in 2011.

20. Development Initiatives, "Global Humanitarian Assistance Report 2013," Wells, UK: Development Initiatives, 2013.

21. S. Lautze et al., "Early Warning, Late Response (Again): The 2011 Famine in Somalia," *Global Food Security*, 1, 1 (2012), pp. 43–9, N. Haan, S. Devereux, and D. Maxwell, "Global Implications of Somalia 2011 for Famine Prevention, Mitigation and Response," *Global Food Security* 1, 1 (2012), pp. 74–9.

22. IPC Global Partners, "Integrated Food Security Phase Classification: Technical Manual Version 2.0," Rome: UN Food and Agriculture Organization, 2012. This version came out in 2012 after the famine was declared. An earlier version of this document was used to declare the famine of 2011.

23. M. Buchanan Smith and S. Davies, *Famine Early Warning and Response—The Missing Link*, London: IT Publications, 1995.

24. S. Devereux, *The New Famines: Why Famines Persist in an Era of Globalization*, London: Routledge, 2006.

2. THE PROBLEM OF FAMINES

1. A. de Waal, *Famine Crimes: Politics and the Disaster Relief Industry*, Oxford: James Currey, 1997, p. 7.
2. Some of this chapter draws on an article by one of the authors written for Oxford Bibliographies Online: D. Maxwell and M. Fitzpatrick, "Famine," Oxford: Oxford Bibliographies Online, 2012.
3. D. Maxwell and K. Sadler, "Responding to Food Insecurity and Malnutrition in Crises," World Disaster Report 2011, Geneva: International Federation of Red Cross and Red Crescent Societies, 2011.
4. M. Buchanan Smith and S. Davies, *Famine Early Warning and Response—The Missing Link*, London: IT Publications, 1995.
5. S. Devereux, *The New Famines: Why Famines Persist in an Era of Globalisation*, Oxon: Routledge, 2007.
6. Ibid. See also, J. Dreze and A. Sen, *Hunger and Public Action*, Oxford: Clarendon Press, 1989.
7. T. Malthus, *An Essay on the Principle of Population*, Oxford: Oxford University Press, 1993 [1809].
8. A. Sen, *Poverty and Famines: An Essay on Entitlement and Deprivation*, New York: Oxford University Press, 1981.
9. D. Keen, *The Benefits of Famine: A Political Economy of Famine and Relief in Southwestern Sudan 1983–1989*, Princeton, NJ: Princeton University Press, 1994.
10. L.B. Deng, "The Sudan Famine of 1998," *IDS Bulletin*, 33, 4 (2002), pp. 28–38. S. Lautze and A. Raven-Roberts, "Violence and Complex Humanitarian Emergencies: Implications for Livelihoods Models," *Disasters*, 30, 4 (2006), pp. 383–401.
11. De Waal, *Famine Crimes*.
12. A. Sen, *Development as Freedom*, New York: Random House, 1999.
13. J. Macrae and A.B. Zwi, "Food as an Instrument of War in Contemporary African Famines: A Review of the Evidence," *Disasters*, 16, 4 (1992), pp. 299–321.
14. I. Smillie, *The Alms Bazaar: Altruism under Fire—Non-Profit Organizations and International Development*, London: Intermediate Technology Publications, 1995.
15. Deng, "Sudan Famine of 1998."
16. C. Ó Gráda, "Making Famine History," *Journal of Economic Literature*, 45, 1 (2007), pp. 5–38.
17. F. Dikötter, *Mao's Great Famine: The History of China's Most Devastating Catastrophe, 1958–1962*, New York: Walker and Co., 2010.
18. S. Haggard and M. Noland, *Famine in North Korea: Markets, Aid, and Reform*, New York: Columbia University Press, 2007.
19. A. de Waal and A. Whiteside, "New Variant Famine: AIDS and Food Crisis in Southern Africa," *Lancet*, 362, 9391 (2003), pp. 1234–7.

20. Maxwell and Fitzpatrick, "Famine."

21. "Food security" is a term used a lot in technical analysis, but not in common parlance. Food security "exists when all people, at all times, have physical and economic access to sufficient, safe and nutritious food that meets their dietary needs and food preferences for an active and healthy life" (World Food Summit, 1996). Food insecurity is what happens when some of these conditions are not met, and obviously can vary from very slight food insecurity to very severe. Famine is broadly understood as the most severe manifestation of food insecurity.

22. A. de Waal, *Famine That Kills*, New York: Oxford University Press, 2005. See also, M. Handino, "Green Famine in Ethiopia: Understanding the Causes of Increasing Vulnerability to Food Insecurity and Policy Responses in the Southern Ethiopian Highlands," PhD thesis, University of Sussex, 2014.

23. M.J. Toole and R.J. Waldman, "The Association between Inadequate Rations, Undernutrition Prevalence, and Mortality in Refugee Camps: Case Studies of Refugee Popluations in Eastern Thailand, 1979–1980, and Eastern Sudan, 1984–1985," *Journal of Tropical Pediatrics*, 34 (1988), pp. 218–24. P.A. Hakewill and A. Moren, "Monitoring and Evaluation of Relief Programs," *Tropical Doctor*, 21, 1 (1991), pp. 24–8. H. Kloos and B. Lindtjorn, "Malnutrition and Mortality during Recent Famines in Ethiopia: Implications for Food Aid and Rehabilitation," *Disasters*, 18, 2 (1994), pp. 130–9.

24. D.G. Maxwell, "Why Do Famines Persist? A Brief Review of Ethiopia, 1999–2000," *IDS Bulletin*, 33, 4 (2002), pp. 48–54. P. Howe and S. Devereux, "Famine Intensity and Magnitude Scales: A Proposal for an Instrumental Definition of Famine," *Disasters*, 28, 4 (2004), pp. 353–72.

25. Howe and Devereux acknowledge that they owe some intellectual debt for their insights to the work of Jeremy Swift on the Turkana District Early Warning System and indeed to the Indian Famine Codes of late nineteenth-century India (Dreze and Sen, *Hunger and Public Action*).

26. IPC Global Partners, "Integrated Food Security Phase Classification: Technical Manual Version 2.0," Rome: UN Food and Agriculture Organization, 2012.

27. See information on IPC coverage at: www.ipcinfo.org

28. H. Young and S. Jaspars, "Review of Nutrition and Mortality Indicators for the Integrated Food Security Phase Classification (IPC): Reference Levels and Decision-Making," New York: Nutrition Cluster, Inter-Agency Standing Committee, 2009.

29. H. Kloos and B. Lindtjorn, "Malnutrition and Mortality during Recent Famines in Ethiopia: Implications for Food Aid and Rehabilitation," *Disasters*, 18, 2 (1994), pp. 130–9.

30. De Waal, *Famine That Kills*. Handino, "Green Famine in Ethiopia."

31. It should be noted that FEWSNET and FSNAU are institutions (technically they are donor-funded projects, but they have become institutionalized); the IPC is

an analytical tool for aggregating data. It was developed by FSNAU, and is now being used globally by FEWSNET. A variety of food security indicators are used by the IPC and by early warning systems more broadly. But it is important not to conflate all of these into a mish-mash of indicators, tools, and institutions—as some contemporary analysts seem to do.

32. Smith and Davies, *Famine Early Warning and Response.*

33. L. Hammond and D. Maxwell, "The Ethiopian Crisis of 1999–2000: Lessons Learned, Questions Unanswered," *Disasters*, 26, 3 (2002), pp. 262–79. S. Lautze and D. Maxwell, "Why Do Famines Persist in the Horn of Africa? Ethiopia, 1999–2003," S. Devereux, *The "New Famines": Why Famines Persist in an Era of Globalization*, London: Routledge, 2006.

34. Humanitarian Policy Group, "Saving Lives through Livelihoods: Critical Gaps in the Response to the Drought in the Greater Horn of Africa," London: Humanitarian Policy Group, 2006.

35. K. Glenzer, "We Aren't the World: Discourses on the Sahel, Partnership, and the Institutional Production of Partial Success," in X. Crombé and J.-H. Jézéque (eds), *Une Catastrophe Si Naturelle: Niger 2005*, Paris: Medicins sans Frontiere, 2007.

36. L. Hammond and D. Maxwell, "The Ethiopian Crisis of 1999–2000: Lessons Learned, Questions Unanswered," *Disasters*, 26, 3 (2002), pp. 262–79, S. Devereux, "The Malawi Famine of 2002," *IDS Bulletin*, 33, 4 (2002), pp. 70–8.

37. S. Levine and C. Chastre, "Missing the Point: An Analysis of Food Security Interventions in the Great Lakes," London: Overseas Development Institute, Humanitarian Policy Group, 2004.

38. J. Dreze and A. Sen, *Hunger and Public Action*, Oxford: Clarenden Press, 1989.

39. C.B. Barrett and D.G. Maxwell, *Food Aid after Fifty Years: Recasting Its Role*, London: Routledge, 2005.

40. D. Maxwell, J. Parker, and H. Stobaugh, "What Drives Program Choice in Food Security Crises? Examining the 'Response Analysis' Question," *World Development*, 49 (Sep. 2013), pp. 68–79.

41. LEGS, *Livestock Emergency Guidelines and Standards*, Warwickshire: Practical Action, 2009.

42. D. Maxwell and K. Sadler, "Responding to Food Insecurity and Malnutrition in Crises," World Disaster Report 2011, Geneva: International Federation of Red Cross and Red Crescent Societies, 2011.

43. L. De Haan and A. Zoomers, "Development Geography at the Crossroads of Livelihoods and Globalisation," *Ijdschrift voor Economishe en Socialie Geografie*, 94, 3 (2003), pp. 350–62.

44. L. Hammond, "Family Ties: Remittances and Livelihood Support in Puntland and Somaliland," Nairobi, Kenya: FSNAU, 2013.

45. UNDP, "Human Development Report: Somalia," Nairobi/New York: UN Development Programme, 2001.

46. J. Edkins, "Mass Starvations and the Limitations of Famine Theorising," *IDS Bulletin*, 33, 4 (2002), pp. 12–18.

47. ICISS, "The Responsibility to Protect: Report of the International Commission on Intervention and State Sovereignty," New York: International Commission on Intervention and State Sovereignty, 2001.

48. K. Annan, "We the Peoples: The Role of the United Nations in the 21st Century (Millennium Report of the Secretary-General)," New York: United Nations, 2000.

49. A. de Waal, *Famine Crimes: Politics and the Disaster Relief Industry in Africa*, London: James Currey, 1997.

50. United Nations, "Background Information on the Responsibility to Protect," n.d., http://www.un.org/en/preventgenocide/rwanda/about/bgresponsibility.shtml

51. P. Howe and S. Devereux, "Famine Intensity and Magnitude Scales: A Proposal for an Instrumental Definition of Famine," *Disasters*, 28, 4 (2004), pp. 353–72.

52. N. Haan, S. Devereux, and D. Maxwell, "Global Implications of Somalia 2011 for Famine Prevention, Mitigation and Response," *Global Food Security*, 1, 1 (2012), pp. 74–9.

53. Stephen Devereux originally posed this question in 2006. We are only repeating it here.

54. S. Devereux, *The New Famines: Why Famines Persist in an Era of Globalization*, London: Routledge, 2006.

3. SOMALIA AND EXTERNAL INTERVENTION IN THE GREATER HORN OF AFRICA: 1970–2010

1. I.M. Lewis, *A Modern History of Somalia—Nation and State in the Horn of Africa*, London: Longman, 1980.

2. Ibid.

3. Ibid.

4. Mark Bradbury, *Becoming Somaliland*, Oxford: James Currey, 2008.

5. K. Menkhaus, H. Sheikh, S. Quinn, and I. Farah, "Somalia: Civil Society in a Collapsed State," in Thania Paffenholz (ed.), *Civil Society and Peacebuilding: A Critical Assessment*, Boulder, CO: Lynne Rienner, 2010.

6. K. Menkhaus, "Getting Out vs. Getting Through: US and UN Policies in Somalia," *Middle East Policy*, 3 (1994), pp. 146–63.

7. Ibid., p. 147

8. Ibid.

9. UNDP, "Human Development Report: Somalia," Nairobi/New York: UN Development Programme, 2001.

10. Ibid.

11. Menkhaus, "Getting Out vs. Getting Through," pp. 146–63. The annual budget of UNOSOM II was over $1.5bn.

12. *Hawala*, or *xawilaad* in Somali, are the money transfer enterprises that move money between their offices around the world very cheaply and quickly.

13. A. Lindley, "The Early Morning Phone Call: Remittances from a Refugee Diaspora Perspective: Working Paper No. 47," Oxford: Centre on Migration, Policy and Society, 2007.

14. UNDP, "Human Development Report: Somalia."

15. Ibid.

16. Menkhaus, Sheikh, Quinn, and Farah, "Somalia: Civil Society in a Collapsed State."

17. C. Besteman and L. Cassanelli, *The Struggle for Land in Southern Somalia: The War behind the War*, Boulder, CO: Westview Press, 2000.

18. R. Marchal, "A Survey of Mogadishu's Economy," Nairobi/Brussels: European Commission, 2002.

19. T. Hagmann and M. Hoehne, "Failures of the State Failure Debate: Evidence from the Somali Territories," *Journal of International Development*, 21, 1 (2009), pp. 42–57.

20. T. Hagmann, "From State Collapse to Duty-Free Shop: Somalia's Path to Modernity," *African Affairs*, 104, 416 (2005), pp. 525–35.

21. J. Gundel, "The Predicament of the Oday: The Role of Traditional Structures in Security, Rights, Law and Development," Copenhagen: Danish Refugee Coucil and NOVIB/Oxfam, 2006.

22. M. Bradbury, "State-Building, Counterterrorism, and Licencing Humanitarianism in Somalia," Somerville: Feinstein International Center, Tufts University, 2010.

23. K. Menkhaus, "There and Back Again in Somalia," Middle East Research and Information Report, Feb. 11, 2007, http://www.merip.org/mero/mero021107

24. Ibid. No page number.

25. Menkhaus, Sheikh, Quinn, and Farah, "Somalia: Civil Society in a Collapsed State."

26. I.I. Ahmed and R.H. Green, "The Heritage of War and State Collapse in Somalia and Somaliland: Local-Level Effects, External Interventions and Reconstruction," *Third World Quarterly*, 20, 1 (1999), pp. 113–27.

27. I. Lewis, *Abaar: The Somali Drought*, International African Institute, 1975.

28. G. Haaland and W. Keddeman, "Poverty Analysis: The Case of Rural Somalia," *Economic Development and Cultural Change*, 32, 4 (1984), pp. 843–60.

29. B. Davidson, "Review of *ABAAR: The Somali Drought* by I.M. Lewis," *Review of African Political Economy*, 6 (1976), pp. 110–12.

30. P. Webb, J. von Braun, and Y. Yohannes, "Famine in Ethiopia: Policy Implications of Coping Failure at National and Household Levels," Washington: IFPRI, 1992.

31. A. de Waal, "Dangerous Precedents? Famine Relief in Somalia 1991–93," in J. Macrae and A. Zwi (eds), *War and Hunger: Rethinking International Responses to Complex Emergencies*, London: Zed Books 1994.

32. A. de Waal, *Famine Crimes: Politics and the Disaster Relief Industry in Africa*, London: James Currey, 1997.

33. N. Majid and S. McDowell, "Hidden Dimensons of the Somalia Famine," *Global Food Security*, 1, 1 (2012), pp. 36–42.

34. The two languages are Af-Maay and Maxatiir—the latter often just referred to as "Somali." The difference between them is described as equivalent to the difference between Italian and French. See, Lewis, *A Modern History Of Somalia*.

35. K. Menkhaus, "Getting Out vs. Getting Through," p. 148.

36. De Waal, *Famine Crimes*.

37. Ibid., p. 166. Throughout these areas, the fighting, looting, and killing were driven by attempted alliances formed by local populations. Initially, the "liberators"—the Hawiye militia—overthrew the Barre/Darood/Marehan forces, only to themselves also take land and plunder local resources. Then the Darood took revenge in the to-ing and fro-ing of territorial fluidity. Rahanweyn militias were also active participants taking their own share along the way.

38. Ibid. p. 165.

39. De Waal, "Dangerous Precedents?".

40. Ibid.

41. J. Prendergast, "Preventing Future Famine in Somalia," in H.M. Adam and R. Ford (eds), *Mending Rips in the Sky: Options for Somali Communities in the 21st Century*, Lawrenceville and Asmara: Red Sea Press, 1997.

42. L. Hammond and D. Maxwell, "The Ethiopian Crisis of 1999–2000: Lessons Learned, Questions Unanswered," *Disasters*, 26, 3 (2002), pp. 262–79.

43. FEWSNET and CARE, "Greater Horn of Africa Food Security Update," Nairobi: FEWSNET and CARE, 2001.

44. Humanitarian Policy Group, "Saving Lives through Livelihoods: Critical Gaps in the Response to the Drought in the Greater Horn of Africa," London: Humanitarian Policy Group, 2006.

45. S. Pantuliano and M. Wekesa, "Improving Drought Response in Pastoral Areas of Ethiopia," London: Humanitarian Policy Group, Overseas Development Institute, 2008.

46. Humanitarian Policy Group, "Saving Lives through Livelihoods."

47. LEGS, *Livestock Emergency Guidelines and Standards*, Warwickshire: Practical Action, 2009.

48. Ken Menkhaus, "Somalia: They Created a Desert and Called it Peace(Building)," *Review of African Political Economy*, 36, 120 (2009), pp. 223–33.

49. Ibid.

50. N. Majid and S. McDowell, "Hidden Dimensons of the Somalia Famine," *Global Food Security*, 1, 1 (2012), 36–42.

51. A. Simons, *Networks of Dissolution: Somalia Undone*, New York: Westview Press, 1995.

52. Ibid.

53. UNDP, "Human Development Report: Somalia," Nairobi/New York: UN Development Programme, 2001.

54. Ibid., p. 141.

55. L. Cassanelli, "Explaining the Somali Crisis," in C. Besteman and L. Cassanelli (eds), *The Struggle for Land in Southern Somalia: The War behind the War*, Boulder, CO: Westview Press, 2000.

56. UN Monitoring Group, "Report of the Monitoring Group on Somalia Pursuant to Security Council Resolution 1853 (2008) (2010, March 10). UN Security Council (S/2010/91)," New York: UN, 2010.

57. M. Bradbury, "Normalising the Crisis in Africa," *Disasters*, 22, 4 (1998), pp. 328–38.

58. Ibid.

59. The oil boom is associated with the creation of a parallel remittance economy in the 1970s and 1980s and the commonplace condition of a member of the family abroad. See J. Gardner and J. El Bushra, *Somalia—The Untold Story*, London: CIIR and Pluto Press, 2004. Many Somalis displaced from Ethiopia further migrated to the West during the 1990s.

60. UNDP, "Human Development Report: Somalia."

61. L.A. Hammond et al., "Cash and Compassion: The Role of the Somali Diaspora in Relief, Development and Peace-Building," Nairobi: UNDP Somalia, 2011. '

62. K. Menkhaus, "The Role and Impact of the Somali Diaspora in Peace-Building," in R. Bardouille, M. Ndulo, and M. Grieco (eds), *Africa's Finances: The Contribution of Remittances*, Cambridge: Cambridge Scholars Publishing, 2008.

63. UNDP, "In Search of Somalia's Missing Million: The Somali Diaspora and Its Role in Development," Nairobi: UNDP, 2009.

64. K. Menkhaus, "The Role and Impact of the Somali Diaspora in Peace-Building."

65. S.J. Hansen, *Al-Shabaab in Somalia: The History and Ideology of a Militant Islamist Group 2005–2012*, London and New York: Hurst/Oxford University Press, 2013.

66. Ibid., p. 23.

67. No analysis of the 2011 famine would be complete without analyzing the role of Al-Shabaab in both the causes of the crisis and the complications arising in responding to it. But this section is not intended as a complete history of the role of Al-Shabaab more broadly in recent Somali history. For that, the reader is referred to Hansen (2013), Marchal (2012), Menkhaus (2010 and 2012), or Pham (2013) among other more authoritative accounts than this one.

68. Hansen, *Al-Shabaab in Somalia*. Hansen also notes that, over time, Al-Shabaab developed relations with different groups of maritime pirates, although it had initially been quite independent of pirate groups.

69. A. Seal and R. Bailey, "The 2011 Famine in Somalia: Lesson Learnt from a Failed Response?" *Conflict and Health*, 7, 22 (2013), pp. 1–5.

70. Hansen, *Al-Shabaab in Somalia*.

71. Ibid.

72. Human Rights Watch, "Harsh War, Harsh Peace. Abuses by Al Shabaab, the Transitional Federal Government and AMISOM in Somalia," New York: Human Rights Watch, 2010, p. 21.

73. Ibid. Interview data from our study tends to suggest that perhaps women had more freedom than suggested here, but these restrictions likely varied from place to place.

74. Jeffrey Gettleman, "For Somali Women, Pain of Being a Spoil of War," *New York Times*, Dec. 27, 2011.

75. Human Rights Watch, "Harsh War, Harsh Peace."

76. Field interviews, 2013–14.

77. Field interviews, 2013–14.

78. Field interviews, 2013.

79. J.P. Pham, "State Collapse, Insurgency and Counter-Insurgency: Lessons from Somalia," Carlisle, PA: Strategic Studies Institute and U.S. Army War College Press, 2013.

80. *Zakat* is a mandatory contribution for the poor—one of the five pillars of Islam.

81. Field interviews, 2014.

82. K. Menkhaus, "No Access: Critical Bottlenecks in the 2011 Somali Famine," *Global Food Security*, 1, 1 (2012), pp. 29–35, p. 30.

83. Field interviews, 2012–14.

84. Field interviews, 2013–14.

85. N. Majid and S. McDowell, "Hidden Dimensons of the Somalia Famine," *Global Food Security*, 1, 1 (2012), pp. 36–42. '

86. M. Bryden, "Somalia's Famine is Not Just a Catastrophe, It's a Crime," The Enough Project, 2011. L. Hammond and H. Vaughan-Lee, "Humanitarian Space in Somalia: A Scarce Commodity," London: Humanitarian Policy Group, 2012.

87. M. Bradbury and M. Kleinman, "Winning Hearts and Minds? Examining the Relationship between Aid and Security in Kenya," Medford, MA: Feinstein International Center, Tufts University 2010, p. 4.

88. Hansen, *Al-Shabaab in Somalia*.

89. K. Mackintosh and P. Duplat, "Study of the Impact of Donor Counter-Terrorism Measures on Principled Humanitarian Action," New York: OCHA and Norwegian Refugee Council, 2013, p. 75.

90. Ibid. WFP officially cited security concerns, and Al-Shabaab had killed a number of their staff by this time. However, in a widely cited cable posted later on WikiLeaks, the UN special representative of the secretary general to Somalia, noted that WFP's withdrawal had been driven by its need to demonstrate that it was distancing itself from Al-Shabaab, given the legal risks. The cable is labeled 10USUNNEWYORK27, UN SRSG FOR SOMALIA PLEADS FOR

FUNDING TO THWART SOMALI TERRORISM. As of Aug. 3, 2014, it was found at http://wikileaks.org/cable/2010/01/10USUNNEWYORK27.html. The cable was published in the UK by DEVEX and by *The Telegraph* but was subsequently removed from the website of the latter. Our interviews and the research conducted for the OCHA/NRC report confirmed many of the same reasons.

91. UN Monitoring Group, "Report of the Monitoring Group on Somalia Pursuant to Security Council Resolution 1853 (2008), (2010, March 10). UN Security Council (S/2010/91)," New York: UN, 2010.

92. Jeffrey Gettleman, "U.N. Criticizes U.S. Restrictions on Aid for Somalia," *New York Times*, Feb. 17, 2010; Gettleman, "U.N. to End Some Deals for Food to Somalia," *New York Times*, March 12, 2010; and Gettleman, "Somalia's President Assails U.N. Report on Corruption," *New York Times*, March 17, 2010. Field interviews, 2014.

93. In particular, the International Committee of the Red Cross, and Médecins sans Frontières, although other agencies also tried hard to operate under humanitarian principles. Field interviews, 2012–14.

94. The Kurdistan Workers' Party (PKK) in Turkey and the Liberation Tigers of Tamil Eelam (the "Tamil Tigers") in Sri Lanka. Neither had direct links to Somalia.

95. Adam Liptak, "Court Affirms Ban on Aiding Groups Tied to Terror," *New York Times*, June 21, 2010.

96. K. Mackintosh and P. Duplat, "Study of the Impact of Donor Counter-Terrorism Measures on Principled Humanitarian Action," New York: OCHA and Norwegian Refugee Council, 2013.

97. This refers to Phase 4 ("Humanitarian Emergency") in IPC terms.

4. THE WORSENING CRISIS, THE DELAY, AND THE IMPACT OF THE FAMINE

1. J. Darcy, P. Bonard, and S. Dini, "IASC Real Time Evaluation of the Humanitarian Response to the Horn of Africa Drought Crisis: Somalia 2011–2012," New York: IASC, 2012.

2. ICAI, "DFID's Humanitarian Emergency Response in the Horn of Africa," Independent Comission for Aid Impact, 2012; Field interviews, 2013–14.

3. C. Hillbruner and G. Moloney, "When Early Warning Is Not Enough—Lessons Learned from the 2011 Somalia Famine," *Global Food Security*, 1, 1 (2012), pp. 20–8.

4. Chris Hillbruner, personal communication.

5. See the Integrated Food Security Phase Classification maps for early 2011 at the FSNAU website: www.fsnau.org

6. Field Interviews, 2012–13.

7. Field interviews, 2012–14. See also K. Menkhaus, "No Access: Critical Bottlenecks in the 2011 Somali Famine," *Global Food Security*, 1, 1 (2012), pp. 29–35.

8. Figures 4.2 and 4.2 rely on the combined average of the price per kilogram of white maize and red sorghum—the two most commonly consumed staple food of low-income people in rural Somalia.

9. Field interviews, 2012–14.

10. E.M. Rebelo et al., "Nutritional Response to the 2011 Famine in Somalia," *Global Food Security*, 1, 1 (2012), pp. 64–73, p. 66.

11. ICAI, "DFID's Humanitarian Emergency Response in the Horn of Africa," Independent Comission for Aid Impact, 2012. Numerous key informant interviews.

12. M. Bradbury, "Normalising the Crisis in Africa," *Disasters*, 22, 4 (1998), pp. 328–38.

13. J. Paul et al., "IASC Real-Time Evaluation of the Humanitarian Response to the Horn of Africa Drought Crisis Kenya," IASC, 2012.

14. Field interviews, 2013–14.

15. L. Sida, B. Gray, and E. Asmare, "IASC Real-Time Evaluation of the Humanitarian Response to the Horn of Africa Drought Crisis Ethiopia February 2011," IASC, 2012.

16. Darcy, Bonard, and Dini, "IASC Real Time Evaluation of the Humanitarian Response to the Horn of Africa Drought Crisis: Somalia 2011–2012."

17. P. Salama et al., "Famine in Somalia: Evidence for a Declaration," *Global Food Security*, 1, 1 (2012), pp. 13–19.

18. F. Checchi and C. Robinson, "Mortality among Populations of Southern and Central Somalia Affected by Severe Food Insecurity and Famine during 2010–2012," Rome and Washington, DC: FAO/FEWSNET, 2013.

19. J.P. Pham, "State Collapse, Insurgency and Counter-Insurgency: Lessons from Somalia," Carlisle, PA: Strategic Studies Institute and U.S. Army War College Press, 2013.

20. A. Jackson and A. Aynte, "Talking to the Other Side: Humanitarian Negotiations with Al-Shabaab in Somalia: HPG Working Paper," London: Humanitarian Policy Group, ODI, 2013.

21. Ibid., p. 7.

22. See: http://www.criticalthreats.org/somalia/zimmerman-shabaab-humanitarian-assistance-somalia-july-27-2011; and http://ent.siteintelgroup.com/Jihadist-News/shabaab-bans-un-mine-action.html

23. Field interviews, 2012–14.

24. See Chapter 3.

25. Field interviews, 2012–14.

26. S.J. Hansen, *Al-Shabaab in Somalia: The History and Ideology of a Militant Islamist Group 2005–2012*, London and New York: Hurst/Oxford University Press, 2013.

27. R. Marchal, "The Rise of a Jihadi Movement in a Country at War: Harakat Al Shabaab Al Mujaheddin in Somalia," Paris: SciencesPo Paris, 2011, p. 74.

28. Hansen, *Al-Shabaab in Somalia*.

29. Ibid.

30. Ibid., p. 114.

31. Pham, "State Collapse, Insurgency and Counter-Insurgency."

32. BBC News, "Somalia Islamists Lift Ban on Aid to Drought Victims," BBC News Africa, July 6, 2011; http://www.bbc.co.uk/news/world-africa-14046267

33. BBC News, "Somali Islamists Maintain Aid Ban and Deny Famine," BBC News Africa, July 22, 2011; http://www.bbc.co.uk/news/world-africa-14246764

34. Jackson and Aynte, "Talking to the Other Side," p. 15.

35. A. Seal and R. Bailey, "The 2011 Famine in Somalia: Lesson Learnt from a Failed Response?" *Conflict and Health*, 7, 22 (2013), pp. 1–5, p. 3.

36. Menkhaus, "No Access," pp. 29–35.

37. Jackson and Aynte, "Talking to the Other Side." The issue of paying fees was highly controversial because, of course, it would have been considered a criminal offense under the counter-terrorism laws of the United States and other Western donor countries. Nevertheless, Jackson and Aynte recount fairly specific requirements.

38. Field interviews, 2011–14.

39. Data from OCHA Financial Tracking Service. See: http://fts.unocha.org/

40. K. Mackintosh and P. Duplat, "Study of the Impact of Donor Counter-Terrorism Measures on Principled Humanitarian Action," New York: OCHA and Norwegian Refugee Council, 2013. OCHA Financial Tracking Service records confirm no new US grants for Somalia between October 2010 and May 2011.

41. Field interviews, 2012–14.

42. Field interviews, 2012–14.

43. Menkhaus, "No Access," pp. 29–35. Menkhaus went on to note that US officials thought they were being "scapegoated" by the humanitarian sector because of the increased linkage of US humanitarian assistance to security objectives more generally.

44. Statement of Jeremy Konyndyk, director of policy and advocacy, Mercy Corps, to the US Senate Subcommittee on Africa, hearing entitled "Responding to the Drought and Famine in the Horn of Africa," August 3, 2011, p. 7. http://relief-web.int/report/somalia/statement-jeremy-konyndyk-director-policy-and-advocacy-mercy-corps

45. Ibid. Some key informants gave another interpretation to this interlude, that the intent was to draw people out of Al-Shabaab-controlled areas, to underline the incompetence of Al-Shabaab in handling the crisis. Confirming which story was true was not possible but, either way, the effect was the same: the window of opportunity to mitigate a massive humanitarian catastrophe was wasted. If the attempt was to draw people out of Al-Shabaab-controlled areas, the preparations made in Kenya, Ethiopia, and Mogadishu were also too little, too late.

46. The OFAC license issued to USAID on July 28, 2011 exempts humanitarian assistance in Somalia from some of the legal consequences in the event that some aid inadvertently ended up in the hands of Al-Shabaab. Nevertheless, the license did not exempt US agencies, citizens, or agencies receiving US funding from complying in full with sanctions in place against terrorist organizations.

47. Field interviews, 2013–14.

48. Field interviews, 2014.

49. Mackintosh and Duplat, "Study of the Impact of Donor Counter-Terrorism Measures on Principled Humanitarian Action," p. 85.

50. Menkhaus, "No Access," pp. 29–35.

51. Field interviews, 2013–14.

52. Jackson and Aynte, "Talking to the Other Side."

53. Seal and Bailey, "2011 Famine in Somalia," p. 3.

54. "Excess mortality" figures are in addition to the underlying "baseline" mortality for any given year. For example, the baseline crude death rate (CDR) was estimated to be between 0.5 and 0.8 per 10,000 people per day in southern and central Somalia, while the 2010 sub-Saharan Africa average was 0.37 and baseline mortality in Somali-speaking areas of Kenya and Ethiopia ranged in the same area. See Checchi and Robinson "Mortality among Populations of Southern and Central Somalia Affected by Severe Food Insecurity and Famine," and UNICEF Kenya 2014 data on baseline mortality (personal communication).

55. P. Salama et al., "Famine in Somalia: Evidence for a Declaration," pp. 13–19.

56. IPC Global Partners, "Integrated Food Security Phase Classification: Technical Manual Version 1.1," Rome: FAO, 2008. Note that the IPC manual was updated to Version 2.0 shortly thereafter, but Version 1.1 was the operative tool for declaring the famine.

57. Meaning, technically, that at least 30 percent of all children under the age of five years register a ratio of weight to height that is more than two standard deviations below the median of a global reference standard.

58. Defined as number of people dying per day per 10,000 people.

59. FSNAU market information. Accessed August 14, 2014; http://www.fsnau.org/ids/trade/index.php

60. Darcy, Bonard and Dini, "IASC Real Time Evaluation of the Humanitarian Response to the Horn of Africa Drought Crisis: Somalia."

61. FSNAU, "Post Deyr 2010–2011 Technical Report and the Post Gu 2011," Nairobi: FSNAU, 2011.

62. Field interviews, 2013–14.

63. FSNAU, "Subsistence Farming in Lower Shabelle Riverine Zone," Nairobi: FSNAU, 2013.

64. Field interviews, 2013–14.

65. FSNAU, "Subsistence Farming in Lower Shabelle Riverine Zone."

66. N. Majid and S. McDowell, "Hidden Dimensons of the Somalia Famine," *Global Food Security*, 1, 1 (2012), pp. 36–42. Field interviews, 2013–14.

67. This is called Household Economy Analysis (or HEA—originally called Food Economy Analysis) developed by Save the Children (UK) in the 1990s. The FSNAU baseline analyses for food security were built on HEA assessments. The figures cited are for poor households in the Bay Agro-Pastoral Low Potential livelihood zone. See FSNAU/FEWSNET, "Famine Persists, Improvements Noted," November 18, 2011, Nairobi: FSNAU/FEWSNET.

68. See, for instance, the report of the Unconditional Cash Transfer Program: K. Hedlund et al., "Final Evaluation of the Unconditional Cash and Voucher Response to the 2011–12 Crisis in Southern and Central Somalia," London: Humanitarian Outcomes, 2013.

69. K. Menkhaus, "Somalia: They Created a Desert and Called it Peace(Building)," *Review of African Political Economy*, 36, 120 (2009), pp. 223–33.

70. C. Robinson, L. Zimmerman, and F. Checchi, "Internal and External Displacement among Populations of Southern and Central Somalia Affected by Severe Food Insecurity and Famine during 2010–2012," Washington, DC: FEWS NET, 2014.

71. FSNAU, "Food Security and Nutrition Analysis Post Deyr 2011/2012," Nairobi: FSNAU, 2012.

72. Robinson, Zimmerman and F. Checchi, "Internal and External Displacement among Populations of Southern and Central Somalia." Of note is that reports have a variety of monthly totals for refugees arriving in both Dadaab and Dollo-Ado—even reports that claim to be using the same basic data from UNHCR. Our own team calculated total arrivals in Dollo-Ado from monthly UNHCR reports obtained in Dollo-Ado, and while the trends were the same, the monthly totals were rather different. We chose to report Robinson's data here since it is the most authoritative single report on the topic.

73. Refugee Consortium of Kenya, "Asylum under Threat: Assessing the Protection of Somali Refugees in Dadaab Refugee Camp and along the Migration Corridor," Nairobi: Refugee Consortium of Kenya, 2012.

74. Field interviews, 2013–14.

75. L. Sida, B. Gray, and E. Asmare, "IASC Real-Time Evaluation of the Humanitarian Response to the Horn of Africa Drought Crisis Ethiopia February 2011," IASC, 2012.

76. Field interviews, 2014.

77. A. Bhattacharjee, "IASC Real Time Evaluation of the Humanitarian Response to the Horn of Africa Drought Crisis 2011: Regional Mechanisms and Support during the Response," New York: IASC, 2012.

78. UNHCR, "Report of Nutrition and Health Survey in Kobe and Hileweyn Camps of Dollo Ado, Somali Region of Ethiopia during Mid October to Early November 2011," Addis Ababa: UNHCR, 2011.

79. Sida, Gray, and Asmare, "IASC Real-Time Evaluation of the Humanitarian Response to the Horn of Africa Drought Crisis."

80. Field interviews, 2014

81. UNHCR data. Field interviews, 2014. A number of veteran humanitarian aid workers said they had never seen conditions like those prevailing in the transit camp in June 2011.

82. UNHCR, "Population Tracking Movement Unit, Kenya: Dadaab," 2011. Retrieved Jan. 2014, from http://data.unhcr.org/horn-of-africa/region. php?id=3&country=110; C. Robinson, L. Zimmerman, and F. Checchi, "Internal and External Displacement among Populations of Southern and Central Somalia Affected by Severe Food Insecurity and Famine during 2010–2012," Washington, DC: FEWS NET, 2014.

83. C. Horst, *Transnational Nomads: How Somalis Cope with Refugee Life in the Dadaab Camps of Kenya*, New York and Oxford: Berghahn Books, 2006.

84. Defined as more than three standard deviations below the global reference standard median. Elevated levels of severe acute malnutrition (SAM) are strongly associated with high child mortality. See H. Young and S. Jaspars, "Review of Nutrition and Mortality Indicators for the Integrated Food Security Phase Classification (IPC): Reference Levels and Decision-Making," New York: Nutrition Cluster, Inter-Agency Standing Committee, 2009.

85. E.M. Rebelo et al., "Nutritional Response to the 2011 Famine in Somalia," *Global Food Security*, 1, 1 (2012), pp. 64–73.

86. IPC Global Partners, "Integrated Food Security Phase Classification: Technical Manual Version 1.1."

87. Salama et al., "Famine in Somalia," pp. 13–19.

88. Rebelo et al., "Nutritional Response to the 2011 Famine in Somalia," pp. 64–73.

89. Checchi and Robinson, "Mortality among Populations of Southern and Central Somalia."

90. Ibid.

91. To understand the mortality figures, the original report by Checchi and Robinson (ibid.) must be read, and the serious reader is strongly encouraged to do so. Measuring mortality in a famine is an extremely fraught enterprise, and as Checchi and Robinson note, much of the estimated excess mortality is just that—estimates based on the best extrapolation of data that they could manage, given the actual mortality survey data available. Their estimate of total mortality was met with hostility in some quarters when the report came out in 2013. We report their data here because our judgment is that this is the best data we have on the famine—they were honest in reporting the constraints they faced, and transparent in their methods. There is certainly no better data on mortality during the famine from any other source.

92. FSNAU, "FSNAU Evidence for Updated Famine Declaration," Nairobi: FSNAU, 2011.

93. The graph in Figure 4.7 varies slightly from the graph in the widely read publication by Checchi and Robinson, but only because "excess mortality" is graphed here. The Checchi and Robinson report graphs "baseline" and total mortality. "Excess mortality" is the difference between these two measures.

94. Field interviews, 2013–14.

95. Checchi and Robinson, "Mortality among Populations of Southern and Central Somalia."

96. P. Salama et al., "Malnutrition, Measles, Mortality, and the Humanitarian Response during a Famine in Ethiopia," *Journal of the American Medical Association*, 286, 5 (2001), pp. 563–71.

97. Checchi and Robinson, "Mortality among Populations of Southern and Central Somalia," FSNAU, "Food Security and Nutrition Analysis Post Deyr 2011/2012."

98. K. Menkhaus, "Kenya–Somalia Border Conflict Analysis: Report to USAID," Washington, DC: Development Alternatives Incorporated, 2005).

99. A slight circularity to the argument here should be pointed out, however. Terms of trade was one of the factors that Checchi and Robinson used to estimate mortality throughout the crisis. But they also used seven other predictor variables, so terms of trade wasn't by any means the sole determinant of their estimation. See Checchi and Robinson, "Mortality among Populations of Southern and Central Somalia," pp. 26–7.

5. "NO ONE TO CRY TO": A SOMALI NARRATIVE OF THE FAMINE

1. This chapter draws on over 400 interviews that were conducted with people from affected communities in Somalia, Ethiopia, and Kenya in 2013 and 2014, both in person and by telephone.

2. See M. Duffield, "Challenging Environments: Danger, Resilience and the Aid Industry," *Security Dialogue*, 43, 5 (2012), pp. 475–92. See also A. Donini and D. Maxwell, "From Face-to-Face to Face-to-Screen: Implications of Remote Management for the Effectiveness and Accountability of Humanitarian Action in Insecure Environments," *International Review of the Red Cross*, 95, 980 (2014), pp. 383–414.

3. The Rahanweyn are a large clan family divided into many sub-clans. They are primarily agro-pastoral (although with significant differences between agricultural and livestock dependence within them). They are considered a marginalized social group. Clan identities and structures will be explained in more detail in the following chapter.

4. *Deyr* is the shorter, secondary rainy season, running from October to November. *Gu* is the main rainy season, running from April to June. *Jilaal* is the long dry season between the *deyr* and *gu*. *Hagai* is the dry season between the *gu* and the *deyr*.

5. Having someone "to cry to" means having someone to call upon to help in times of difficulty.

6. The Yantar, Hubeer, and Gelidle are sub-clans of the Rahanweyn, who mainly reside in Dinsor and Qansaxdheere Districts in Bay Region. The Jareer are Somali Bantu, not ethnically Somali, and have minority status throughout Somalia.

7. In general, the Rahanweyn are not considered wealthy or well diversified in comparison to the "major" clans.

8. For an overview of this population group, see, K. Menkaus, "The Question of Ethnicity in Somali Studies: The Case of Somali Bantu Identity," in M. Hoehne and V. Luling (eds), *Peace and Milk, Drought and War. Somali Culture, Society and Politics—Essays in Honor of I.M. Lewis*, London: Hurst, 2010.

9. Kilometer 50 or K50 is a commonly used reference to a location 50 kilometers northwest of Mogadishu on the road to Kismayu.

10. ICU refers to the Islamic Courts Union, who controlled Mogadishu and most of southern Somalia from June to December 2006. Hizbul-Islam is a militant Islamic group that turned against Al-Shabaab.

11. Minority groups, such as the Jareer, often form alliances with one of the local dominant clans.

12. This is an important dynamic referred to in other interviews and explained in the following chapter.

13. The naming of these clans is significant as they are associated with certain characteristics and territories.

14. This is explained further in Chapter 6.

15. This interviewee made the following point after he was contacted (by telephone): "If I don't address any of your questions it means I don't want to address it so don't repeat it to me." This reflects his concern about Al-Shabaab presence.

16. The relative importance of different livestock types is discussed in the following chapter.

17. The Jiddo and Garre are Somali clans. The former are predominantly cattle pastoralists, while the Garre are also pastoralists but some have mixed herds, while others have either only cattle or only camels (with sheep and/or goats). See the following chapter for more discussion on clan identities and their livelihood and vulnerability characteristics.

18. This probably refers to Kenya's military engagement with Al-Shabaab in this area of southern Somalia.

19. This is an issue taken up in greater detail in Chapter 6.

20. This money came from a variety of sources, but notably a substantial proportion of it was reportedly from Somaliland, including business and diaspora interests.

21. See Chapter 4.

22. "Sadaka" is voluntary charity to the poor.

6. DIVERSIFICATION, FLEXIBILITY, AND SOCIAL CONNECTEDNESS: UNDERSTANDING THE NARRATIVES

1. L. Cassanelli, "Speculations on the Historical Origins of the 'Total Somali Genealogy,'" in M. Hoehne and V. Luling (eds), *Milk and Peace, Drought and War: Somali Culture, Society and Politics*, London: Hurst, 2009.

2. I. Lewis, *A Pastoral Democracy: A Study of Pastoralism and Politics among the Northern Somali of the Horn of Africa*, London: James Currey, 1961.

3. V. Luling, "Genealogy as Theory, Genealogy as Tool: Aspects of Somali 'Clanship,'" *Social Identities*, 12, 4 (2006), pp. 471–85.

4. Lewis, *Pastoral Democracy*.

5. A. de Waal, *Famine Crimes: Politics and the Disaster Relief Industry*, Oxford: James Currey, 1997.

6. Ibid.

7. K. Menkaus, "The Question of Ethnicity in Somali Studies: The Case of Somali Bantu Identity," in Hoehne and Luling, *Peace and Milk*.

8. J. Gundel, "The Migration–Development Nexus: Somalia Case Study," *International Migration*, 40, 5 (2002), pp. 255–81.

9. J. Gardner and J. El Bushra, *Somalia—The Untold Story*, London: CIIR and Pluto Press, 2004, p. 100.

10. Menkaus, "Question of Ethnicity in Somali Studies."

11. Field interviews, 2013–14.

12. J. Corbett, "Famine and Household Coping Strategies," *World Development*, 16, 9 (1988), pp. 1099–112.

13. The resilience literature is vast, and has grown rapidly since the famine—indeed, the Somalia famine of 2011 and a regional crisis in the Sahel in 2012 were the events that gave rise to much of the current policy discourse on resilience. For the most important conceptual work on this, see C.B. Barrett and M.A. Constas, "Toward a Theory of Resilience for International Development Applications," *Proceedings of the National Academy of Sciences*, 111, 40 (2014), pp. 14625–30. In terms of programmatic applications, see T. Frankenberger et al., "Community Resilience: Conceptual Framework and Measurement Feed the Future Learning Agenda," Rockville, MD: USAID Feed the Future FEEDBACK Project, 2013.

14. Gardner and El Bushra, *Somalia—The Untold Story*.

15. Ibid. See also S.J. Hansen, *Al-Shabaab in Somalia: The History and Ideology of a Militant Islamist Group 2005–2012*, London and New York: Hurst/Oxford University Press, 2013.

16. Ibid. Human Rights Watch, "Harsh War, Harsh Peace: Abuses by Al Shabaab, the Transitional Federal Government and AMISOM in Somalia," New York: Human Rights Watch, 2010.

17. The most complete evidence on this question is mostly for Somaliland. See L. Hammond et al., "Cash and Compassion: The Role of the Somali Diaspora in Relief, Development and Peace-Building," Nairobi: UNDP, 2011.

18. Field interviews, 2013–14.

19. Field interviews, 2013–14.

20. Field interviews, 2013–14.

21. UN Monitoring Group, "Report of the Monitoring Group on Somalia Pursuant to Security Council Resolution 1853 (2008)," New York: United Nations, 2010, pp. 6–7.

22. Ibid.

23. Field interview, 2014.

24. K. Menkhaus, "No Access: Critical Bottlenecks in the 2011 Somali Famine," *Global Food Security*, 1, 1 (2012), pp. 29–35.

25. E. Bryld, C. Kamau, and D. Sinigallia, "Gatekeepers in Mogadishu," Nairobi: Somalia Cash Consortium, 2013, p. 12.

26. Ibid., p. 10.

27. Human Rights Watch, "Hostages of the Gatekeepers: Abuses against Internally Displaced in Mogadishu, Somalia," New York: Human Rights Watch, 2013.

28. Ibid.

29. M. Bradbury, "State-Building, Counterterrorism, and Licensing Humanitarianism in Somalia," Boston: Feinstein International Center, 2010.

30. Menkhaus, "No Access," p. 33.

31. Field interviews, 2012–14.

32. Menkhaus, "No Access."

33. Ibid., pp. 34–5.

7. THE RESPONSE OF THE (WESTERN) INTERNATIONAL "HUMANITARIAN COMMUNITY"

1. C. Hillbruner and G. Moloney, "When Early Warning Is Not Enough—Lessons Learned from the 2011 Somalia Famine," *Global Food Security*, 1, 1 (2012), pp. 20–8.

2. A. Martínez-Piqueras and M.R. Bascarán, "External Evaluation of ACF International's Response to the Horn of Africa Crisis, 2011," Nairobi: ACF, 2012. This is only one example of many, and the intent is not to single out individual agencies. Indeed, it was the courageous agencies that admitted some internal problems in the aftermath of the crisis—most simply blamed donors for the late response.

3. J. Darcy, P. Bonard, and S. Dini, "IASC Real Time Evaluation of the Humanitarian Response to the Horn of Africa Drought Crisis: Somalia 2011–2012," New York: IASC, 2012.

4. M. Buchanan Smith and S. Davies, *Famine Early Warning and Response—The Missing Link*, London: IT Publications, 1995. And R. Bailey, "Managing Famine Risk: Linking Early Warning to Early Action—A Chatham House Report," London: Chatham House, 2013.

5. S. Levine, A. Crosskey, and M. Abdinoor, "System Failure? Revisiting the Problems of Timely Response to Crises in the Horn of Africa," London: Humanitarian Practice Network, 2011.

6. R. Polastro et al., "DARA IASC Evaluation of the Humanitarian Response in South Central Somalia 2005–2010," IASC, 2011.

7. Bailey, "Managing Famine Risk."

8. C.C. Venton et al., "The Economics of Early Response and Disaster Resilience: Lessons from Kenya and Ethiopia," London: DFID, Conflict, Humanitarian, and Security Department, 2012.

9. OCHA Financial Tracking Service 2013.

10. Field interviews, 2013–14.

11. Darcy, Bonard, and Dini, "IASC Real Time Evaluation of the Humanitarian Response to the Horn of Africa Drought Crisis: Somalia."

12. Field interviews, 2013–14.

13. K. Menkhaus, "No Access: Critical Bottlenecks in the 2011 Somali Famine," *Global Food Security*, 1, 1 (2012), pp. 29–35.

14. ICAI, "DFID's Humanitarian Emergency Response in the Horn of Africa," Independent Comission for Aid Impact, 2012.

15. D. Hillier and B. Dempsey, "A Dangerous Delay: The Cost of Late Response to Early Warnings in the 2011 Drought in the Horn of Africa," Oxford, UK: Oxfam UK and Save the Children UK, 2012.

16. Field interviews, 2013–14. Recall (from Chapter 2), the argument of K. Glenzer, "We Aren't the World: Discourses on the Sahel, Partnership, and the Institutional Production of Partial Success," in X. Crombé and J.-H. Jézéque (eds), *Une Catastrophe Si Naturelle: Niger 2005*, Paris: Medicins sans Frontiere, 2007.

17. This claim came to light mainly after the fact, for example in a speech given by the UN humanitarian coordinator in a speech to an Inter-Agency Working Group meeting on Mar. 2, 2012.

18. Even though not physically present, WFP could have done more to promote mitigation of the worsening drought had it had a good contingency plan. It did not have such a plan, and neither did much of the rest of the humanitarian community. See WFP, "Summary Evaluation Report—Somalia Country Portfolio," Rome: WFP Office of Evaluation, 2012.

19. Darcy, Bonard and Dini, "IASC Real Time Evaluation of the Humanitarian Response to the Horn of Africa Drought Crisis: Somalia."

20. There were many reasons for Al-Shabaab's opposition to food aid: first, for the most part, they just didn't trust the humanitarian agencies. Second, they wanted people in the area they controlled to be self-sufficient, and believed that food aid undermined self-sufficiency. Third, they saw food aid as something foreign that promoted foreign control and manipulation. Fourth, it was something they did not fully control and it gave people a sort of independence from Al-Shabaab's control. See S. J. Hansen, *Al-Shabaab in Somalia. The History and Ideology of a Militant Islamist Group 2005–2012*, London and New York: Hurst/Oxford University Press, 2013.

21. D. Ali and K. Gelsdorf, "Risk-Averse to Risk-Willing: Learning from the 2011 Somalia Cash Response," *Global Food Security*, 1, 1 (2012), pp. 57–63.

22. Field interviews, 2012–13.

23. See, for example, C.B. Barrett et al., "Market Information and Food Insecurity Response Analysis," *Food Security*, 1, 2 (2009), pp. 151–68.

24. K. Hedlund et al., "Final Evaluation of the Unconditional Cash and Voucher Response to the 2011–12 Crisis in Southern and Central Somalia," London: Humanitarian Outcomes, 2013, p. 5.

25. FEWSNET, "Markets Functioning in Southern Somalia," Nairobi: FEWSNET, 2011, WFP, "Food Market and Supply Situation in Southern Somalia," Rome: World Food Programme, 2011.

26. FSNAU, "How to Increase Food Access in Southern Somalia: Cash Interventions and Local Market Responses in Somalia: Roundtable Discussion, March 4," Nairobi: FSNAU, 2011.

27. The preliminary findings were available in July, right at the time of the declaration. See FEWSNET, "Markets Functioning in Southern Somalia."

28. Field interviews, 2012.

29. FEWSNET, "Markets Functioning in Southern Somalia."

30. Field interviews, 2012

31. WFP, "WFP Extraordinary Briefing on the Horn of Africa," Rome, July 15, 2011.

32. See D. Maxwell et al., "Response Analysis and Response Choice in Food Security Crises: A Roadmap," London: Humanitarian Practice Network, 2012.

33. J. Egeland, A. Harmer, and A. Stoddard, "To Stay and Deliver: Good Practice for Humanitarians in Complex Security Environments," New York: OCHA, 2011, p. xv.

34. A. Donini and D. Maxwell, "From Face-to-Face to Face-to-Screen: Implications of Remote Management for the Effectiveness and Accountability of Humanitarian Action in Insecure Environments," *International Review of the Red Cross*, First View Articles (July 2014), pp 1–31.

35. L. Hammond and H. Vaughan-Lee, "Humanitarian Space in Somalia: A Scarce Commodity," London: Humanitarian Policy Group, 2012, Humanitarian Outcomes, "Aid Worker Security Report 2013," London: Humanitarian Outcomes, 2013.

36. Egeland, Harmer and A. Stoddard, "To Stay and Deliver," p. 2.

37. Field interviews, 2013–14.

38. A.S. DiDomenico and V.A. Harmer, "Providing Aid in Insecure Environments: 2009 Update—Trends in Violence against Aid Workers and the Operational Response," London: Overseas Development Institute, 2009.

39. Humanitarian Outcomes, "Aid Worker Security Report 2013," London: Humanitarian Outcomes 2013.

40. J. Belliveau, "'Remote Management' in Somalia," Humanitarian Practice Network, 2013.

41. Donini and Maxwell, "From Face-to-Face to Face-to-Screen."

42. Field interviews, 2013–14.

43. Field interviews, 2013–14.

44. Fortunately, the latter did not happen. The use of drones has been associated with external (particularly American) military intervention, and the introduction of drones for humanitarian purposes simply runs too many risks of being misperceived.

45. Field interviews, 2012–14.

46. This included using cellphone technology and Somali diaspora networks to interview recipients in inaccessible areas—a methodology improved and used in the research for this book. For a brief description, see Hedlund et al., "Final Evaluation of the Unconditional Cash and Voucher Response."

47. Donini and Maxwell, "From Face-to-Face to Face-to-Screen."

48. Menkhaus, "No Access."

49. FSNAU, "How to Increase Food Access in Southern Somalia," p. 8.

50. The "no sector/unknown" category in Table 6.1 simply means that either a program addressed multiple sectors and could not be categorized, or else none was specified in the FTS data.

51. C.B. Barrett and D.G. Maxwell, *Food Aid after Fifty Years: Recasting Its Role*, London: Routledge, 2005.

52. D. Ali and K. Gelsdorf, "Risk-Averse to Risk-Willing: Learning from the 2011 Somalia Cash Response," *Global Food Security*, 1, 1 (2012), pp. 57–63.

53. Ibid. See also, N. Majid, I. Hussein, and H. Shuria, "Evaluation of the Cash Consortium in Southern Somalia," Oxfam/Horn Relief, 2007.

54. K. Hedlund et al., "Final Evaluation of the Unconditional Cash and Voucher Response to the 2011–12 Crisis in Southern and Central Somalia," UNICEF, 2013.

55. FAO Office of Evaluation, "Evaluation of FAO's Cooperation in Somalia," Rome: FAO, 2013.

56. There is some evidence that cash transfers were shared among recipients, meaning that indirectly the program probably reached a greater number of people, but there are no numbers on this. Field interviews, 2012–14.

57. Hedlund et al., "Final Evaluation of the Unconditional Cash and Voucher Response." See also, C. Longley, S. Dunn, and M. Brewin, "Final Monitoring Report of the Somalia Cash and Voucher Transfer Programme—Phase I: September 2011–March 2012, Cash and Voucher Monitoring Group," London: Humanitarian Policy Group, Overseas Development Institute, 2012.

58. For full disclosure, the authors were part of the evaluation team.

59. Field interviews, 2011–13.

60. Field interviews, 2012–14.

61. Hedlund et al., "Final Evaluation of the Unconditional Cash and Voucher Response."

62. Longley, Dunn, and Brewin, "Final Monitoring Report of the Somalia Cash and Voucher Transfer Programme—Phase I." Hedlund et al., "Final Evaluation of the Unconditional Cash and Voucher Response."

63. FSNAU, "Food Security and Nutrition Analysis Post Deyr 2011/2012," Nairobi: FSNAU, 2012. It is a bit dangerous to play "what if?" games retrospectively, but if food prices had remained high, at a minimum, larger cash transfers would have been required to achieve the same food security outcomes, but even had this been the case, the evidence was clear that the intended supply response was induced by the cash transfers.

64. Hedlund et al., "Final Evaluation of the Unconditional Cash and Voucher Response."

65. Although already underway before the famine, much of this continued throughout 2011 and 2012 under the auspices of CaLP—the Cash Learning Partnership. The very fact that donors were willing to invest $3 million on the monitoring and evaluation of the unconditional cash transfer program was also testament to this observation.

66. Hedlund et al., "Final Evaluation of the Unconditional Cash and Voucher Response," p. 4.

67. Field interviews, 2012.

68. D. Ali and K. Gelsdorf, "Risk-Averse to Risk-Willing: Learning from the 2011 Somalia Cash Response," *Global Food Security*, 1, 1 (2012), pp. 57–63.

69. J. Darcy, P. Bonard, and S. Dini, "IASC Real Time Evaluation of the Humanitarian Response to the Horn of Africa Drought Crisis: Somalia 2011–2012," New York: IASC, 2012.

70. Field interviews, 2011–12.

71. Hedlund et al., "Final Evaluation of the Unconditional Cash and Voucher Response."

72. Ibid.

73. Field interviews, 2013–14. None of our respondents had been able to see the results of these audits.

74. FAO, "'Like a Good Trip to Town without Selling Your Animals': A Study of FAO Somalia's Cash for Work Programme, Impact Evaluation Report," Rome: FAO Office of Evaluation, 2013.

75. FAO Office of Evaluation, "Evaluation of FAO's Cooperation in Somalia," Rome: FAO, 2013, FAO, "'Like a Good Trip to Town without Selling Your Animals.'"

76. FAO, "'Like a Good Trip to Town without Selling Your Animals.'"

77. Field interviews, 2012–13.

78. FAO Office of Evaluation, "Evaluation of FAO's Cooperation in Somalia."

79. Field interviews, 2012–14.

80. Field interviews, 2011–13.

81. L. Alinovi, G. Hemrich, and L. Russo, *Beyond Relief: Food Security in Protracted Crises*, Rugby, UK: Practical Action Publishing, 2008.

82. FAO/UNICEF/WFP, "A Common Way Forward on Resilience in Eastern and Central Africa, Workshop Report," Nairobi: FAO/UNICEF/WFP, 2013.

83. A handful of local and international NGOs had been advocating for a large-scale cash response throughout the first half of 2011, and they played a lead role in implementing programs on the ground. However, their calls were largely ignored in early 2011. See Ali and Gelsdorf, "Risk-Averse to Risk-Willing."

84. WFP Food Aid Information System, http://www.wfp.org/fais/

85. UN Monitoring Group, "Report of the Monitoring Group on Somalia Pursuant to Security Council Resolution 1853 (2008)," New York: United Nations, 2010. See also M. Bradbury, "State-Building, Counterterrorism, and Licensing Humanitarianism in Somalia," Boston: Feinstein International Center, 2010, D. Maxwell, "Those with Guns Never Go Hungry: The Instrumental Manipulation of Food Assistance in Conflict," in A. Donini (ed.), *The Golden Fleece: Manipulation and Independence in Humanitarian Action*, Sterling: Kumarian Press, 2012.

86. These reasons had more to do with corruption and diversion, rather than the likelihood of causing price inflation. Field interviews, 2012–13.

87. Field interviews, 2012–13.

88. "Somali Islamists Ban Red Cross," *The Guardian*, Jan. 31, 2012.

89. UN OCHA figures. See: https://fts.unocha.org/reports/daily/ocha_R4_A948_1212201156

90. Field interviews, 2012–14.

91. Field interviews, 2011–13.

92. Moderate acute malnutrition refers to children (sometimes under the age of five years, sometimes more specifically aged six to thirty-six months) whose weight compared to height places them between two and three standard deviations below the median weight for height for their sex. Severe acute malnutrition refers to children more than three standard deviations below the median. The combination of these two (i.e., all those less than two standard deviations below the median) is referred to as global acute malnutrition—often referred to in humanitarian-speak as "GAM" (or "SAM" to denote severe acute malnutrition). The prevalence of GAM or SAM (i.e., the proportion of the population of children of these ages that fall into these categories) is the most frequently used general indicator of severity in humanitarian crises.

93. Rebelo et al., "Nutritional Response to the 2011 Famine in Somalia," *Global Food Security*, 1, 1 (2012), pp. 64–73.

94. Salama, et al., "Famine in Somalia: Evidence for a Declaration," pp. 13–19.

95. Rebelo et al., "Nutritional Response to the 2011 Famine in Somalia," pp. 64–73.

96. For a much more complete technical discussion of the nutrition situation, see ibid.

97. The IASC was a body set up by UN General Assembly Resolution 46/182 in 1992 to coordinate humanitarian policy and preparedness among UN agencies, the Red Cross, the International Organization on Migration, and international NGOs.

98. R. Polastro, et al., "DARA IASC Evaluation of the Humanitarian Response in South Central Somalia 2005–2010," IASC, 2011, p. 9.

99. S. Truelove and J. Duncalf, "Humanitarian Coalition East Africa Drought Appeal—Final Evaluation—Somalia (Oxfam and SCF)," Humanitarian Coalition, 2012, p. 3.

100. A.M. Hassan, "ACTED Emergency Project to Mitigate the Effects of La Niña Drought in Middle Juba Region, South Somalia—ECHO Funded Emergency Food Security and Livelihood Project Implemented in Sakow District—Final External Evaluation Report," ACTED, 2011, pp. ii–iii.

101. D. Guillemois and M.S. Mohamed, "Final Report—Final Evaluation of Famine Response Banadir, Bay and Lower Shabelle Somalia for NRC," NRC, 2012, p. 4. All of these quotes are reviewed in greater depth in the desk review conducted for this research. See: D. Maxwell et al., "Lessons Learned from the Somalia Famine and the Greater Horn of Africa Crisis 2011–2012: Desk Review of Literature," Medford, MA, USA: Feinstein Internaitonal Center, Tufts University, 2014.

102. Darcy, Bonard, and Dini, "IASC Real Time Evaluation of the Humanitarian Response to the Horn of Africa Drought Crisis: Somalia"; Hedlund et al., "Final Evaluation of the Unconditional Cash and Voucher Response"; Longley, Dunn, and Brewin, "Final Monitoring Report of the Somalia Cash and Voucher Transfer Programme—Phase I."

103. WFP, "Somalia: An Evaluation of WFP's Portfolio Vol. 1—Full Report May 2012," Rome: WFP Office of Evaluation, 2012, p. 19.

104. WFP, "Summary Evaluation Report—Somalia Country Portfolio," (Rome: WFP Office of Evaluation, 2012).

105. WFP, "Somalia: An Evaluation of WFP's Portfolio Vol. II—Annexes May 2012," Rome: WFP Office of Evaluation, 2012.

106. N. Majid and S. McDowell, "Hidden Dimensons of the Somalia Famine," *Global Food Security*, 1, 1 (2012), pp. 36–42.

107. Hedlund et al., "Final Evaluation of the Unconditional Cash and Voucher Response"; FAO, "'Like a Good Trip to Town without Selling Your Animals.'"

108. UN Monitoring Group, "Report of the Monitoring Group on Somalia."

109. Darcy, Bonard, and Dini, "IASC Real Time Evaluation of the Humanitarian Response to the Horn of Africa Drought Crisis: Somalia."

110. A. Haider and S. Dini, "Real Time Evaluation (RTE) of CARE Somalia's Response to the Drought, Food Security and Displacement Emergency 2011 South-Central and Puntland Regions of Somalia," 2012.

8. THE SHIFTING INTERNATIONAL DYNAMICS OF THE HUMANITARIAN RESPONSE

1. These were the terms used to describe this whole category of actors by the (mostly Western) humanitarian community in Somalia in 2011–12. But some of these

agencies (such as the Kizilay—the Turkish Red Crescent Society) have been around for as long as organized humanitarianism or have been working in Somalia for some time, but mostly not in a specifically humanitarian mode.

2. One group of Islamic humanitarian agencies, based mostly in Europe, has some characteristics that overlap with the group analyzed here, but also has an identity that closely resembles that of Western NGOs. This chapter is about a different category of actor.

3. A. Whiting, "New Donors Chip Away at Aid Industry Status Quo," Thomson Reuters Foundation, 2012.

4. M. Kroessin, "Worlds Apart? Muslim Donors and International Humanitarianism," *Forced Migration Review*, 29 (Dec. 2007), pp. 36–7.

5. Development Initiatives, "Global Humanitarian Assistance Report 2013," Wells, UK: Development Initiatives, 2013.

6. A. Binder, C. Meier, and J. Steets, "Humanitarian Assistance: Truly Universal? A Mapping Study of Non-Western Donors. GPPi Research Paper No. 12," Berlin: GPPI, 2010.

7. Ibid. p. 4.

8. Kroessin, "Worlds Apart?" Of course, the OIC only coordinates aid from Islamic countries. In the case of Somalia, this effectively covered all of the non-Western actors, but it doesn't cover donors like China and India (who were not particularly active in Somalia in 2011).

9. See http://www.oic-un.org/forum/OIC-ICHAD.pdf

10. Development Initiatives, "Global Humanitarian Assistance Report 2013."

11. For further information on the history of Islamic and Muslim charities and NGOs, see J. Bellion-Jourdan, "Islamic Relief Organizations: Between 'Islamism' and 'Humanitarianism,'" Leiden: International Institute for the Study of Islam in the Modern World, 2000. For a discussion of Saudi Arabian official aid and national charities and how 'relations have changed over the years, see L. Barasi, "Saudi Arabia's Humanitarian Aid: A Political Takeover?" *Humanitarian Exchange*, 29 (2005), pp. 41–5.

12. In the Somalia response, technical experts from the Istanbul municipality and experts from different ministries were engaged in fieldwork.

13. See, for examples: www.ihc.ae/ for the International Humanitarian City in Dubai; http://qcri.com/our-research/social-innovation/social-innovation for the Qatar Foundation's social innovation work in humanitarian contexts; https://www.icrc.org/eng/resources/documents/news-release/2014/05–06-kuwait-forum-principles-challenges-face-humanitarian-work.htm and https://www.icrc.org/eng/resources/documents/news-release/2012/kuwait-news-2012–10–08.htm for examples of other humanitarian gatherings.

14. The following website gives an outline of the UAE's foreign aid: http://www.uaeinteract.com/government/development_aid.asp

15. Kuwait and Qatar are now advisory members of the United Nations Central Emergency Response Fund: http://www.irinnews.org/indepthmain.aspx?indepthid=91&reportid=94010

16. One small Somali NGO interviewed had worked closely with a large international Islamic charity during 2011 and reported receiving funds from individual and organizational donors in seven countries including Saudi Arabia, Kuwait, Qatar, UAE, Bahrain, Egypt, and the UK, with several donors named from each of Kuwait, Qatar, and Saudi Arabia.

17. Field interviews, 2012–13.

18. See Jonathan Benthall, "Red Crescent Politics," in J. Benthall and J. Bellion-Jourdan (eds), *The Charitable Crescent: Politics of Aid in the Muslim World*, London and New York: I.B. Tauris, 2009, pp. 45–68.

19. M. Abuarqub and I. Phillips, "A Brief History of Humanitarianism in the Muslim World," Birmingham: Islamic Relief Worldwide, 2009.

20. IRIN, "The Rise of the 'New' Donors: Arab and Muslim Aid and the West—Two China Elephants," Nairobi: IRIN, 2011.

21. Kroessin, "Worlds Apart?"

22. Islamic Relief, "Back from the Brink: 10 Ways the International Community Must Address Somalia's Humanitarian Crisis," Birmingham: Islamic Relief Worldwide, 2012.

23. There are also many other hadith (the body of teachings and practices of the Prophet Muhammad) and concepts of charity that are essential parts of Islamic morals, laws, and practice. See J. Moussa, "Ancient Origins, Modern Actors: Defining Arabic Meanings of Humanitarianism," London: ODI, 2014. J. Krafess, "The Influence of the Muslim Religion in Humanitarian Aid," *International Review of the Red Cross*, 87, 585 (2005).

24. Moussa, "Ancient Origins, Modern Actors."

25. For a discussion of "civil society" in the Gulf, see J. Benthall, "NGOs in the Contemporary Muslim World," in J. Benthall and J. Bellion-Jourdan (eds), *The Charitable Crescent: Politics of Aid in the Muslim World*, London and New York: I.B.Tauris, 2009. And, Benthall, "Red Crescent Politics." ''

26. K. Kirisci, "Turkey's 'Demonstrative' Effect and the Transformation of the Middle East," *Insight Turkey*, 13, 2 (2011), pp. 33–55.

27. See T. Murphy and O. Sazak, "Turkey's Civilian Capacity in post-Conflict Reconstruction," Istanbul: Istanbul Policy Centre, Sabanci University, 2012.

28. Field interviews. 2012–13.'

29. P. Tank, "Turkey's New Humanitarian Approach in Somalia," Oslo: Norwegian Peace-Building Resource Centre, 2013.

30. It should be noted that Turkish NGOs have different political positions vis-à-vis the state, with some considered in the "opposition" camp.

31. For a discussion of the Saudi Arabian aid and aid agencies, see L. Barasi, "Saudi Arabia's Humanitarian Aid: A Political Takeover?" *Humanitarian Exchange*, 29 (2005), pp. 41–5.

32. For an analysis of Qatari interests at home and abroad, see B. Haykel, "Qatar and Islamism," Oslo: Norwegian Peacebuilding Resource Centre, 2013.

33. A. Le Sage, "Somalia and the War on Terrorism: Political Islamic Movements and US Counter-Terrorism Efforts," PhD thesis, Cambridge University, 2004.

34. J. Benthall and J. Bellion-Jourdan (eds), *The Charitable Crescent: Politics of Aid in the Muslim World*, London and New York: I.B. Tauris, 2009, p. 85.

35. Field interviews, 2012–13.

36. Field interview, 2014.

37. "Why Are Muslim Charities Guilty until Proven Innocent?" Huffington Post, November 4, 2014, http://www.huffingtonpost.co.uk/abdurahman-sharif/why-are-muslim-charities-guilty-til-proven-innocent_b_6093956.html

38. Field interviews, 2014–15. One key informant called this the "worst nightmare" for Islamic NGOs—forcing the closure of many excellent programs. '

39. Tank, "Turkey's New Humanitarian approach in Somalia."

40. Field interview, 2014.

41. Field interviews, 2014.

42. Development Initiatives, "Global Humanitarian Assistance Report 2013."

43. Field interviews, 2013–14.

44. IRIN, "Rise of the 'New' Donors."

45. Royal Embassy of Saudi Arabia, "Saudi King Launches Fundraising Campaign for Somali People," 2011.

46. See: http://reliefweb.int/report/somalia/qatar-relief-alliance-charitable-societies-initiates-phase-ii-somalia-and-philippine

47. One of the largest NGOs from the Global South, Mercy Malaysia, sent a three-person team in late August 2011, using a Somali volunteer student (many in Malaysia), and reported to be partnering with Muslim Aid. They were part of a group of three Malaysian NGOs that came together soon after the famine declaration to mobilize funds and organize a response and who appear to still be working in Somalia in 2013; http://www.perdana4peace.org/aiding-somalia-en-masse/

48. Oxfam, "Crises in a New World Order: Challenging the Humanitarian Project," Oxford: Oxfam, 2012.

49. IRIN, "Rise of the 'New' Donors."

50. OCHA Somalia, Weekly Humanitarian Bulletin, Issue 48, 2010; http://relief-web.int/sites/reliefweb.int/files/resources/11D75DB74E09A838C12577F50 04C8590-Full_Report.pdf

51. Oxfam, "Crises in a New World Order."

52. Field interviews, 2013–14.

53. Field interviews, 2012–13.

54. Field interview, 2014.

55. Field interviews, 2013–14.

56. IRIN, "Rise of the 'New' Donors."

57. Refugees International, "Horn of Africa: Not the Time to Look Away—Field Report," Washington, DC: Refugees International, 2011.

58. See, S. Jaspars and D. Maxwell, "Targeting in Complex Emergencies: Somalia Case Study," 2008. Also see UN Monitoring Group, "Report of the Monitoring Group on Somalia Pursuant to Security Council Resolution 1853 (2008), (2010, March 10). UN Security Council (S/2010/91)," New York: UN, 2010.

59. Le Sage, "Somalia and the War on Terrorism."

60. Field interviews, 2014.

61. Jaspars and Maxwell, "Targeting in Complex Emergencies."

62. Le Sage, "Somalia and the War on Terrorism."

63. Field interviews, 2014.

64. Field interviews, 2014.

65. Humanitarian Forum (HF) seconded a member of staff and sent several visitors to Mogadishu from mid-2011 (field interviews, 2014). In 2011, in partnership with Muslim Charities Forum, HF helped to establish the Somali Relief and Development Forum (SRDF), bringing together NGOs based in the UK that operated in or with Somalia in response to the deteriorating conditions in Somalia See, Islamic Relief, "Back from the Brink."

66. Field interviews, 2014.

67. IRIN, "Rise of the 'New' Donors."

68. Field interviews, 2013–14.

69. Field interviews, 2014

70. Field interviews, 2014.

71. Field interviews, 2014.

72. Field interviews, 2013–14.

73. M. Kroessin, "Islamic Charities and the 'War on Terror': Dispelling the Myths," *Humanitarian Exchange*, 38 (June 2007).

74. Field interview, 2014

75. Field interview, 2014.

76. Field interviews, 2013–14.

77. Field interviews, 2014.

78. D. Jorgic and T. Karadeniz, "Biggest donor Turkey stops direct budget support to Somalia," Reuters, 2014.

79. Field interview, 2014.

80. Field interview, 2014.

81. Field interviews, 2013–14.

82. Field interviews, 2013–14.

83. Field interviews, 2014.

84. Field interview, 2014.

9. 2012–14 AND THE AFTERMATH OF THE FAMINE

1. M. Bryden, "Somalia Redux: Assessing the New Somali Federal Government," Center for Strategic and International Studies, 2013.
2. BBC News, "Somalia Profile," http://www.bbc.com/news/world-africa-14094 632
3. Bryden, "Somalia Redux," p. 1.
4. D. Balthazar, "Thinking Beyond Roadmaps in Somalia: Expanding Policy Options for Statebuilding," Center for Strategic and International Studies: Center for Strategic and International Studies, 2014.
5. Although diaspora returns and political and economic investment were already significant prior to this. K. Menkhaus, "The Role and Impact of the Somali Diaspora in Peace-Building, Governance and Development," *Africa's Finances: The Contribution of Remittances*, 16 (2008), pp. 187–202.
6. Field interviews, 2012–14. Bryden, "Somalia Redux," See also: International Crisis Group, "Jubaland in Jeopardy: The Uneasy Path to State-Building in Somalia," Brussels: International Crisis Group, 2013.
7. S.J. Hansen, *Al-Shabaab in Somalia: The History and Ideology of a Militant Islamist Group 2005–2012*, London and New York: Hurst/Oxford University Press, 2013.
8. J.P. Pham, "State Collapse, Insurgency and Counter-Insurgency: Lessons from Somalia," Carlisle, PA: Strategic Studies Institute and U.S. Army War College Press, 2013, p. 44.
9. A. Seal and R. Bailey, "The 2011 Famine in Somalia: Lesson Learnt from a Failed Response?" *Conflict and Health*, 7, 22 (2013), pp. 1–5.
10. R. Marchal, "The Rise of a Jihadi Movement in a Country at War: Harakat Al Shabaab Al Mujaheddin in Somalia," Paris: SciencesPo Paris, 2011.
11. Ibid.
12. "Will the Famine Weaken Somalia's al Shabaab Militants?" France 24, Jan. 17, 2014.
13. Hansen, Al-Shabaab in Somalia.
14. A. Jackson and A. Aynte, "Talking to the Other Side: Humanitarian Negotiations with Al-Shabaab in Somalia, HPG Working Paper," London: Humanitarian Policy Group, ODI, 2013.
15. Hansen, *Al-Shabaab in Somalia*.
16. BBC News, "Somalia Profile," http://www.bbc.com/news/world-africa-1409 4632
17. Ibid.
18. D. Balthazar, "Thinking Beyond Roadmaps," p. 1.
19. Oxfam, "Risk of Relapse: Somalia Crisis Update," Oxfam International, 2014.
20. D. Maxwell and N. Majid, "Another Humanitarian Crisis in Somalia? Learning from the 2011 Famine," Medford, MA: Feinstein International Center, Tufts University, 2014.

21. C.B. Barrett and M.A. Constas, "Toward a Theory of Resilience for International Development Applications," *Proceedings of the National Academy of Sciences*, 111, 40 (2014), pp. 14625–30.

22. DFID, "Defining Disaster Resilience: A DFID Approach Paper," London: DFID, 2011; T. Frankenberger, "Building Resilience to Food Security Shocks in the Horn of Africa—Discussion Note," Washington, DC: USAID/DFID, 2012.

23. S. Levine et al., "The Relevance of 'Resilience'?" London: Humanitarian Policy Group, Overseas Development Institute, 2012.

24. DFID, "Defining Disaster Resilience," p. 6.

25. Barrett and Constas, "Toward a Theory of Resilience."

26. Kenya Drought Management Authority, "Drought Risk Management and Ending Drought Emergencies Medium Term Plan 2013–2017," Nairobi: National Disaster Management Authority, 2013. '

27. M. Hobson and L. Campbell, "How Ethiopia's Productive Safety Net Programme (PSNP) is Responding to the Current Humanitarian Crisis in the Horn," *Humanitarian Exchange*, 53 (Mar. 2012), pp. 3–4.

28. FAO/UNICEF/WFP, "A Common Way Forward on Resilience in Eastern and Central Africa, Workshop Report," Nairobi: FAO/UNICEF/WFP, 2013.

29. V. Tilstone, "Resilience in the Drylands of the Horn of Africa: What It Means for Practice?" Regional Learning and Advocacy Program for Vulnerable Dryland Communities, 2013.

30. Levine et al., "Relevance of 'Resilience'?" London: Humanitarian Policy Group, Overseas Development Institute, 2012.

31. Some of this documentation was in the public domain, and some was not. Eventually, with the permission of (some) donors and (some) agencies, we obtained and reviewed some proposals and calls for proposals. Several key donors ultimately did not allow us to review any proposals, others only with the explicit permission of the implementing partner. These proposals were all for annual program cycles or, in some cases, for multi-year funding, but nevertheless were for work in the Somalia context where protracted crisis is a fact of life. Hence, although not all of them said so explicitly, most were in some way dealing with the question of "resilience" in a risk-prone context and with the constant threat of renewed humanitarian emergency. A scoring protocol for assessing the proposals was developed and the results of the scoring were recorded. The proposals were anonymized. The point of the analysis was to get a sense of the degree to which the essential lessons learned had been incorporated into the programming of the humanitarian community at large—it was not about which agency had the best proposal. Several caveats regarding this analysis should be mentioned. First, the reviewed proposals were, of course, only a fraction of those written and submitted for funding in the post-famine period, and the particular batch of reviewed proposals do not necessarily represent the larger body of programming ideas. Second, many of the cri-

teria noted below could arguably have been incorporated into programming long before 2011—the point of including them here is that the 2011–12 crisis made them explicit—irrespective of whether they were already part of the programming portfolio. Third, some of these criteria were not necessarily explicitly spelled out in program proposals. Fourth (and conversely), just because something is mentioned in a proposal does not necessarily mean that it will be implemented on the ground.

32. Dissemination meeting, 2015.

33. This fear of "getting out ahead of crowd" and perhaps being accused of "chicken-little" style false alarms was raised by several respondents as one reason for the delayed response in 2010 and 2011. However, there are few actual examples of major responses triggered by early warning in which the crisis turned out not to be severe as predicted. The late-response problem is much more prevalent than any kind of "over-response."

34. H. Slim, "IASC Real-Time Evaluation of the Humanitarian Response to the Horn of Africa Drought Crisis in Somalia, Ethiopia, and Kenya," IASC, 2012.

35. Field interviews, 2013–14.

36. K. Menkhaus, "No Access: Critical Bottlenecks in the 2011 Somali Famine," *Global Food Security*, 1, 1 (2012), pp. 29–35, K. Menkhaus, "Stabilisation and Humanitarian Access in a Collapsed State: The Somali Case," *Disasters*, 34 (2010), pp. S320–S341. Seal and Bailey, "2011 Famine in Somalia."

37. A limited number of donors and agencies recognized the problem with this, and continued to search for ways of working in the most conflict affected or Al-Shabaab-controlled areas, but many simply switched their attention to other, less fraught environments as long as there was no major crisis going on.

38. As noted in Chapter 9, some donors strongly disagree with the contention that the risk of financial loss is outsourced to agencies—be they international or local. There were cases in which donors forced agencies, or attempted to force them, to repay, but there were also cases in which the donors did not do this. Much of the evidence on this question is in forensic audits undertaken after the famine ended that are not in the public domain, and which, despite requests, we have never been able to see.

39. Hedlund et al., "Final Evaluation of the Unconditional Cash and Voucher Response." FAO, "'Like a Good Trip to Town without Selling Your Animals': A study of FAO Somalia's Cash for Work programme, Impact Evaluation Report," Rome: FAO Office of Evaluation, 2013. Numerous agency-specific evaluations of the cash transfer program were reviewed—too many to list here.

40. Field interviews, 2012–14.

41. For more on response analysis, see, D. Maxwell, J. Parker, and H. Stobaugh, "What Drives Program Choice in Food Security Crises? Examining the 'Response Analysis' Question," *World Development*, 49 (Sep. 2013), pp. 68–79.

42. The pre-positioning of food aid in or near chronically vulnerable countries is increasingly practiced, and has reduced response times in other crises. Given the absence of WFP and the antipathy of Al-Shabaab to food aid, this practice had a limited impact in Somalia in 2011.

43. Hedlund et al., "Final Evaluation of the Unconditional Cash and Voucher Response."

44. During the course of the research, we encountered numerous examples of the way independent consultants are put under considerable pressure to be lenient in evaluations; it is not clear how open many agencies are to critical evaluations.

45. Field interviews, 2012–13.

46. C.C. Venton et al., "The Economics of Early Response and Disaster Resilience: Lessons from Kenya and Ethiopia," London: DFID, Conflict, Humanitarian and Security Department, 2012.

47. Field interviews, 2014.

48. Field interviews, 2013–14. But see also, Food and Agriculture Organization, "Evaluation of FAO's Cooperation in Somalia: 2007 to 2012," Rome: FAO Office of Evaluation, 2013. Much of the leadership issue is well analyzed in M. Buchanan Smith and K. Scriven, "Leadership in Action: Leading Effectively in Humanitarian Operations," London: ALNAP, 2011.

49. One of the most obvious is to recognize the critical importance of remittances. Western governments have repeatedly tried to close down the Western bank accounts of remittance companies because of the possibility that they may be used to channel money to Al-Shabaab—most notably the Barclay's Bank account of Dahabshiil, one of the largest Somali *hawalas*. From the point of view of supporting resilience, this is completely counter-productive.

50. K. Mackintosh and P. Duplat, "Study of the Impact of Donor Counter-Terrorism Measures on Principled Humanitarian Action," New York: OCHA and Norwegian Refugee Council, 2013, pp. 102–3.

51. See also J. Burniske, N. Modirzadeh, and D. Lewis, "Counter-Terrorism Laws and Regulations: What Aid Agencies Need to Know," London: Humanitarian Practice Network, Overseas Development Institute, 2014.

52. A. Jackson and A. Aynte, "Al-Shabaab Engagement with Aid Agencies," London: Humanitarian Policy Group. Overseas Development Institution, 2013.

53. Field interviews, 2013–14.

54. Jackson and Aynte, "Al-Shabaab Engagement with Aid Agencies."

55. Burniske, Modirzadeh, and Lewis, "Counter-Terrorism Laws and Regulations."

10. PREVENTING FAMINE: AN UNFINISHED AGENDA?

1. Field interviews, 2013–14.

2. Field interviews, 2011–12.

3. Field interviews, 2012–14.

4. Numerous requests for data from the research team—data that was collected using donor funds and for which reports were in the public domain—were simply ignored. In twenty years of research, we have never seen people act so stingily with data. Promises would be made—and then simply ignored. Occasionally, people would say the data was too sensitive, and might constitute a protection problem, but of course the data did not include personal identifiers—or if it did, they could have been easily removed.

5. For the most flagrant cases, see, UN Monitoring Group, "Report of the Monitoring Group on Somalia Pursuant to Security Council Resolution 1853 (2008)," New York: United Nations, 2010. That report noted that as much as half of the food aid in Somalia at the time was being diverted to non-humanitarian uses.

6. This refers to aid that ended up in the hands of wealthier and more powerful people who didn't really need it.

7. For a more in-depth discussion on aid targeting in Somalia, see S. Jaspars and D. Maxwell, "Targeting in Complex Emergencies: Somalia Case Study," 2008). See also D. Maxwell et al., "Targeting and Distribution in Complex Emergencies: Participatory Management of Humanitarian Food Assistance," *Food Policy*, 36, 4 (2011), pp. 535–43.

8. A. Jackson and A. Aynte, "Talking to the Other Side: Humanitarian Negotiations with Al-Shabaab in Somalia, HPG Working Paper," London: Humanitarian Policy Group, ODI, 2013; C. Horst, *Transnational Nomads: How Somalis Cope with Refugee Life in the Dadaab Camps of Kenya*, New York and Oxford: Berghahn Books, 2006.

9. Some donors chafed at the suggestion that risk was not shared jointly, noting that they were aware of aid going astray but did not insist that the agency repay the value of the lost aid. But the risks were not just about diversion, but included security, legal, and reputational threats to operational agencies, and agency staff felt that they were pretty much on their own in terms of managing those risks. Nevertheless, many donor agencies did run their own risks by continuing to provide funding support. The very fact that it was a sort of "us against them" dynamic only highlighted the depth of the fragmentation and malaise.

10. This was not a one-off comment from one agency—it was repeated many times in interviews. The intent of the research team was not to identify specific instances of diversion, but rather to get a general sense of the problem.

11. By 2014, many agencies had new risk management approaches; the NGO Consortium for Somalia had recently come out with a joint risk management framework. While its adoption was not mandatory, it represented a good attempt to work jointly on a joint problem.

12. Field interviews, 2014.

13. Field interviews, 2014.

14. K. Menkhaus, "No Access: Critical Bottlenecks in the 2011 Somali Famine," *Global Food Security*, 1, 1 (2012), pp. 29–35.

15. Field interviews, 2012–14.
16. Field interviews, 2013–14.
17. By 2014, Turkey had become the fourth largest humanitarian donor country in the world, according to the Financial Tracking Service of OCHA: http://fts. unocha.org/. Turkish NGOs were adding considerable additional resources to the mix, mostly raised independently of the Turkish government. Field interviews, 2014.
18. That said, much of the on-the-ground presence of many non-Western agencies in 2011 was limited to Mogadishu.
19. For a general discussion of this topic, see, A. Donini, "The Golden Fleece: Manipulation and Independence in Humanitarian Action," Sterling: Kumarian Press, 2012.
20. F. Terry, *Condemned to Repeat? The Paradox of Humanitarian Action*, Ithaca, NY: Cornell University Press, 2002.
21. DFID, "Humanitarian Emergency Response Review: UK Government Response," London: DFID, 2011.
22. N. Haan, S. Devereux, and D. Maxwell, "Global Implications of Somalia 2011 for Famine Prevention, Mitigation and Response," *Global Food Security*, 1, 1 (2012), pp. 74–9.
23. See J. Darcy, P. Bonard, and S. Dini, "IASC Real Time Evaluation of the Humanitarian Response to the Horn of Africa Drought Crisis: Somalia 2011–2012," New York: IASC, 2012. See also, WFP, "Somalia: An Evaluation of WFP's Portfolio Vol. 1—Full Report May 2012," Rome: WFP Office of Evaluation, 2012.
24. Recent government composition and even Al-Shabaab's policies are changing this to some extent
25. This is reminiscent of Kapteijns's accusation that there is no internal acknowledgement of how clan identities were politicized to mobilize clans against each other in the civil wars of the early 1990s. See, L. Kapteijns, *Clan Cleansing in Somalia: The Ruinous Legacy of 1991*, Philadelphia: University of Pennsylvania Press, 2013.
26. Menkhaus, "No Access," p. 34.
27. For the classic view on this, see A. de Waal, *Famine Crimes: Politics and the Disaster Relief Industry in Africa*, London James Currey, 1997. For an analysis focused on the 2011 famine in Somalia, see Haan, Devereux, and Maxwell, "Global Implications of Somalia 2011," pp. 74–9.
28. ICISS, "The Responsibility to Protect: Report of the International Commission on Intervention and State Sovereignty," New York: International Commission on Intervention and State Sovereignty, 2001. For an example involving famines, see S. Devereux, *The New Famines: Why Famines Persist in an Era of Globalization*, London: Routledge, 2006.
29. J. Darcy, P. Bonard, and S. Dini, "IASC Real-Time Evaluation of the Humanitarian Response to the Horn of Africa Drought Crisis Somalia 2011–2012," IASC, 2012, p. 10.

30. WFP, "Somalia: An Evaluation of WFP's Portfolio Vol. 1," p. vii.

31. Devereux, *New Famines*. S. Lautze et al., "Early Warning, Late Response (Again): The 2011 Famine in Somalia," *Global Food Security*, 1, 1 (2012), pp. 43–39; Haan, Devereux, and Maxwell, "Global Implications of Somalia 2011," pp. 74–9.

32. P. Howe and S. Devereux, "Famine Intensity and Magnitude Scales: A Proposal for an Instrumental Definition of Famine," *Disasters*, 28, 4 (2004), pp. 353–72.

33. Haan, Devereux, and Maxwell, "Global Implications of Somalia 2011."

34. Lautze et al., "Early warning, Late Response."

35. Field interviews, 2012–14.

36. Kapteijns, *Clan Cleansing in Somalia*.

37. R. Polastro et al., "DARA IASC Evaluation of the Humanitarian Response in South Central Somalia 2005–2010," IASC, 2011.

38. K. Glenzer, "We Aren't the World: Discourses on the Sahel, Partnership, and the Institutional Production of Partial Success," in X. Crombé and J.-H. Jézéque (eds), *Une Catastrophe Si Naturelle: Niger 2005*, Paris: Medicins sans Frontiere, 2007.

39. UNDP, "Human Development Report: Somalia," Nairobi/New York: UN Development Programme, 2001.

40. UN Monitoring Group, "Report of the Monitoring Group on Somalia Pursuant to Security Council Resolution 1853 (2008)," New York: United Nations, 2010.

41. A. Donini, "The Far Side: The Meta Functions of Humanitarianism in a Globalised World," *Disasters*, 34, 2 (2010), pp. S220–S237.

42. While empirical examples of these phenomena have been presented here, a more theoretical or generic discussion of these can be found in T.G. Weiss and P. J. Hoffman, "The Fog of Humanitarianism: Collective Action Problems and Learning-Challenged Organizations," *Journal of Intervention and Statebuilding*, 1, 1 (2007), pp. 47–65. And in A. Cooley and J. Ron, "The NGO Scramble: Organizational Insecurity and the Political Economy of Transnational Action," *International Security*, 27, 1 (2002), pp. 5–39.

43. Field Interview, 2014.

44. The authors are admittedly not counter-terrorism experts, but the experts we interviewed about Somalia never suggested that the eventual response to the famine—delayed by counter-terrorism objectives though it might have been—in any way undermined those objectives.

45. It was clear from both interviews and the daylong seminar in Nairobi at the end of the research that there are deep disagreements about this.

46. M.N. Barnett, "Humanitarianism Transformed," *Perspectives on Politics*, 3, 4 (2005), pp. 723–40.

47. P. Walker and C. Russ, "Professionalising the Humanitarian Sector: A Scoping Study," Medford, MA: ELHRA, RED-R, and Feinstein International Center, Tufts University, 2010.

48. M. Maren, *The Road to Hell: The Ravaging Effects of Foreign Aid and International Charity*, New York: Free Press, 1997. L. Polman, *The Crisis Caravan: What's Wrong with Humanitarian Aid?* New York: Henry Holt, 2010. D. Moyo, *Dead Aid: Why Aid Is Not Working and How There Is a Better Way for Africa*, New York: Farrar, Strauss and Giroux, 2009.

49. M.B. Anderson, *Do No Harm: How Aid Can Support Peace—Or War*, Boulder, CO: Lynne Rienner, 1999.

50. Sphere Project, *The Sphere Project Handbook*, Sphere Project, 2011.

51. HAP, Sphere Project, People in Aid, and ALNAP, "Horn of Africa Crisis—A Call for Program Quality, Accountability and Effectiveness," London and Geneva: ALNAP/HAP, 2011.

52. S. Graves and V. Wheeler, "Good Humanitarian Donorship: Overcoming Obstacles to Improved Collective Donor Performance," London: Overseas Development Institute, 2006.

53. Field interviews, 2013–14.

54. A. Le Sage, "Somalia and the War on Terrorism: Political Islamic Movements & US Counter-Terrorism Efforts," PhD thesis, University of Cambridge, 2004; K. Menkhaus, "The Role and Impact of the Somali Diaspora in Peace-Building," in R. Bardouille, M. Ndulo, and M. Grieco (eds), *Africa's Finances: The Contribution of Remittances*, Cambridge: Cambridge Scholars Publishing, 2008.

55. Inter-Agency Standing Committee, "Concept Paper on 'Empowered Leadership,'" New York: IASC, 2014.

56. Paraphrased from many key informant interviews.

57. M. Handino, "Green Famine in Ethiopia: Understanding the Causes of Increasing Vulnerability to Food Insecurity and Policy Responses in the Southern Ethiopian Highlands," PhD thesis, University of Sussex, 2014. Handino cites a long history of experimentation with indigenous indicators and interpretations—little of which has been successfully incorporated into current practice.

58. K. Menkhaus, "No Access: Critical Bottlenecks in the 2011 Somali Famine," *Global Food Security*, 1, 1 (2012), pp. 29–35.

59. See Handino, "Green Famine in Ethiopia." Still, one of the innovations of this research (and growing out of the experience itself) is much greater reliance on the merger of twenty-first-century technology (cellphones) with long-existing Somali social networks, to identify key informants in inaccessible areas who could narrate local experiences there. The possibilities for improving this kind of information are enormous.

ANNEX: METHODOLOGICAL NOTE

1. See D. Maxwell, J. Parker, and H. Stobaugh, "What Drives Program Choice in Food Security Crises? Examining the 'Response Analysis' Question," *World Development*,

49 (Sep. 2013), pp. 68–79. This research had been planned in advance of the events of 2011, but the Horn of Africa was selected as the context. So somewhat by coincidence, some of the evidence—particularly the debate of the appropriateness of the cash response and the various alternative forms of food assistance—comes from this study.

BIBLIOGRAPHY

Abuarqub, Mamoun, and Isabel Phillips, "A Brief History of Humanitarianism in the Muslim World," Birmingham: Islamic Relief Worldwide, 2009.

Ahmed, Ismail I., and Reginald Herbold Green, "The Heritage of War and State Collapse in Somalia and Somaliland: Local-Level Effects, External Interventions and Reconstruction," *Third World Quarterly*, 20, 1 (1999), pp. 113–27.

Ali, Degan, and Kirsten Gelsdorf, "Risk-Averse to Risk-Willing: Learning from the 2011 Somalia Cash Response," *Global Food Security*, 1, 1 (Nov. 2012), pp. 57–63.

Alinovi, Luca, Günter Hemrich, and Luca Russo, *Beyond Relief: Food Security in Protracted Crises*, Rugby, UK: Practical Action Publishing, 2008.

Anderson, Mary B., *Do No Harm: How Aid Can Support Peace—Or War*, Boulder, CO: Lynne Rienner, 1999.

Annan, Kofi, "We the Peoples: The Role of the United Nations in the 21st Century (Millennium Report of the Secretary-General)," New York: United Nations, 2000.

Associated Press, "Somali Militants Shut Down Red Cross Food Aid," *The Guardian*, London, 2012.

Bailey, Rob, "Managing Famine Risk: Linking Early Warning to Early Action—A Chatham House Report," London: Chatham House, 2013.

Balthazar, Dominic, "Thinking Beyond Roadmaps in Somalia: Expanding Policy Options for Statebuilding," Washington, DC: Center for Strategic and International Studies, 2014.

Barasi, Leo, "Saudi Arabia's Humanitarian Aid: A Political Takeover?" *Humanitarian Exchange*, 29 (2005), pp. 41–45.

Barnett, Michael N., "Humanitarianism Transformed," *Perspectives on Politics*, 3, 4 (2005), pp. 723–40.

Barrett, Christopher B., Robert Bell, Erin C. Lentz, and Daniel G. Maxwell, "Market Information and Food Insecurity Response Analysis," *Food Security*, 1, 2 (2009), pp. 151–68.

Barrett, Christopher B., and Mark A. Constas, "Toward a Theory of Resilience for

International Development Applications," *Proceedings of the National Academy of Sciences*, 111, 40 (Oct. 7, 2014), pp. 14625–30.

Barrett, Christopher B., and Daniel G. Maxwell, *Food Aid after Fifty Years: Recasting Its Role*, London: Routledge, 2005.

Bellion-Jourdan, Jerome, "Islamic Relief Organizations: Between 'Islamism' and 'Humanitarianism,'" *ISIM Newsletter*, Leiden: International Institute for the Study of Islam in the Modern World, 2000.

Belliveau, Joe, "'Remote Management' in Somalia," *Humanitarian Exchange Magazine*, Humanitarian Practice Network, 2013.

Benthall, Jonathan, "Ngos in the Contemporary Muslim World," in Jonathan Benthall and Jerome Bellion-Jourdan (eds), *The Charitable Crescent: Politics of Aid in the Muslim World*, pp. 85–110, London and New York: I.B.Tauris, 2009.

——— "Red Crescent Politics," in Jonathan Benthall and Jerome Bellion-Jourdan (eds), *The Charitable Crescent: Politics of Aid in the Muslim World*, pp. 45–68, London and New York: I.B. Tauris, 2009.

Benthall, Jonathan, and Jerome Bellion-Jourdan (eds), *The Charitable Crescent: Politics of Aid in the Muslim World*, London and New York: I.B. Tauris, 2009.

Besteman, Catherine, and Lee Cassanelli, *The Struggle for Land in Southern Somalia: The War Behind the War*, Boulder, CO: Westview Press, 2000.

Bhattacharjee, Abhijit, "IASC Real Time Evaluation of the Humanitarian Response to the Horn of Africa Drought Crisis 2011: Regional Mechanisms and Support during the Response," New York: IASC, 2012.

Binder, Andrea, Claudia Meier, and Julia Steets, "Humanitarian Assistance: Truly Universal? A Mapping Study of Non-Western Donors. Gppi Research Paper No. 12," Berlin: GPPI, 2010.

Bradbury, Mark, "Normalising the Crisis in Africa," *Disasters*, 22, 4 (Dec. 1998), pp. 328–38.

——— "State-Building, Counterterrorism, and Licencing Humanitarianism in Somalia," Somerville: Feinstein International Center, Tufts University, 2010.

——— "State-Building, Counterterrorism, and Licensing Humanitarianism in Somalia," Medford, MA: Feinstein International Center, Tufts University, 2010.

Bradbury, Mark, and Michael Kleinman, "Winning Hearts and Minds? Examining the Relationship between Aid and Security in Kenya," Medford MA: Feinstein International Center, Tufts University 2010.

Bryden, Matt, "Somalia Redux: Assessing the New Somali Federal Government," Center for Strategic and International Studies, 2013.

——— "Somalia's Famine Is Not Just a Catastrophe, It's a Crime," Published electronically, Oct. 3, 2011. http://www.enoughproject.org/publications/somalia%E2%80%99s-famine-not-just-catastrophe-it%E2%80%99s-crime

Bryld, Erik, Christine Kamau, and Dina Sinigallia, "Gatekeepers in Mogadishu," Nairobi: Somalia Cash Consortium, 2013.

Buchanan Smith, M., and S. Davies, *Famine Early Warning and Response—The Missing Link*, London: IT Publications, 1995.

Buchanan Smith, Margaret, and Kim Scriven, "Leadership in Action: Leading Effectively in Humanitarian Operations," London: ALNAP, 2011.

Burniske, Jessica, Naz Modirzadeh, and Dustin Lewis, "Counter-Terrorism Laws and Regulations: What Aid Agencies Need to Know," London: Humanitarian Practice Network, Overseas Development Institute, 2014.

CARE and FEWSNET, "Greater Horn of Africa Food Security Update," Nairobi: FEWSNET and CARE, 2001.

Cassanelli, Lee, "Explaining the Somali Crisis," in Catherine Besteman and Lee Cassanelli (eds), *The Struggle for Land in Southern Somalia: The War Behind the War*, Boulder CO: Westview Press, 2000.

——— "Speculations on the Historical Origins of the 'Total Somali Genealogy,'" in Markus Hoehne and Virginia Luling (eds), *Milk and Peace, Drought and War: Somali Culture, Society and Politics*, pp. 51–66, London: Hurst, 2009.

Checchi, Francesco, and Courtland Robinson, "Mortality among Populations of Southern and Central Somalia Affected by Severe Food Insecurity and Famine during 2010–2012," Rome and Washington: FAO/FEWSNET, 2013.

Cooley, Alexander, and James Ron, "The NGO Scramble: Organizational Insecurity and the Political Economy of Transnational Action," *International Security*, 27, 1 (2002), pp. 5–39.

Corbett, Jane, "Famine and Household Coping Strategies," *World Development*, 16, 9 (1988), pp. 1099–112.

Darcy, James, Paul Bonard, and Shukria Dini, "IASC Real Time Evaluation of the Humanitarian Response to the Horn of Africa Drought Crisis: Somalia 2011–2012," New York: IASC, 2012.

Davidson, Basil, "Review of *Abaar: The Somali Drought* by I.M. Lewis," *Review of African Political Economy*, 6 (1976), pp. 110–12.

De Haan, Leo, and Annelies Zoomers, "Development Geography at the Crossroads of Livelihoods and Globalisation," *Ijdschrift voor Economishe en Socialie Geografie*, 94, 3 (2003), pp. 350–62.

De Waal, Alex, "Dangerous Precedents? Famine Relief in Somalia 1991–93," in Joanna Macrae and Anthony Zwi (eds), *War and Hunger: Rethinking International Responses to Complex Emergencies*, London: Zed Books 1994.

——— *Famine Crimes: Politics and the Disaster Relief Industry*, Oxford: James Currey, 1997.

——— *Famine Crimes: Politics and the Disaster Relief Industry in Africa*, African Issues. London James Currey, 1997.

——— *Famine That Kills*, New York: Oxford University Press, 2005.

De Waal, Alex, and Alan Whiteside, "New Variant Famine: Aids and Food Crisis in Southern Africa," *Lancet*, 362, 9391 (2003), 1234–7.

Deng, Luka Biong, "The Sudan Famine of 1998," *IDS Bulletin*, 33, 4 (2002), pp. 28–38.

Development Initiatives, "Global Humanitarian Assistance Report 2013," 2013.

Devereux, Stephen, "The Malawi Famine of 2002," *IDS Bulletin*, 33, 4 (2002), pp. 70–8.

—— *The New Famines: Why Famines Persist in an Era of Globalisation*, Oxon: Routledge, 2007.

—— *The New Famines: Why Famines Persist in an Era of Globalization*, London: Routledge, 2006.

DFID, "Defining Disaster Resilience: A DFID Approach Paper," London: DFID, 2011.

—— "Humanitarian Emergency Response Review: UK Government Response," London: DFID, 2011.

DiDomenico, Victoria, Abby Stoddard and Adele Harmer, "Providing Aid in Insecure Environments: 2009 Update—Trends in Violence against Aid Workers and the Operational Response," *HPG Policy Brief*, London: Overseas Development Institute, 2009.

Dikötter, Frank, *Mao's Great Famine: The History of China's Most Devastating Catastrophe, 1958–1962*, New York: Walker and Co., 2010.

Donini, Antonio, "The Far Side: The Meta Functions of Humanitarianism in a Globalised World," *Disasters*, 34, 2 (2010), S220–S37.

Donini, Antonio, and Daniel Maxwell, "From Face-to-Face to Face-to-Screen: Implications of Remote Management for the Effectiveness and Accountability of Humanitarian Action in Insecure Environments," *International Review of the Red Cross*, 95, 980 (2014), pp. 383–414.

Dreze, Jan, and Amartya Sen, *Hunger and Public Action*, Oxford: Clarenden Press, 1989.

Duffield, Mark, "Challenging Environments: Danger, Resilience and the Aid Industry," *Security Dialogue*, 43, 5 (2012), pp. 475–92.

Edkins, Jenny, "Mass Starvations and the Limitations of Famine Theorising," *IDS Bulletin*, 33, 4 (2002), pp. 12–18.

Egeland, Jan, Adele Harmer, and Abby Stoddard, "To Stay and Deliver: Good Practice for Humanitarians in Complex Security Environments," New York: OCHA, 2011.

Elhawary, Samir, and Sarah Collinson, "Humanitarian Space: A Review of Trends and Issues," 36, London, United Kingdom: Overseas Development Institute, 2012.

FAO, "Evaluation of FAO's Cooperation in Somalia," Rome: FAO Office of Evaluation, 2013.

—— "'Like a Good Trip to Town without Selling Your Animals': A Study of FAO Somalia's Cash for Work Programme—Impact Evaluation Report," Rome: FAO Office of Evaluation, 2013.

FAO/UNICEF/WFP, "A Common Way Forward on Resilience in Eastern and Central Africa. Workshop Report," Nairobi: FAO/UNICEF/WFP, 2013.

FEWSNET, "Markets Functioning in Southern Somalia," Nairobi: FEWSNET, 2011.

Frankenberger, Tim, "Building Resilience to Food Security Shocks in the Horn of Africa—Discussion Note," Washington, DC: USAID/DFID, 2012.

Frankenberger, Tim, Monica Mueller, Tom Spangler, and Sara Alexander, "Community Resilience: Conceptual Framework and Measurement Feed the Future Learning Agenda," Rockville, MD: USAID Feed the Future FEEDBACK Project, 2013.

FSNAU, "Food Security and Nutrition Analysis Post Deyr 2011/2012," *Technical Series*, Nairobi: FSNAU, 2012.

―― "FSNAU Evidence for Updated Famine Declaration," Nairobi: FSNAU, 2011.

―― "How to Increase Food Access in Southern Somalia: Cash Interventions and Local Market Responses in Somalia. Roundtable Discussion. March 4," Nairobi: FSNAU, 2011.

―― "Post Deyr 2010–2011 Technical Report and the Post Gu 2011," *Technical Report*, Nairobi: FSNAU, 2011.

―― "Subsistence Farming in Lower Shabelle Riverine Zone," Nairobi: FSNAU, 2013.

FSNAU, and FEWSNET, "Food Security and Nutrition Analysis Unit (Somalia), Fewsnet July 20, 2011 Press Release," Nairobi: Food Security and Nutrition Analysis Unit (Somalia), 2011.

Gardner, Judith, and Judy El Bushra (eds), *Somalia—The Untold Story*, London: CIIR and Pluto Press, 2004.

Gettleman, Jeffrey, "For Somali Women, Pain of Being a Spoil of War," *New York Times*, Dec. 27, 2011.

Glenzer, Kent, "We Aren't the World: Discourses on the Sahel, Partnership, and the Institutional Production of Partial Success," in X. Crombé and J.-H. Jézéque (eds), *Une Catastrophe Si Naturelle: Niger 2005*, Paris: Medicins sans Frontiere, 2007.

Graves, Sue, and Victoria Wheeler, "Good Humanitarian Donorship: Overcoming Obstacles to Improved Collective Donor Performance," *HPG Discussion Paper*, London: Overseas Development Institute, 2006.

Guillemois, David, and Muktar Sheikh Mohamed, "Final Report—Final Evaluation of Famine Response Banadir, Bay and Lower Shabelle Somalia for NRC," NRC, 2012.

Gundel, Joakim, "The Migration–Development Nexus: Somalia Case Study," *International Migration*, 40, 5 (2002), pp. 255–81.

―― "The Predicament of the Oday: The Role of Traditional Structures in Security, Rights, Law and Development," Copenhagen: Danish Refugee Council and NOVIB/Oxfam, 2006.

Haaland, Gunnar, and Willem Keddeman, "Poverty Analysis: The Case of Rural Somalia," *Economic Development and Cultural Change*, 32, 4 (1984), pp. 843–60.

Haan, Nicholas, Stephen Devereux, and Daniel Maxwell, "Global Implications of

Somalia 2011 for Famine Prevention, Mitigation and Response," *Global Food Security*, 1, 1 (2012), pp. 74–9.

Haggard, Stephan, and Marcus Noland, *Famine in North Korea: Markets, Aid, and Reform*, New York: Columbia University Press, 2007.

Hagmann, Tobias, "From State Collapse to Duty-Free Shop: Somalia's Path to Modernity," *African Affairs*, 104, 416 (2005), pp. 525–35.

Hagmann, Tobias, and Markus Hoehne, "Failures of the State Failure Debate: Evidence from the Somali Territories," *Journal of International Development*, 21, 1 (2009), pp. 42–57.

Haider, Abdullahi, and Shukria Dini, "Real Time Evaluation (RTE) of Care Somalia's Response to the Drought, Food Security and Displacement Emergency 2011 South–Central and Puntland Regions of Somalia," 2012.

Hakewill, P.A., and A. Moren, "Monitoring and Evaluation of Relief Programs," *Tropical Doctor*, 21, 1 (1991), pp. 24–8.

Hammond, Laura, "Family Ties: Remittances and Livelihood Support in Puntland and Somaliland," Nairobi, Kenya: FSNAU, 2013.

Hammond, Laura, Mustafa Awad, Ali Ibrahim Dagane, Peter Hansen, Cindy Horst, Ken Menkhaus, and Lynette Obare, "Cash and Compassion: The Role of the Somali Diaspora in Relief, Development and Peace-Building," Nairobi: UNDP, 2011.

Hammond, Laura, and Daniel Maxwell, "The Ethiopian Crisis of 1999–2000: Lessons Learned, Questions Unanswered," *Disasters*, 26, 3 (2002), pp. 262–79.

Hammond, Laura, and Hannah Vaughan-Lee, "Humanitarian Space in Somalia: A Scarce Commodity," London: Humanitarian Policy Group, 2012.

Handino, Mulugeta, "Green Famine in Ethiopia: Understanding the Causes of Increasing Vulnerability to Food Insecurity and Policy Responses in the Southern Ethiopian Highlands," PhD thesis, University of Sussex, 2014.

Hansen, Stig Jarle, *Al-Shabaab in Somalia: The History and Ideology of a Militant Islamist Group 2005–2012*, London and New York: Hurst/Oxford University Press, 2013.

HAP, The Sphere Project, People in Aid, and ALNAP, "Horn of Africa Crisis—A Call for Program Quality, Accountability and Effectiveness," London and Geneva: ALNAP/HAP, 2011.

Hassan, Abdi Maalim, "Acted Emergency Project to Mitigate the Effects of La Niña Drought in Middle Juba Region, South Somalia—Echo Funded Emergency Food Security and Livelihood Project Implemented in Sakow District: Final External Evaluation Report," ACTED, 2011.

Haykel, Bernard, "Qatar and Islamism," Oslo: Norwegian Peacebuilding Resource Centre, 2013.

Healy, Sean, and Sandrine Tiller, "Where Is Everyone? Responding to Emergencies in the Most Difficult Places," Paris: Medicins sans Frontieres, 2014.

Hedlund, Kerren, Nisar Majid, Daniel Maxwell, and Nigel Nicholson, "Final Evaluation of the Unconditional Cash and Voucher Response to the 2011–12 Crisis in Southern and Central Somalia," UNICEF, 2013.

——— "Final Evaluation of the Unconditional Cash and Voucher Response to the 2011–12 Crisis in Southern and Central Somalia," London: Humanitarian Outcomes, 2013.

Hillbruner, Christopher, and Grainne Moloney, "When Early Warning Is Not Enough—Lessons Learned from the 2011 Somalia Famine," *Global Food Security*, 1, 1 (Nov. 2012), pp. 20–8.

Hillier, Debbie, and Benedict Dempsey, "A Dangerous Delay: The Cost of Late Response to Early Warnings in the 2011 Drought in the Horn of Africa," Oxford: Oxfam UK, Save the Children UK, 2012.

Hobson, Matt, and Laura Campbell, "How Ethiopia's Productive Safety Net Programme (PSNP) Is Responding to the Current Humanitarian Crisis in the Horn." *Humanitarian Exchange*, 53 (Mar. 2012), pp. 3–4.

Horst, Cindy, *Transnational Nomads: How Somalis Cope with Refugee Life in the Dadaab Camps of Kenya*, New York and Oxford: Berghahn Books, 2006

Howe, Paul, and Stephen Devereux, "Famine Intensity and Magnitude Scales: A Proposal for an Instrumental Definition of Famine," *Disasters*, 28, 4 (Oct. 2004), pp. 353–72.

Human Rights Watch, "Harsh War, Harsh Peace: Abuses by Al Shabaab, the Transitional Federal Government and Amisom in Somalia," New York: Human Rights Watch, 2010.

——— "Hostages of the Gatekeepers: Abuses against Internally Displaced in Mogadishu, Somalia," New York: Human Rights Watch, 2013.

Humanitarian Outcomes, "Aid Worker Security Report 2013," London: Humanitarian Outcomes, 2013.

Humanitarian Policy Group, "Saving Lives through Livelihoods: Critical Gaps in the Response to the Drought in the Greater Horn of Africa," London: Humanitarian Policy Group, 2006.

ICAI, "DFID's Humanitarian Emergency Response in the Horn of Africa," Independent Comission for Aid Impact, 2012.

ICISS, "The Responsibility to Protect: Report of the International Commission on Intervention and State Sovereignty," New York: International Commission on Intervention and State Sovereignty, 2001.

Inter Agency Standing Committee, "Concept Paper on 'Empowered Leadership'," *Transformative Agenda Reference Document*, New York: IASC, 2014.

International Crisis Group, "Jubaland in Jeopardy: The Uneasy Path to State-Building in Somalia," Brussels: International Crisis Group, 2013.

IPC Global Partners, "Integrated Food Security Phase Classification: Technical Manual Version 1.1," Rome: FAO, 2008.

BIBLIOGRAPHY

—— "Integrated Food Security Phase Classification: Technical Manual Version 2.0," Rome: UN Food and Agriculture Organization, 2012.

IRIN, "The Rise of the 'New' Donors: Arab and Muslim Aid and the West—Two China Elephants," news release, 2011, http://www.irinnews.org/indepthmain.asp x?indepthid=91&reportid=94010

Islamic Relief, "Back from the Brink: 10 Ways the International Community Must Address Somalia's Humanitarian Crisis," Birmingham: Islamic Relief Worldwide, 2012.

Jacinto, Leela, "Will the Famine Weaken Somalia's Al Shabaab Militants?" France 24, Jan. 17, 2012.

Jackson, Ashley, and Abdi Aynte, "Al-Shabaab Engagement with Aid Agencies," London: Humanitarian Policy Group/Overseas Development Institution, 2013.

—— "Talking to the Other Side: Humanitarian Negotiations with Al-Shabaab in Somalia. Hpg Working Paper," London: Humanitarian Policy Group, ODI, 2013.

Jaspars, Susanne, and Daniel Maxwell, "Targeting in Complex Emergencies: Somalia Case Study," 2008.

Jorgic, D., and T. Karadeniz, "Biggest Donor Turkey Stops Direct Budget Support to Somalia," Reuters, 2014.

Kapteijns, Lidwien, *Clan Cleansing in Somalia: The Ruinous Legacy of 1991*, Philadelphia: University of Pennsylvania Press, 2013.

Keen, David, *The Benefits of Famine: A Political Economy of Famine and Relief in Southwestern Sudan 1983–1989*, Princeton, NJ: Princeton University Press, 1994.

Kenya Drought Management Authority, "Drought Risk Management and Ending Drought Emergencies Medium Term Plan 2013–2017," Nairobi: National Disaster Management Authority, 2013.

Kirisci, Kemal, "Turkey's 'Demonstrative' Effect and the Transformation of the Middle East," *Insight Turkey*, 13, 2 (2011), pp. 33–55.

Kloos, Helmut, and Bernt Lindtjorn, "Malnutrition and Mortality during Recent Famines in Ethiopia: Implications for Food Aid and Rehabilitation," *Disasters*, 18, 2 (June 1994 1994), pp. 130–9.

Krafess, Jamal, "The Influence of the Muslim Religion in Humanitarian Aid," *International Review of the Red Cross*, 87, 585 (2005).

Kroessin, Mohamed, "Islamic Charities and the 'War on Terror': Dispelling the Myths," *Humanitarian Exchange*, 38 (June 2007).

—— "Worlds Apart? Muslim Donors and International Humanitarianism," *Forced Migration Review*, 29 (Dec. 2007), pp. 36–7.

Lautze, Sue, Winnie Bell, Luca Alinovi, and Luca Russo, "Early Warning, Late Response (Again): The 2011 Famine in Somalia," *Global Food Security*, 1, 1 (Nov. 2012), pp. 43–9.

Lautze, Sue, and Daniel Maxwell, "Why Do Famines Persist in the Horn of Africa? Ethiopia, 1999–2003," in Stephen Devereux (ed.), *The 'New Famines': Why Famines Persist in an Era of Globalization*, pp. 222–44. London: Routledge, 2006.

Lautze, Sue, and Angela Raven-Roberts, "Violence and Complex Humanitarian Emergencies: Implications for Livelihoods Models," *Disasters*, 30, 4 (2006), pp. 383–401.

Le Sage, Andre, "Somalia and the War on Terrorism: Political Islamic Movements and US Counter-Terrorism Efforts," Cambridge University, 2004.

LEGS, *Livestock Emergency Guidelines and Standards*, Warwickshire: Practical Action, 2009.

Levine, Simon, and Claire Chastre, "Missing the Point: An Analysis of Food Security Interventions in the Great Lakes," London: Overseas Development Institute, Humanitarian Policy Group, 2004.

Levine, Simon, Alexandra Crosskey, and Mohammed Abdinoor, "System Failure? Revisiting the Problems of Timely Response to Crises in the Horn of Africa," London: Humanitarian Practice Network, 2011.

Levine, Simon, Adam Pain, Sarah Bailey, and Liliane Fan, "The Relevance of 'Resilience'?" London: Humanitarian Policy Group, Overseas Development Institute, 2012.

Lewis, Ioan, *Abaar: The Somali Drought*, International African Institute, 1975.

—— *A Modern History of Somalia—Nation and State in the Horn of Africa*, 4th Edition, London: Longman, 1980.

—— *A Pastoral Democracy: A Study of Pastoralism and Politics among the Northern Somali of the Horn of Africa*, London: James Currey, 1961.

Lindley, Anna, "The Early Morning Phone Call: Remittances from a Refugee Diaspora Perspective, Working Paper No. 47," Oxford: Centre on Migration, Policy and Society, 2007.

Little, Peter, "Somalia: Economy without State," *Review of African Political Economy*, 30, 97 (Sep. 2003), p. 4.

—— *Somalia: Economy without State*, Bloomington: Indiana University Press 2003.

Longley, Catherine, Sophia Dunn, and Mike Brewin, "Final Monitoring Report of the Somalia Cash and Voucher Transfer Programme. Phase I: September 2011–March 2012. Cash and Voucher Monitoring Group," London: Humanitarian Policy Group, Overseas Development Institute, 2012.

Luling, Virginia, "Genealogy as Theory, Genealogy as Tool: Aspects of Somali 'Clanship'," *Social Identities*, 12, 4 (2006), pp. 471–85.

Mackintosh, Kate, and Patrick Duplat, "Study of the Impact of Donor Counter-Terrorism Measures on Principled Humanitarian Action," New York: OCHA and Norwegian Refugee Council, 2013.

Macrae, Joanna, and Anthony B. Zwi, "Food as an Instrument of War in Contemporary African Famines: A Review of the Evidence," *Disasters*, 16, 4 (Oct. 1992), pp. 299–321.

Majid, N., I Hussein, and H. Shuria, "Evaluation of the Cash Consortium in Southern Somalia," Oxfam/Horn Relief, 2007.

Majid, Nisar, and Stephen McDowell, "Hidden Dimensons of the Somalia Famine," *Global Food Security*, 1, 1 (Nov. 2012), pp. 36–42.

Malthus, Thomas, *An Essay on the Principle of Population*, Oxford: Oxford University Press, 1993 [1809].

Marchal, Roland, "The Rise of a Jihadi Movement in a Country at War: Harakat Al Shabaab Al Mujaheddin in Somalia," Paris: SciencesPo Paris, 2011.

——— "A Survey of Mogadishu's Economy," Nairobi/Brussels: European Commission, 2002.

Maren, Michael, *The Road to Hell: The Ravaging Effects of Foreign Aid and International Charity*, New York: Free Press, 1997.

Martínez-Piqueras, Antonio, and María Ruiz Bascarán, "External Evaluation of Acf International's Response to the Horn of Africa Crisis, 2011," Nairobi: ACF, 2012.

Maxwell, Daniel, "Those with Guns Never Go Hungry: The Instrumental Manipulation of Food Assistance in Conflict," in Antonio Donini (ed.), *The Golden Fleece: Manipulation and Independence in Humanitarian Action*, Sterling: Kumarian Press, 2012.

——— "Why Do Famines Persist? A Brief Review of Ethiopia 1999–2000," *IDS Bulletin*, 33, 4 (2002), pp. 48–54.

Maxwell, Daniel, and Merry Fitzpatrick, "Famine," in African Studies, Oxford: Oxford Bibliographies Online, 2012.

Maxwell, Daniel, and Nisar Majid, "Another Humanitarian Crisis in Somalia? Learning from the 2011 Famine," Medford, MA: Feinstein International Center, Tufts University, 2014.

Maxwell, Daniel, Nisar Majid, Heather Stobaugh, Jeeyon Janet Kim, Jacqueline Lauer, and Eliza Paul, "Lessons Learned from the Somalia Famine and the Greater Horn of Africa Crisis 2011–2012. Desk Review of Literature," Medford, MA: Feinstein Internaitonal Center, Tufts University, 2014.

Maxwell, Daniel, John Parker, and Heather Stobaugh, "What Drives Program Choice in Food Security Crises? Examining the 'Response Analysis' Question," *World Development*, 49 (Sep. 2013), pp. 68–79.

Maxwell, Daniel, and Kate Sadler, "Responding to Food Insecurity and Malnutrition in Crises," in *World Disaster Report 2011*, pp. 124–45, Geneva: International Federation of Red Cross and Red Crescent Societies, 2011.

Maxwell, Daniel, Heather Stobaugh, John Parker, and Megan McGlinchy, "Response Analysis and Response Choice in Food Security Crises: A Roadmap," London: Humanitarian Practice Network, 2012.

Maxwell, Daniel, Helen Young, Susanne Jaspars, Jacqueline Frize, and John Burns, "Targeting and Distribution in Complex Emergencies: Participatory Management of Humanitarian Food Assistance," *Food Policy*, 36, 4 (2011), pp. 535–43.

Menkhaus, Ken, "Getting out vs. Getting Through: US and UN Policies in Somalia," *Middle East Policy*, 3 (1994), pp. 146–63.

—— "Kenya–Somalia Border Conflict Analysis: Report to USAID," Washington, DC: Development Alternatives Incorporated, 2005.

—— "No Access: Critical Bottlenecks in the 2011 Somali Famine," *Global Food Security*, 1, 1 (Nov. 2012), pp. 29–35.

—— "The Question of Ethnicity in Somali Studies: The Case of Somali Bantu Identity," in Markus Hoehne and Virginia Luling (eds), *Peace and Milk, Drought and War: Somali Culture, Society and Politics—Essays in Honor of I.M. Lewis*, London: Hurst, 2010.

—— "The Role and Impact of the Somali Diaspora in Peace-Building," in R. Bardouille, M. Ndulo, and M. Grieco (eds), *Africa's Finances: The Contribution of Remittances*, pp. 187–202. Cambridge: Cambridge Scholars Publishing, 2008.

—— "The Role and Impact of the Somali Diaspora in Peace-Building, Governance and Development," *Africa's Finances: The Contribution of Remittances*, 16 (2008), pp. 187–202.

—— "Somalia: They Created a Desert and Called It Peace(Building)," *Review of African Political Economy*, 36, 120 (2009), pp. 223–33.

—— "Stabilisation and Humanitarian Access in a Collapsed State: The Somali Case," *Disasters*, 34 (2010), pp. S320–S41.

—— "Vicious Circles and Security-Development Nexus in Somalia," *Security and Development*, 4, 2 (2004), pp. 149–65.

Menkhaus, Ken, H. Sheikh, S. Quinn, and I. Farah, "Somalia: Civil Society in a Collapsed State," in Thania Paffenholz (ed.), *Civil Society and Peacebuilding: A Critical Assessment*, pp. 321–50. Boulder, CO: Lynne Rienner, 2010.

Moussa, Jasmine, "Ancient Origins, Modern Actors: Defining Arabic Meanings of Humanitarianism," HPG Working Paper, London: ODI, 2014.

Moyo, Dambisa, *Dead Aid: Why Aid Is Not Working and How There Is a Better Way for Africa*, New York: Farrar, Strauss and Giroux, 2009.

Murphy, Teri, and Onur Sazak, "Turkey's Civilian Capacity in Post-Conflict Reconstruction," Istanbul: Istanbul Policy Centre, Sabanci University, 2012.

Ó Gráda, Cormac, "Making Famine History," *Journal of Economic Literature*, 45, 1 (2007), pp. 5–38.

Oxfam, "Crises in a New World Order: Challenging the Humanitarian Project," *Oxfam Briefing Paper 158*, Oxford: Oxfam, 2012.

—— "Risk of Relapse: Somalia Crisis Update," Oxfam International, 2014.

Pantuliano, Sara, and Mike Wekesa, "Improving Drought Response in Pastoral Areas of Ethiopia," London: Humanitarian Policy Group, Overseas Development Institute, 2008.

Paul, Jock, Jeff Duncalf, Langdon Greenhalgh, Hadijah Mohammed, Marco Marroni, and Bernard Maina, "IASC Real-Time Evaluation of the Humanitarian Response to the Horn of Africa Drought Crisis Kenya," IASC, 2012.

Pham, J. Peter, "State Collapse, Insurgency and Counter-Insurgency: Lessons from

Somalia," Carlisle, PA: Strategic Studies Institute and U.S. Army War College Press, 2013.

Polastro, Riccardo, Mohamed Abdirahman Khalif, Magda Ninaber van Eyben, Soledad Posada, Abduskadir Sh Mohamoud Salah, Nicolai Steen, and Erik Toft, "Dara IASC Evaluation of the Humanitarian Response in South Central Somalia 2005–2010," IASC, 2011.

Polman, Linda, *The Crisis Caravan: What's Wrong with Humanitarian Aid?* New York: Henry Holt, 2010.

Prendergast, John, "Preventing Future Famine in Somalia," in Hussein M. Adam and Richard Ford (eds), *Mending Rips in the Sky: Options for Somali Communities in the 21st Century*, Lawrenceville and Asmara: Red Sea Press, 1997.

Rebelo, Erin McCloskey, Marc-André Prost, Simon Renk, Shalini Guduri, and Peter Hailey, "Nutritional Response to the 2011 Famine in Somalia," *Global Food Security*, 1, 1 (Nov. 2012), pp. 64–73.

Refugee Consortium of Kenya, "Asylum under Threat: Assessing the Protection of Somali Refugees in Dadaab Refugee Camp and Along the Migration Corridor," Nairobi: Refugee Consortium of Kenya, 2012.

Refugees International, "Horn of Africa: Not the Time to Look Away—Field Report," Washington, DC: Refugees International, 2011.

Robinson, Courtland, Linnea Zimmerman, and Francesco Checchi, "Internal and External Displacement among Populations of Southern and Central Somalia Affected by Severe Food Insecurity and Famine during 2010–2012," Washington, DC: FEWSNET, 2014.

Royal Embassy of Saudi Arabia, "Saudi King Launches Fundraising Campaign for Somali People," 2011.

Salama, Peter, Fitsum Assefa, Leisel Taley, Paul Spiegel, Albertien van der Veen, and Carol A. Gotway, "Malnutrition, Measles, Mortality, and the Humanitarian Response during a Famine in Ethiopia," *Journal of the American Medical Association*, 286, 5 (Aug. 1 2001), pp. 563–71.

Salama, Peter, Grainne Moloney, Oleg O. Bilukha, Leisel Talley, Daniel Maxwell, Peter Hailey, Christopher Hillbruner, "Famine in Somalia: Evidence for a Declaration," *Global Food Security*, 1, 1 (Nov. 2012), pp. 13–19.

Seal, Andrew, and Rob Bailey, "The 2011 Famine in Somalia: Lesson Learnt from a Failed Response?" *Conflict and Health*, 7, 22 (2013), pp. 1–5.

Sen, Amartya, *Development as Freedom*, New York: Random House, 1999.

———— *Poverty and Famines: An Essay on Entitlement and Deprivation*, New York: Oxford University Press, 1981.

Sida, Lewis, Bill Gray, and Eleni Asmare, "IASC Real-Time Evaluation of the Humanitarian Response to the Horn of Africa Drought Crisis Ethiopia February 2011," IASC, 2012.

Simons, A., *Networks of Dissolution: Somalia Undone*, New York: Westview Press, 1995.

Slim, Hugo, "IASC Real-Time Evaluation of the Humanitarian Response to the Horn of Africa Drought Crisis in Somalia, Ethiopia, and Kenya," IASC, 2012.

Smillie, Ian, *The Alms Bazaar: Altruism under Fire—Non-Profit Organizations and International Development*, London: Intermediate Technology Publications, 1995.

Sphere Project, *The Sphere Project Handbook*, Sphere Project, 2011.

Tank, Pinar, "Turkey's New Humanitarian Approach in Somalia," *Policy Brief*, Oslo: Norwegian Peace-Building Resource Centre, 2013.

Terry, Fiona, *Condemned to Repeat? The Paradox of Humanitarian Action*, Ithaca, NY: Cornell University Press, 2002.

Tilstone, Vanessa, "Resilience in the Drylands of the Horn of Africa: What It Means for Practice?" Regional Learning and Advocacy Program for Vulnerable Dryland Communities, 2013.

Toole, Michael J., and Ronald J. Waldman, "The Association between Inadequate Rations, Undernutrition Prevalence, and Mortality in Refugee Camps: Case Studies of Refugee Poplulations in Eastern Thailand, 1979–1980, and Eastern Sudan, 1984–1985," *Journal of Tropical Pediatrics*, 34 (Oct. 1988), pp. 218–24.

Truelove, Sharon, and Jeff Duncalf, "Humanitarian Coalition East Africa Drought Appeal—Final Evaluation: Somalia (Oxfam and SCF)," Humanitarian Coalition, 2012.

UN Monitoring Group, "Report of the Monitoring Group on Somalia Pursuant to Security Council Resolution 1853 (2008)," New York: United Nations, 2010.

UNDP, "Human Development Report: Somalia," Nairobi/New York: UN Development Programme, 2001.

—— "In Search of Somalia's Missing Million: The Somali Diaspora and Its Role in Development," Nairobi: UNDP, 2009.

UNHCR, "Report of Nutrition and Health Survey in Kobe and Hileweyn Camps of Dollo Ado, Somali Region of Ethiopia during Mid October to Early November 2011," Addis Ababa: UNHCR, 2011.

Venton, Courtenay Cabot, Catherine Fitzgibbon, Tenna Shitarek, Lorraine Coulter, and Olivia Dooley, "The Economics of Early Response and Disaster Resilience: Lessons from Kenya and Ethiopia," London: DFID, Conflict, Humanitarian and Security Department, 2012.

Walker, Peter, and Catherine Russ, "Professionalising the Humanitarian Sector: A Scoping Study," Medford, MA: ELRHA, RED-R, and Feinstein International Center, Tufts University, 2010.

Webb, Patrick, Joachim von Braun, and Yisehac Yohannes, "Famine in Ethiopia: Policy Implications of Coping Failure at National and Household Levels," Research Report no. 92, Washington: IFPRI, 1992.

Weiss, Thomas G., and Peter J. Hoffman, "The Fog of Humanitarianism: Collective Action Problems and Learning-Challenged Organizations," *Journal of Intervention and Statebuilding*, 1, 1 (2007), pp. 47–65.

BIBLIOGRAPHY

WFP, "Food Market and Supply Situation in Southern Somalia," Rome: World Food Programme, 2011.

——— "Somalia: An Evaluation of WFP's Portfolio Vol. 1—Full Report May 2012," Rome: WFP Office of Evaluation, 2012.

——— "Somalia: An Evaluation of WFP's Portfolio Vol. II—Annexes May 2012," Rome: WFP Office of Evaluation, 2012.

——— "Somalia: An Evaluation of WFP's Portfolio," Rome: World Food Programme, 2012.

——— "Summary Evaluation Report—Somalia Country Portfolio," Rome: WFP Office of Evaluation, 2012.

Whiting, Alex, "New Donors Chip Away at Aid Industry Status Quo," Thomson Reuters Foundation, http://www.trust.org/item/?map=new-donors-chip-away-at-aid-industry-status-quo

Young, Helen, and Susanne Jaspars, "Review of Nutrition and Mortality Indicators for the Integrated Food Security Phase Classification (IPC): Reference Levels and Decision-Making," New York: Nutrition Cluster, Inter-Agency Standing Committee, 2009.

INDEX